M000207620

Geckos & Guns:
THE PAKISTAN YEARS

Sharon Bazant

BookLocker
Saint Petersburg, Florida

Print ISBN: 978-1-64719-318-8
Epub ISBN: 978-1-64719-319-5
Mobi ISBN: 978-1-64719-320-1

Published by BookLocker.com, Inc., St. Petersburg, Florida.

Printed on acid-free paper.

As a memoir, this book reflects the author's present recollections of experiences over time. Some names and characteristics have been changed, some events have been compressed, and some dialogue has been recreated.

BookLocker.com, Inc.
2021

First Edition

Cover Design: Kim Davis
Cover Photo: Used with kind permission of the Asian Studies Group, Islamabad, Pakistan
Maps: Davey Villalobos
Gecko illustration: Davey Villalobos
Author Photograph: Wayne Bazant

Library of Congress Cataloguing in Publication Data
Bazant, Sharon
Geckos & Guns: The Pakistan Years by Sharon Bazant
Library of Congress Control Number: 2021900320

Dedication

For my greatest treasures
Max, Jack, and Ben.

Khyber
Pakhtunkhwa
(North West
Frontier Province)

Gilgit
Baltistan

Skardu

Mingora
Saidu Sharif
Peshawar

Azad
Kashmir

Islamabad
Rawalpindi

Tribal
Areas

Lahore

Quetta

Punjab

Balochistan

Sindh

Hyderabad

Karachi

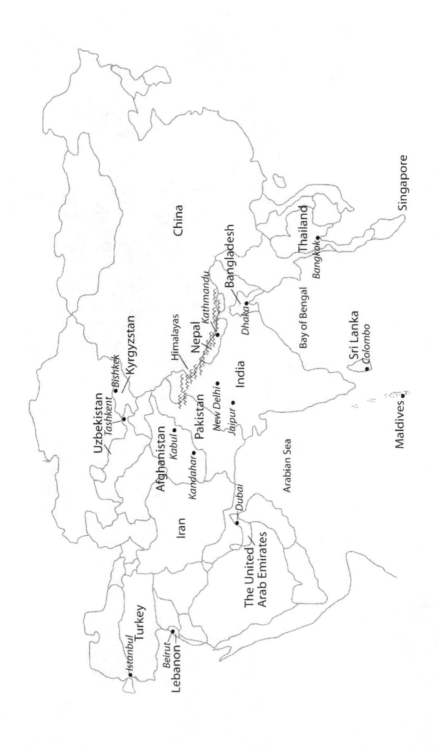

Acknowledgments

I would like to thank Lynne Allen for being my first reader and editor. Your continuous support and listening ear have been invaluable to me. I am grateful to my family for their endless love and encouragement of the wife, mother and grandmother who has decided to write books in her autumn years. A special thanks goes to my son, Colin for keeping me true to his story.

A big thank you to my Beta readers: Norma Sparks, Tom Sparks, Ayesha Bashir, Doris Gallan, Laurel Tokuda, and Shairshah Bayan for fact-checking and providing helpful critiques. I appreciate the time all of you took to help me elevate my story. Kudos to my Islamabad storytellers, Norma Sparks, Tom Sparks, Catherine and Barry Brown, Cindy Pavlos, and Gail Seay for their expat tales. Thanks to Kim Davis for final editing, marketing assistance, book cover design and answering my many questions. It is a joy to work with you. A shout out to my launch team for helping me get my book out there. And, finally, I would like to thank Angela Hoy and the team at BookLocker for their continued support and services in publishing my books.

Table of Contents

PART 1
BEGINNINGS

CHAPTER 1—DISPLACED

I opened my eyes and gradually adjusted to my surroundings. The watch on my bedside table registered 8 a.m. A cool, artificial breeze blew through the cavernous room. Where was I? I breathed in the sharp odor of ripe fruit mixed with sweat. Faint shards of light pierced the cracks in the heavy draperies. The bed was large, hard, and flat. I stretched, rolled over, and there was Wayne sprawled out peacefully beside me. Suddenly, something green slithered across the wall and I jolted upright.

Wayne was instantly awake. "What is it, Sharon?"

"An animal is darting around the room."

He took my hand and brushed my hair out of my eyes. "It's only a gecko—a little lizard. They're everywhere and completely harmless. They eat insects."

With that, he folded me into his arms. "Oh Sharon, I've missed you so much. I thank God that our family is together again."

Then it came flooding back, all the reasons that I found myself in this godforsaken guesthouse in Pakistan on a sunny February morning. I felt a sudden tremor in my gut. What were we doing here? Maybe our friends in Canada had been right after all. Maybe we were crazy to make such a drastic move at our age. Behind slatted wooden doors slept two resentful and disoriented teenagers who would have wholeheartedly attested to the craziness of their parents at this moment.

Yet it was something we had wanted to do—a new start, something all our own. Life in Canada had become lackluster, predictable. We had sheltered ourselves in the bosom of a sleepy, tree-lined suburban community for almost 15 years. I was teaching, taking university courses, and acting in a small theatre group with friends.

Wayne had worked for the Alberta government for years—21 to be exact—and was stuck reinventing the wheel in what seemed like an endless cyclical pattern. His boss was mean-spirited and difficult, never giving credit or the slightest ray of hope for the future. Wayne needed to get out from under this oppressive glass ceiling.

Sure, we had good jobs, the promise of a pension, medical coverage, vacation time, a "3-bedroom bungalow with developed basement in maturing and stable neighborhood," friends, family. Many people would have given their right arm for this kind of life— to sail into old age on this secure and conventional vessel. Not us!

Or should I say, not me. Sometimes I think that Wayne would never have attempted to apply for this UN job—which happened to come across his desk like so many other bits and pieces—if it hadn't been for my constant and infectious sense of adventure. However, that may be unfair. Maybe we had both just reached a pivotal point in our lives.

I was 42, Wayne 44. God knows we were working on our demons. I'd been in therapy for two years dealing with family of origin and personal issues. Wayne was dealing with baggage from his past as well and our marriage of 22 years had hit some rocky roads that merited counseling. Just to add more spice, our sixteen-year-old son, Jason, was rebellious, stubborn, and out of reach much of the time. We felt helpless in the face of this tall, skinny enigma.

We needed a change. We needed to eat together again, exchange ideas, and expand our minds beyond our tight little circle. Why Pakistan? Well, as they say in Pakistan, "Why not?"

We spent the better part of a year getting ready: negotiating the deal, selling things we could no longer keep, including the house and the car, deciding what to put in storage, giving away the cat. Jason stayed firmly in denial, talking for hours on the phone, shutting himself away in his bedroom, and going out with friends.

He wasn't interested in being removed from his comfort zone. Our daughter, Julie, at fourteen, was a different story, conscientiously and quietly negotiating the landmines of her parents' passionate and sometimes stormy relationship and her brother's burgeoning anger and rebellion.

On January 15 of 1991, after months of deliberation and preparation, Jason, Julie, and I found ourselves sitting on our beds with two suitcases each and the clothes on our backs, poised to fly away. Wayne was already in New York for work orientation and we were to join him in London, then travel together to Islamabad.

Two teenagers and one mom had found their patience strained in the threadbare highway motel with the greasy spoon restaurant where we waited out our final Canadian moments. Then, just hours before we were scheduled to leave, the telephone rang.

"Hi Sharon!"

"Wayne? What's going on? Why are you calling? We're just about ready to head for the airport."

"I'm so sorry, hon. I'm calling from the UN offices in New York to let you know that the UN has canceled your flight. The Gulf War has started, and it's been deemed unsafe for you to travel."

My heart stopped. "What? What do you mean? What are we supposed to do? When will they let us travel?"

I put down the phone, stunned. What to do? How long would this war with the Iraqi dictator, Saddam Hussein, last? We unpacked. I rented a car. Days passed. Wayne moved on to London and then to headquarters in Vienna. More days passed.

Jason and Julie went to stay with friends. Finally, they went back to school, mortified after all the goodbyes and best wishes. They were in Limbo School—there but never really there. Weeks passed. Should I go back to work? Should I rent an apartment? Saddam was running my life.

Finally, Wayne was flown into Islamabad. Life there was tense. Many Americans had been evacuated and all remaining *expats*[1] were warned to stay inside their homes and shelter in place. "Hate Americans" and "Kill Jews" slogans were painted on walls; *mullahs*[2] screeched over the loudspeakers, tension pulsed in the air. People were afraid of being attacked or even killed by angry mobs. Saddam was running their lives too.

The UN Resident Representative in Islamabad at that time was a powerful and rather formidable German. Wayne started regularly showing up at his office and insisting that the rest of our family be sent to Pakistan despite the Gulf War. The separation and uncertainty were affecting all of us. Wayne, in particular, felt like he had been parachuted into an alien land without a compass. We needed to be together during this time of stress and change.

After a month of exasperation, Wayne's steady stream of visits and threats of returning to Canada were wearing down the resolve of the local UN authorities. Meanwhile, the three of us back in Canada were trying to decide what to do about creating more permanent circumstances. Then, one frigid February morning, after five weeks of anxiety, the call came through. The kids and I could fly to Islamabad!

Awash in the teary goodbyes of Jason and Julie's teenage friends, we boarded the plane in Edmonton, Alberta, Canada, bound for Islamabad by way of London. As we soared through the clouds, each of us absorbed in private thoughts, I don't think we had any idea that we were flying into another dimension of life from which we would never return. As individuals and as a family we would be profoundly altered by our sojourn into the subcontinent and beyond. But we knew none of this then.

---

[1] An expat is a person living outside of their native country.

[2] A mullah is an Islamic cleric.

Meanwhile, our stopover in London offered a temporary distraction from fear of the future. The city would be our halfway port for many trips to come, but this visit was special. It was the first!

The first time we learned how to hail an elegant black London cab complete with dapper driver, our first time attending London theatre and dancing in the aisles, the first time we discovered Oxford Street and Piccadilly Circus, the first time I would run behind my two young, cool consumers shouting, "Don't buy anything. It's too expensive!" and the first time for *Sale e Pepe*, our favorite Italian restaurant, where the waiters burst into arias as they served us. Those first London memories would always belong to the three of us—warm smiles in the corners of our minds.

But our smiles slowly faded as we packed our bags and prepared for the next leg of our journey. Security was tight, cases were searched, and batteries were confiscated. Now we take these measures for granted, but in 1991, this kind of airport security was highly unusual. Very few people were traveling—the Gulf War had sent shockwaves around the world. It wasn't until a few years later that my mother admitted to me the overpowering anxiety she felt knowing that we were flying toward war and terrorism.

Groggy from a long tense flight, we emerged in Islamabad still hermetically sealed in our protective Canadian façades—safe, ordered, pristine. But for how long? The heat melted away our layers of clothing and we were greeted by a sea of bearded men in loose, flowing trousers and tunics pressing, shouting, and clamoring for attention of one kind or another. As we stood, numb, in the painfully slow customs queue, we were assaulted by a cacophony of smells—body odor, jasmine, urine, pungent fruit, and sewage, all subtly undercut with a hint of *ghee*[3] and curry.

---

[3] Ghee is a type of clarified butter used in the cuisines of India and the Middle East. It is made by heating butter from cow's-milk to gently evaporate the water. The milk solids are strained away to leave behind only the liquid fat.

Heavy-limbed and burdened with luggage, we finally emerged into the blinding sun. As we fought our way through the surging masses, I caught sight of Wayne and a tall, lanky, bearded Pakistani with slicked-back dark hair and the essential beige *shalwar kameez*[4], a *sadri*[5], and sandals. This was Nisar who was to be our driver—both intrepid and irresponsible—for the duration of our stay in this country. He gave me a quick nod and "Hello madam" as Wayne formally made introductions.

I turned to Wayne and my heart dropped as I was hit with a sudden realization that I wouldn't be able to hug, kiss, or otherwise touch my husband until we were in the privacy of our hotel room.

Expressions of affection between men and women were considered inappropriate here.

Thus began my first experience with TIP—This Is Pakistan! There would be many more to come. Steve Martin's roller coaster ride in the movie *Parenthood* could not hold a candle to the one we were about to begin.

---

[4] Shalwar kameez are baggy pajama-like trousers topped with a loose shirt or tunic.

[5] A sadri is a vest.

CHAPTER 2—DELIRIUM

After a few weeks in a guesthouse with peeling brown stains oozing down the walls eating oranges, guavas, and chicken fried rice, drinking innumerable cups of tea, and sleeping under quilts rancid with the odors of previous users—we were finally in our own home. The gigantic, cool white edifice with an ultra-modern design had been Jason's choice. I was so glad that he'd taken ownership of some part of our lives. I hoped acquiring a permanent home might help establish some sense of normalcy for the family.

Because of the Gulf War and the evacuation of many American families, the American International School classes were being held in a few embassy houses. The children were safer there than at the regular campus farther out of town. However, the situation was far from routine. Teachers were doing double and triple duty because some of their colleagues had left. Everyone was wondering if and when the large percentage of students who had been sent away would be coming back.

Jason and Julie, as newbies, had arrived more than halfway through the school year only to find themselves in an entirely different educational system. This caused a lot of fear and frustration. Julie narrowed her focus and worked harder than ever. Jason embarked on a marathon of watching pirated videos—readily available at local markets—while avoiding schoolwork.

I anticipated finding a better sense of balance now that we were in a house, even though its size made it feel more like a hotel. Pakistanis lived in extended families with lots of relatives to occupy the many rooms of their homes, but there were just four of us. Imagine dropping the house from the movie *Sleeping with the Enemy* into Pakistan and covering it with a bit of grunge and grime. That would be the visual for our Park Road home.

Our grand residence was 7000 square feet on three levels with adjoining walkways, swirling overhangs, and tall pillars. There was a "Juliet" balcony off the master bedroom that overlooked most of the house. A series of tiered windows on the west side caused shafts of brilliant sunlight to scatter amongst the pillars at different angles throughout the day. The house was barren and hollow in the beginning, but we planned to fill it with family and fun.

The living room and dining room were joined by a bridge over the solarium and the four of us had five bathrooms and five bedrooms! Our expansive kitchen was pure white as were all the walls of the house both inside and out. The driveway was a bridge over a sunken yard, 10 feet below street level, in which our landlord had planted all kinds of fruit-bearing trees—oranges, lemons, mangoes, guavas, bananas. Rose bushes unfurled their blooms of deep red and creamy alabaster down one side of the garden wall.

Jason and Julie loved their bedrooms, and I gave them carte blanche to design and decorate as they wished. They each had ensuite bathrooms, Julie's room had a large window overlooking the banana tree and Jason's room had a private balcony, as did several other rooms. A large patio outside a sunny glassed-in lounge/solarium on the bottom floor looked out onto the garden.

Our Park Road home was a magnificent structure and more imposing than any house we had ever lived in. We were lucky to find it after looking at many dingy places that had fallen into disrepair. Many houses in Islamabad were huge, stately edifices meant for large families but, in our eyes, they appeared to be depressing rectangles with box-like rooms. Then we found ours—lofty and airy with bright clean lines.

All this magnificence wasn't quite as it appeared at first glance though. Our "marble" floors were composed of a porous off-white stone that absorbed dirt and stains, with just enough marble-like properties to send a piercing cold through the feet and legs during the winter months. Carpets were high on the shopping list! The tiered windows were breathtaking, but a crumbling decay had set in along the casements and down the walls.

There were open wooden shelves in many rooms, which regularly collected dust and bugs, and some of them had cracked and buckled in the humid weather. We were told that, during the rainy winter, mold would collect in all the corners of the house and the folds of the draperies. The outside walls of the "white" house were also collectors of all the tones of brown and gray in the polluted air.

As for the surroundings, the empty lots on both sides of us had overgrown into jungle. After we moved in, some of our new expat friends informed us that "Everyone knows you shouldn't rent a place beside an empty lot in Asia." I guess we didn't fall into the category of "everyone." There were just too many unknowns. Completing this pastoral image was the *nullah*, or small stream, which flowed behind our property. Good in Canada—not so good in Pakistan. The nullah was also a carrier—it carried all the neighborhood sewage and garbage.

The water and dense foliage provided a great environment for snakes, especially the ever-popular cobra. One morning Julie woke up to find an entire mongoose family walking on the wall below her room. At first, she thought they were huge rats, but after calming her down, we explained that these animals were good news—they depleted the cobra population.

On one of our first drives through Islamabad, I was marvelling at the wide streets and boulevards as well as the abundance of trees and flowering bushes.

I noticed what I assumed to be a treed park and exclaimed, "Oh, look that's a perfect place for a picnic!"

Nisar rather stiffly responded, "No madam. No picnic. That is forest." It took me some time to understand why he gave such a terse answer. I later learned that forests and streams provided quite different functions in our new country. No one wishes to dine in the lavatory.

11

Another discovery had been that all our neighbors used empty lots as convenient garbage disposal. The thinking seemed to be that if the garbage wasn't on your private property and if you couldn't see it, then it didn't exist. This afforded our family a new proverb, "smells overpower even the highest of walls."

From there, we entered the realm of things that didn't work. The toilets often leaked or didn't flush, brackish brown water oozed from the faucets, the showers dribbled, there were intermittent gas leaks, and the power went out with great regularity—sometimes for hours at a time as a result of the dreaded *load-shedding*. In essence, there was an imbalance between the demand for electricity and its availability. Therefore, the power was cut in various sectors of the city at different times each day.

As for the telephone, it had a story all its own. We had the remarkable privilege of having an international telephone line in our home, but it came with an unusual price. Pakistani cities are thick with wires and cables that take indiscriminate twists and turns with no regard for efficient usage or safety. In keeping with this tradition, telephone wires are rolled and stuffed into little boxes that pop up here and there along the streets. We discovered that the guts of the telephone box outside our gate were commonly rearranged/reconnected by various passers-by who could then conveniently place calls using our phone line, "borrowing" it for a while. As a result, trying to dial out from our house bore an uncanny resemblance to shooting craps in Las Vegas. If we attempted to call our friends down the street, we might connect with a tailor's shop or military headquarters. Similarly, if someone phoned us, they might be confronted with a flurry of Urdu from a far-flung sector of the city. Often, the wires were just left disconnected and we would wake up in the morning to find the phone dead. Each time, these problems were solved by weaving our way through a labyrinth of bureaucracy and under-the-table payments until someone wandered along and restored the wires. Add to this the regular occurrence of calls being inexplicably cut off in midstream, static and interference overpowering the strongest of voices, or a sleeping telephone operator rendering the connection with anyone overseas impossible (in that small window of time when humans are awake on both sides of the ocean). I got aggravated at times, slamming the receiver down or even throwing the phone across the room.

At that point, if Wayne was home to join me, it was best to go for a little walk and forget that there were workers in my home checking for gas leaks by caressing the length and breadth of all the pipes with a lit match. Or, better yet, ensuring the power supply was working by inserting fingers or utensils into the sockets. After that invigorating walk, which might involve steering clear of rabid dogs or, more often, being ogled by a series of leering men, the cocoon of home would beckon again. I would resign myself to returning to the less intimidating scenarios of the cook preparing tea on the stove leaking gas or the cleaner knocking my precious Canadian ornaments over onto the unforgiving marble floors. That was just the way a regular day went!

Put simply, I was adjusting to a way of life that I had never known and could never have imagined. I had a case of culture shock on steroids. When my patience was stretched to its limit, I sought solitary stillness and humble pleasures. I would sit with a cup of tea and a plate of freshly cut watermelon and watch the afternoon sun dance across the pillars lighting up the sitting room. I might stand on the balcony and behold the rugged, verdant Margalla Hills, the westernmost foothills of the Himalayas, in the distance.

As the drizzly sulkiness of February gave way to sunny spring flowers joyfully emerging in private gardens and boulevards—sweet peas, irises, geraniums, pansies, gladiolas—my spirits lifted. Another embodiment of growth and renewal was the patch of mint in our garden big enough to feed an army.

In the streets, vendors pushed cartloads of plump, juicy oranges, and grapefruit. Others threw raw corn seeds and peanuts onto a hot plate filled with fiery red sand. The resulting delicious puffed-up treats were scooped into brown paper bags and sold for a couple of rupees each. For a few brief moments, my taste buds would be captivated, and my frustrations would melt away. I'd think maybe I could do this.

Chapter 3—Madam of the House

After the initial excitement and the first blows of culture shock wore off, we needed to get organized—hire staff, order furniture, get the house in order. Wayne and the kids were occupied with demanding challenges of their own at work and school. So, the administration of all things "household" fell to me.

Ordering furniture was easy and mostly fun. We drew pictures of what we envisioned, found reputable tradesmen to create handmade pieces for a song compared to prices in Canada, and eagerly awaited the date of delivery. Then came the hard part—the waiting, the calling, and the stalling in endless cycles.

We eventually had to accept that things happen when they happen. I spent hours of every day just waiting for some *thing* to happen. This went against every fiber of my Canadian mindset. However, I needed to hold things together for the family. I felt like a bridge stretched over a bottomless chasm of the unknown—taut, rigid, and weighted down all at once. It would be quite a while before I understood the value of letting go.

Nevertheless, I was propelled forward by the next duty on my list, the hiring of servants—yes, servants. Not a Canadian term by any means, but that is what domestic workers were called in Pakistan in the '90s. I wasn't used to being called Madam or *Memsahib* either but, again, this was the custom in our new country. Wayne was called *Sahib* or Sir and he was considered the undisputed head of the family by all. This dated back to the days of the colonial subcontinent, and the practice was still alive and well in the 1990s.

We learned early on that domestic staff was a necessity. Why? Well, for starters, we lived in a 7000 square foot home! Islamabad was a dusty town in a subtropical climate with no public bathrooms. Interior spaces needed to be kept clean for the sake of everyone's health. Every day the floors had to be cleaned with a solution of Dettol and water to get rid of dirt and bacteria brought in from outside and to protect us from invasion by bugs and pests. All surfaces, ornaments, etc., had to be cleaned and wiped down daily as well. The kitchen and the bathrooms, but particularly the kitchen, had to be thoroughly cleaned and disinfected at least once a day.

We clearly needed a *bearer*. His (household staff in Pakistan were primarily men) job would be to clean the house, help serve food, and assist in washing dishes. It would have been simple if we could have hired one or even two people to perform all the tasks in our home, but we quickly realized that would be impossible, since until 1947, Pakistan had been part of India, and the customs and culture of those bygone days hadn't disappeared. The *caste system*[6] was a prime example. This practice originated in Hinduism and was even more rigidly set in place during the British Raj.

At the time of *Partition*[7], when Pakistan was created, thousands of Muslims migrated to East (now Bangladesh) or West Pakistan and large sectors of the Hindu population migrated to what is now India. Many expected that Muslim Pakistan wouldn't uphold the caste system. However, it was deeply entrenched in their culture. So, while officially, this system no longer existed, in reality, it was very much observed. Duties and jobs were defined by where a person fit in the rigid social order. Because Pakistan was primarily a Muslim society, Christians tended to be the poorest and lowest class in the caste system, having originated from the "untouchable" caste. Many of them lived in colonies surrounded by high walls, and they were most often employed as cleaners, sweepers, etc.—taking care of the "dirty" work.

Sometimes Christians could be cooks and bearers as well. Foreigners would relegate them to these positions when they

---

[6] The caste system is a class structure determined by a person's birth.

[7] Partition refers to the bloody 1947 division of India into separate nations—Muslim and non-Muslim.

recognized a worker's potential. Conversely, Muslims would never take on jobs such as cleaning toilets or sewers. Those occupations were for Christians exclusively, because Christians occupied the lowest strata, but everyone—Muslims, Christians, Hindus, Sikhs—was restricted by the social order. Businesses, trades, and services were handed down in families for generations. If someone was a brass *wallah*[8] then that was his lot in life. Even if he had the intelligence and the resources to procure a law degree, he could never rise above the station of a brass salesman. This would hold true for generation after generation. *Dhobis*[9], *rickshaw*[10] drivers, *chai wallahs*[11] , these jobs weren't just designated for a lifetime, but for all time. For domestic staff, this meant that roles were strictly prescribed. A cook oversaw the kitchen, a bearer was charged with cleaning indoor spaces, a driver took care of the car—each responsibility required hiring someone who could fulfill that duty according to ancient designations. No one could step outside of these parameters. A guard's duty was to open and close the front gate; it would be degrading and shameful for him to be asked to sweep the driveway.

Considering all this, I embarked on the daunting task of hiring a minimum of seven people. Our family in Canada was under the impression that we lived a privileged life of being waited on hand and foot. On the contrary, I quickly came to learn that looking after the household staff was much like overseeing a small class of ninth graders with learning difficulties!

And so, I continued to write my "to hire" list. For outside spaces, we had to have a sweeper. Driveways, walkways, and patios quickly accumulated dust and grime if not cleaned regularly. Gardening was

---

[8] A wallah is a person who has a specific business or service.

[9] Dhobis are laundrymen.

[10] A Rickshaw is a three-wheeled cart.

[11] A Chai wallah is a tea seller.

another matter, and for that, we needed a *mali*[12] who would look after our little patch of garden, cut the grass, prune the trees, plant flowers, and generally attend to the upkeep of our yard.

When I asked why we couldn't work in the garden ourselves, plant vegetable seeds or whatever, I was told that, as foreigners, we didn't understand how to grow and maintain plants in this new environment. And besides that, we might have the bad luck of encountering deadly snakes as we were blissfully working in the soil. In looking back, I think we were dramatically oversold on this narrative so that our staff could take over the garden, which they happily did. The garden patch became the permanent home of their staple choices, okra and mint.

The most important position in the house was that of the cook. He not only shopped for groceries, cleaned the food, prepared meals, and scrubbed the kitchen but he was also considered the de facto head of staff. Why was this a full-time job? In order to understand, we needed a crash course in shopping at local markets and food preparation.

Outdoor food markets in Pakistan were a visual kaleidoscope. One minute we would be tantalized by pyramids of golden spices and the next confronted with stacks of fly blown dates and sweets. Filthy rags swatted at bugs and flies and fought the perpetual dust that settled on everything. The dissonant calls of ubiquitous crows were a constant background to the shouting, haggling, and bargaining of the jostling masses. Strains of Bollywood music blasting from the competing stalls completed the raucous chorus.

Our spotless, spacious, brightly lit local Safeway had been replaced with Friday Market, appropriately named as it was only set up on Fridays. Tomatoes, cucumbers, and all manner of seasonal produce—nothing was available in Pakistan outside of growing season—were displayed on bits of colourful cloth laid out on the ground as far as the eye could see. Fish and chickens were

---

[12] A mali is a gardener.

18

slaughtered and eviscerated, according to customer selection, in prominent corners of this vast open-air market. Imagine breathing in an odorous mixture of raw fish, entrails, and rotting fruit.

A daily shopping alternative was Covered Market where fresh fruits and vegetables were stacked and arranged indoors. It wasn't as crowded or hectic as some of the outdoor markets, but it did have a population of fat rats that skittered in and out of vendor's stalls.

The meat section of Covered Market particularly seized our attention. It was the single greatest reason that Julie suddenly became a vegetarian. Animals were butchered and hung all day in the blistering heat, quickly becoming malodourous flycatchers. Goats were skinned and hung with testicles prominent to assure customers that they were buying cuts of meat from the preferred male. The *coup de grace* was the butcher. He sat on a raised platform thick with blood and gore, slicing raw chunks of meat with a cutting blade between his feet. He always had a smile for passersby.

Sterilized, freeze-wrapped, Canadian supermarkets were a thing of the past. With no time to adjust, we were now confronted by the earthy and often bloody source from whence came our nourishment. Eventually, wandering these markets, heady with the warm-blood scent of ripe meat mingled with the wafting stench of open sewers and rancid smoking oils rising from vendor's deep-fried *samosas*[13] became a way of life for us.

We never got used to the beggars, often at the entrances to the markets, dressed in filthy rags, pointing to massive goiters on their necks or open sores or missing limbs, imploring passersby for money. We were told that many of them were drug addicts or subject to the control of organized criminals. I didn't know what to believe. There was just so much unrelenting poverty.

After a few weeks of searching, we found other stores tucked away here and there—a little shop that sold Laughing Cow cheese,

---

[13] Samosas are fried pastries with a savoury filling.

contraband items like pork hidden at the bottom of a freezer, and Movenpick ice cream. These special treats delighted us beyond words.

Hiring a cook to help with this weekly grocery shopping had to be a number one priority. He would be knowledgeable in navigating the market culture and adept at bargaining. We were hopeless as we had never encountered this bargaining game before. Nothing in Pakistan had a final price tag. Even more important, the cook had the responsibility of cleaning all the food once he arrived home with the groceries. This was a massive job. In Pakistan food was grown using *night soil*[14] as fertilizer. Also, general standards of cleanliness fell well below what was needed for optimal digestive health. As a result, rigorous and lengthy cleaning methods were required for all produce purchased in the markets. This was the routine: First, fruits and vegetables were soaked and scrubbed in regular soapy water and well-rinsed. Then they had to be soaked in a solution of bleach and filtered water. After that, each item was rinsed again with filtered water and set on the counter to dry. The final step was bagging and sealing all items for storage in the refrigerator. Meat, fish, and chicken were immediately placed in the freezer to kill any bacteria.

Ensuring a source of clean water was a process as well. Water-borne illness was prevalent and bottled water wasn't readily available or to be trusted if you could find it. So, we bought a shiny new five-gallon pot. Every morning it was filled with water and set to boil for 20 minutes. After cooling and setting aside some jugs for the refrigerator, this water was used for drinking and cooking. Replacing rusted pipes and keeping the rooftop water tank clean were also part of the efforts required to ensure a good water supply. A lot could and did go wrong. We came to accept that.

Cleaning produce and boiling water added up to hours of work in the kitchen. And that didn't even include the actual preparation or cooking of the food and disinfecting the kitchen a couple of times a

---

[14] Night soil refers to the use of human excrement as fertilizer.

day. We also had teenage children and our son was a bottomless eating pit. Many hours were spent baking and preparing treats for them. In addition to all of this, the cook, as head of the servants, was responsible for listening to any issues brought forward by others on staff and bringing those concerns to us. The lesson here: whoever we hired as our cook would be pivotal to the health and happiness of our home.

I had two more jobs to fill as well—guards, both nighttime and daytime, and *dhobi*. The guards were charged with protecting the house and opening and closing the gate for vehicles. The dhobi was responsible for doing the laundry twice a week.

As I look back, I realize that it was just short of a miracle that we found people to fill all these positions. Most expats had far more support than we did when they moved to a new posting. They occupied the houses of their predecessors which came with an already tried and tested staff. Embassy personnel lived on protected compounds for the most part and the American Embassy and Canadian High Commission had expansive grounds complete with swimming pools, clubhouses, bars, and restaurants. International School staff had designated housing and longer-term staff members to help new teachers get settled.

We, on the other hand, were on our own. We'd had no family orientation prior to arrival, no housing provided, and no support team of any sort. Wayne's bosses were in Vienna and New York and the local UN office had no interest in helping with domestic issues. We'd been dropped into a foreign land and were told to proceed from there on our own.

There we were, sitting on Park Road in the middle of a Pakistani neighborhood where we knew no one. At this point, we knew one Canadian couple who had managed to locate us in early days and invite us for coffee (wow, did I enjoy that cup of coffee when I only had access to guest house tea), a couple of teachers at the kids' school and the UN representative.

One of Jason's teachers told us that their dhobi was looking for more work and that's how we got Rafique. What a character! He was small, dark-skinned, and wiry with thick cataracts on both eyes. The strength of his vocal cords more than compensated for his diminutive physique. Perpetually smiling and cheerful, his normal conversation involved shouting at the top of his lungs. He affectionately referred to Jason as "boy," and every laundry day, we would hear him booming, "Boy, come and get the rupees I found in your pockets!" Naturally, he came from a long line of dhobis dating back to the British Raj and he had mad laundering skills. The washer and dryer we bought were hooked up at the entrance to our servants' quarters which was on the lower level of the house below the street at the back. Our cook and our driver occupied those two rooms and we rarely, if ever, went to that part of the property. We considered this their personal space. Rafique took charge of the machines, the iron, and the entire laundering territory. He wasn't a big fan of the dryer, so on laundry day, we would find our clothing hanging all over the yard, not only on the clothesline but on every tree and bush available. We had to get used to having our underwear on public display.

We still needed to fill out the staff roster but didn't know how to go about the search. Well, it soon became apparent that local Pakistanis received news through a primeval village messaging system, a sort of drumbeat in the streets. When someone new moved in, the word got out that the newcomers were probably looking for servants. And like magic, as soon as I needed to find domestic help, people started knocking on the door. What a great system! But there was one big drawback—we were completely green.

No one had told me what to look for when hiring staff. I'd never done it before. I hired Hamad as our cook as well as a part-time bearer. I don't remember the bearer's name as he didn't last long. In fact, I went through three or four incompetent cleaners before I found a good one. Nisar, our driver, came with Wayne's work but we offered him lodging in our servants' quarters, so he did personal driving for us as well. We also hired a part-time mali/gardener, a daytime *chowkidar*/guard, Mir Abas, a nighttime chowkidar, and a Friday night chowkidar—guards for all occasions!

Finally, our staff was complete, some gorgeous furniture pieces had arrived, we had acquired a few oriental carpets, and our house was becoming a home. We looked forward to smooth sailing ahead. Alas, this was not the case. We'd been looking for adventure in an unknown land. Life was about to get a little too adventurous!

CHAPTER 4—GIRDING OUR LOINS

I remember those early days so well … Julie playing the shiny black baby grand piano we had purchased from a Korean family, the heady fragrance of tuberoses or Queen of the Night, my favourite, permeating the living room. Jason snacking on cookies and watching videos in the family room upstairs. Wayne working at the desk in our massive master bedroom. The talented proficient tailor I had found would be sitting on the floor downstairs creating exquisite pieces of clothing for all of us on an old hand-operated sewing machine. It sounds like the perfect life.

But if you took a stick and turned this idyllic scene over on its head you would find an underbelly of creeping, crawling discontent, and fear. Julie and I were trying to get used to lives of limitation. We always had to be accompanied by a male or face the consequences of being groped or worse. It wasn't considered acceptable for a female to be out alone, although some of the wealthy Pakistani women flouted that rule. For foreign women, it was a much greater problem.

Pakistan was a poor, underdeveloped nation with a high birth rate and low rate of literacy. The wealthy elite ruled over the masses who had no hope of escape from daily grinding poverty. Because of the tight constraints of extreme forms of Islam, the population in the streets was largely composed of men raised in ignorance driven by sexually repressive norms. Many of them secretly watched western sex scenes on pirated videos or gathered in the back of used book shops where they leered at the women's underwear section of old Sears Catalogues. Jason, even as a teenage boy, was astounded by this desperation.

Julie and I fully covered our bodies when we exited the house. We didn't necessarily have to wear *shalwar kameez*[15], although we had several bright-coloured sets made by the tailor. We could wear western clothing such as jeans and a blouse or t-shirt if the sleeves covered the upper arm—skirts were ok if they were long enough to cover most of the leg.

Pakistani women covered their heads with a *dupatta*[16], but western women weren't expected to do this unless they ventured into the more conservative countryside. We wore full shalwar kameez outside of Islamabad. Women from families that adhered to more extreme forms of Islam, often tribal mountain people or Afghan refugees, wore a Burka. This was a piece of heavy cloth fitted from the top of the head and draped down over the entire body with a square of netting over the eyes. In hues of gold, blue, or dark red they resembled colourful one-person pup tents. My heart went out to these women, especially in the sweltering heat of the summer months.

Over and above Pakistan's societal expectations that women should cover their bodies, I found the attitudes about women much more troublesome. Females were considered secondary citizens meant to live under the dominance of males. Almost no women worked in offices or held high-level positions. Poorer women of the lower castes had no choice but to work in the outdoor markets or take jobs as *ayahs*.[17] Teaching and nursing were considered respectable work if the family allowed this, but otherwise, women stayed in their homes. Wife-beating was a fairly common practice as were arranged marriages. According to Islam, men can have multiple wives, but this wasn't the norm in Pakistan.

Our experiences in Pakistani work and social circles were that the wife was mostly considered an ornament or attachment to her

---

[15] Shalwar kameez is a long blouse/tunic worn over loose pajama-like trousers by both men and women.

[16] A dupatta is a shawl-like scarf.

[17] An ayah is a nursemaid who looks after the children of the upper classes.

husband. In the market or even at parties Wayne was deferred to and I was often ignored.

In those early days, regardless of our conscientious attempts to cover ourselves and make sure we always had a male escort, Julie and I were still subjected to constant open-mouth stares, being ogled and leered at everywhere we went. At times, Pakistani men were emboldened enough to point and laugh or make comments in Urdu. The influence of those western movies and Sears catalogues had somehow led many of them to believe that foreign women were fair game. I had friends who were groped even when they were walking with their husbands. This was not common, though. That kind of behaviour was forbidden in Islam, and if other Pakistanis witnessed those actions the perpetrator could be in big trouble. As women, we were expected to look down, ignore the stares, and never make eye contact with men. Julie and I were able to maintain that practice for a year or so. As time went on, though, we got completely fed up with those expectations.

We were soon to find out that these attitudes about women's dress, behaviour, etc. had been, at least partially, absorbed by the expat community. When a family in our neighbourhood invited us to dinner, we were beyond excited. We were anxious to make friends. As Texans who worked for a prestigious oil company, they kindly welcomed us into their charmingly decorated home. We were warm and relaxed after a delicious meal when the conversation took a sharp turn.

The hostess, Pamela, began gossiping about how young women dressed and behaved in Islamabad. Pamela narrowed her eyes, pursed her lips, and proclaimed, "In many cases, when a girl gets raped here it's her own fault. If her body isn't fully covered, she is inviting this sort of thing."

In total shock, I retorted, "I thought this was 1991, not 1946. Why are we still blaming women for being raped?" We were never invited back.

It was clear that both Pakistani and expat women had to live with checks and limitations. As teenagers, Jason and Julie had to live with other constraints as well. Their parents always had to be informed of their whereabouts. While we were living in one of the safest cities in Pakistan—home of the government, diplomats, and foreign service—there were lots of guns, and attitudes about westerners changed with the wind. My kids couldn't run freely like they had in their suburban hometown. Time away from home was spent at school, friends' houses, the Canadian Club, or the American Club. A few more places were added as time went by, but the kids were driven and tracked everywhere they went. We had to be able to locate them in case of an emergency evacuation. Things could get volatile very quickly.

As a memsahib, I moved in my own little circle. I inhabited the same venues as the children, but I also went to the market accompanied by Wayne or Nisar. I was so grateful for Nisar because he escorted me all over town. I felt lonely and isolated most of the time as I wasn't working and knew very few people—expats or Pakistanis. My whole life revolved around the house, the servants, my family, and supervised shopping trips. It was a drastic change from my life in Canada where I drove everywhere, worked, and socialized with friends. In Pakistan, I didn't drive. Driving was dangerous. Well … there was that one time.

"Hey, mom, Julie and I need to go down to the video store to get some new movies. Will you drive us?" I had been enjoying some precious "me time" reading in our newly air-conditioned bedroom and didn't welcome the intrusion. "No Jason, it's been years since I drove a standard transmission vehicle, it's pitch dark out, and driving here is very dangerous at the best of times."

"Oh please, Mom. Dad's away, and we've done all our homework and we deserve to relax with a movie. Please, please!"

"I said no."

"Please, we won't ask for anything else for a month if we can just do this tonight," he pleaded.

"No!"

"Please!"

"Are you going to badger me all night?"

"Yes!"

"Ok then. But I'm warning you, this could turn into a nightmare."

Nightmare didn't even begin to describe the terror of that short drive to the video store and back. It was dark and rainy, I had a sketchy memory of how to operate the gears, and the kids kept shouting "Mom, you almost hit that car." Or "Mom, that car almost hit us." It was a miracle that we got home alive. I vowed never to drive in Pakistan again and I remained true to my word.

We had been warned from the beginning that road accidents were one of the leading causes of death in Pakistan. It was the reason Wayne had been assigned a driver. Wildly decorated buses and Bedford trucks, originally manufactured by Vauxhall in the UK, painted with realistic scenes, elaborate floral art, and calligraphy were a sight to behold. The buses were jammed with passengers and the trucks, driven by anarchistic madmen, often enjoyed a good game of high speed chicken up until the very last minute.

Driving, in general, was an anomaly for green Canadians like us. Everyone drove as fast as possible as there were no speed limits anywhere. Drivers never stopped for pedestrians, and they incessantly honked their horns. Our Canadian neighbours would have been mortified. It was understood that at any time, the largest vehicle ruled the road. Add to this the pedestrian traffic made up of people, various animals, including livestock, scooters, motorbikes, bicycles, and donkey-driven carts on the road and mayhem prevailed.

At first, we were shocked when Nisar drove down the middle of the road, but we quickly came to understand that, at the same time as he was avoiding collisions with other vehicles, he was also avoiding all the slow-moving wandering traffic along the sides of the road that cropped up out of nowhere.

There was another, more far-reaching consequence of driving here. We were told that if we had an accident or even witnessed any kind of accident, we were to keep driving—never stop! This advice went against everything we had ever been taught and tugged at our moral fiber. But accidents immediately raised a crowd. Suddenly, people came out of nowhere to see what had happened and that could instantly translate into mob rule if there was a consensus as to fault. Drivers could be beaten or killed, and foreigners were particularly vulnerable. And even if one escaped this scenario, as an expat, you could be sued or blackmailed for a lot of money regardless of fault. You can imagine how frightened we were when, during our first weeks in Islamabad, Wayne backed out of the Guest House driveway one day when Nisar was off duty and smacked into another car. We were incredibly lucky. The other driver was an accountant from Lahore, and the consequences of the accident were all settled civilly through Wayne's office. Sadly, we wouldn't always be this lucky.

As we were settling in, Wayne was dealing with his own set of restrictions and frustrations. He had traveled across the world to manage a brand-new project that came with some promises. There was the promise of an allocation of vehicles that would be available from a recently phased out project. But, upon arrival, he found that these vehicles had somehow mysteriously vanished into thin air. Questioning the Pakistanis associated with that project drew blank stares. He then proceeded with the long, painfully slow process of ordering a Toyota Cressida, a Land Cruiser, and a jeep. Eventually, we would buy a Honda Accord for personal use.

Next came the promise of workspace. Wayne's project was under the umbrella of the Pakistani government, so he was given office space in their Drug Abuse Prevention Resource Center. Ironically, the largest stand of marijuana we had ever seen was located directly in front of this building. The rooms assigned to Wayne and his team were sparsely furnished with a few desks and chairs plus a telephone line shared with others in the building. None of this was ideal, but Wayne persevered, worked through a pile of bureaucratic paperwork every day, and started to hire staff. One day, two of Wayne's new employees arrived at work to find that all the desks and chairs had been removed from their office space. The Pakistani government staff in the building had left the UN team with nothing but the phone on the floor.

Since these were Pakistani offices, Wayne had no recourse. After a lot of teeth grinding, he decided to make an aggressive plea to the local UN director for a separate building to house his project. Eventually, Wayne was awarded a spacious home. One problem was solved, but there were more to come.

Islamabad was burning hot in the summer months with bone-chilling humidity in the winter. Most homes in Islamabad were constructed of stone, cement, bricks, and cinder blocks. There was no such thing as central heating, so we had to order gas heaters for each room for the colder months and air conditioners for the summer. Hot weather was around the corner, so Wayne proceeded to officially place an order for office and home air conditioners. The Pakistani government administrator in charge of facilitating this was one of the most difficult people we had ever dealt with—a slippery character with a menacing attitude. He was the opposite of a facilitator. He simply refused to sell us air conditioners, telling us repeatedly that there were too many problems with UN staff buying these and then selling them for a profit, a complete fabrication as far as we knew. We went back and forth on this until I was ready to commit murder. Then it finally dawned on us that he wanted *baksheesh*—a bribe.

This was one of our first lessons concerning corruption in Pakistan and how it permeated every level and every walk of life. When we first arrived, we were surprised at how dirty the money was—rupees were consistently crumpled and filthy, often stained with curry and sharp with body odor. Now we had a deeper understanding of "dirty money." We were to learn many more lessons about this in the future.

Even as we became hardened to some of these realities, we were still confronted with incidents that triggered culture shock. A little village of wanderers set up makeshift tents in the empty lot beside us.

The potential for disease from open sewage and degraded living conditions was high. We placed a lot of phone calls and moved mountains to get these new settlers removed—with eventual success. Nevertheless, our compassionate Canadian mentality awarded us a good deal of guilt.

Urdu was the official language of Pakistan, commonly used in the cities, even though the first language of many in Islamabad was Punjabi or Pashto. In Urdu, they use the same word for yesterday and tomorrow. Confusing as that was, the whole "time" issue became an even greater curiosity to us as newcomers to South Asia. No one seemed very bothered about being on time or meeting deadlines. We found this hard to contend with as both Wayne and I were hard-wired to follow these principles.

Another custom went hand-in-hand with the flexibility of time. Pakistani workers rarely said "no." They always acted as if they were perfectly capable of doing anything they were asked, even if it was something they had never done before. A newcomer's failure to understand this practice often led to disappointment at best and total catastrophe at worst.

Searching for advice and information was a further challenge. Since we'd had no orientation regarding day-to-day living, we had to make discoveries by trial and error. Pakistanis were friendly and polite in the marketplace and out and about. However, it wasn't their habit to provide advice to foreigners. We were supposed to ask questions. If we only knew what questions to ask! A conundrum indeed.

One adjustment we didn't have to make was that of learning a new language. This was a saving grace amid so many other shocks to our system. Due to British colonization, Pakistanis generally spoke English, even if it wasn't always perfect. There were lots of funny signs around town. A few blocks from our house was a sign that advertised, "Brains. The School for Smart Kids." And shopkeepers now and then used very unusual turns of phrase. It took me a while to figure out that "geeloo" was glue. For a long time, we wondered what "tyres" were until our British friends explained that Pakistanis had adopted the British spelling for "tires." The first time we drove through Karachi I couldn't understand why there were so many signs indicating where the bathrooms were. It finally came to me that they were rental signs—"To Let" not "Toilet."

There was wondrous evidence everywhere of traditions handed down from the British Raj. Men in shalwar kameez and the ubiquitous Pakistani mushroom hats could always be found along the medians or by the roadside drinking tea out of china cups. Even if the water was dirty and no one bothered with washing up, the decorum of drinking from china cups remained.

CHAPTER 5—CLOSE ENCOUNTERS

"What do you mean they don't celebrate Christmas there?" My mother was shocked by my revelations during one of our first international telephone conversations. "What kind of alien culture is that?" I tried to explain that Muslims, according to their religious beliefs, didn't observe Christmas. They didn't celebrate nearly as many different events as we did in Canada. In a year they would probably celebrate Eid twice and a couple of smaller holidays plus multiple weddings.

On top of that, their holy day of the week was observed on Friday, not Sunday so our weekend was Friday/Saturday. My mom had trouble wrapping her head around all of this. I finally said, "You just have to live here to understand." Even then, it wasn't always easy.

Take alcohol for example ... The upper-class Pakistanis, those with the money and the power, were very worldly, usually educated abroad, and lived a privileged life that allowed them to blur the lines of strict Islam. Even though it was prohibited for Muslims to drink alcohol, wealthy Pakistanis procured it if they could. In Islamabad, it was well-known that the Thai Embassy provided this service after hours. There was a special guard at the back entrance just for this purpose.

You could discover lots of double standards if you scratched the surface of Pakistani society. Despite being illegal, there was widespread use of cannabis. It wasn't hard to imagine what happened following the sudden anonymous harvesting of the many stands of marijuana that dotted Islamabad. *Bhang*[18] was popular in the post-harvest evenings.

---

[18] Bhang is a tea made from the buds and flowers of the cannabis plant.

Prostitution was forbidden, but it was a thriving underground business. Some of our friends told us a story of how they were unexpectedly confronted with this issue. Lucy and Alex arrived in Islamabad and urgently needed an *ayah* for their three-year-old daughter since they were both working at the international school. They hired one immediately. After a few weeks, their cook approached them and complained that the ayah was going home early, leaving him to look after the child. Deeper investigation revealed that the ayah was hurrying home to manage her other business—running a brothel, which included her daughters, out of her home. Of course, this terminated her rather short-lived career as their ayah.

Despite these hiccups of duplicity, most of the population devoutly adhered to Islamic teachings. Alcohol and pork were forbidden. The *muezzin*[19] recited the call to prayer from the minaret loudspeakers five times a day and each person observed this entreaty to the best of his or her ability. The *mullah*[20] inspired everyone with a sermon at Friday prayers, and people purified themselves and went to the mosque regularly. The month-long fasting during *Ramazan*[21] was strictly followed, and the rituals of the *Eid* festival afterward were joyfully carried out.

We had read parts of the *Holy Quran*[22] before we went to Pakistan, so we had some idea of what to expect. We knew there would be no alcohol available locally. Imagine our surprise when we were informed of the booze allotment provided by the UN. Apparently, there was a UN Commissary in Rawalpindi, twin city to Islamabad, where we could get specialty food and alcohol since non-Muslim foreigners were allowed to drink alcohol in Pakistan in the

---

[19] A muezzin is a mosque official.

[20] A mullah is someone educated in Islamic teachings.

[21] Ramazan is the Urdu and Punjabi pronunciation for the month-long Muslim holiday also written as Ramadan, during which fasting and meditation are observed.

[22] The *Holy Quran* is the Islamic sacred book.

privacy of their homes and at licensed venues. A UN peacekeeping force had been in the country for many years due to all the tensions between Pakistan and India since 1947, specifically monitoring the ongoing dispute over the territory of Kashmir. Both India and Pakistan have claimed sovereignty over Kashmir since partition, and the commissary had originally been built for these soldiers but was eventually opened to all UN staff.

Wayne and I excitedly made plans to have Nisar drive us to this magical place. It was a rare treat to get out of Islamabad together and just relax and enjoy the rural scenery. Lulled by the quiet of the countryside, we were suddenly jolted back to reality when a scantily dressed gaunt apparition with wild eyes, crazy hair, and a garland of roses around his neck jumped in front of our car. Nisar screeched to a halt and gave us terse orders to lock the doors and stay in the vehicle. With that, he was out the door. Wayne grabbed my hand. We were both visibly shaking. Would we make it out of this alive? Nisar walked up to this madman and started gesturing and talking to him. After a few minutes, Nisar reached into his pocket, pulled out some rupees, and handed them over. The road warrior disappeared just as quickly as he had appeared.

Nisar sighed as he started the car. We were jabbering, "What just happened?" "Is everything ok?" Nisar smiled and calmly explained that this "crazy guy" lived on the median and regularly stopped cars and asked for money, a kind of bizarre toll-collector. The cost was two rupees, less than five cents.

After this strange encounter, we were happy to finally reach the commissary. It turned out to be a dark, dank warehouse with sparsely stocked food shelves, just a few jars of jam and dated canned items. What a disappointment! Then we entered the "liquor store" section. To put it mildly, we were wowed! This was as well-stocked as any specialty store we had ever seen with wall-to-wall booze. The clerk handed us a slip of paper outlining our liquor allotment: 4 bottles of scotch, 6 bottles of other spirits, 12 bottles of wine, and 10 cases of beer. We assumed that it was for 3 to 6 months. But no, this was our monthly—yes, I said monthly—allotment!

Wayne and I had never been drinkers. We had barely kept one bottle of rum on hand at home in Canada and that would sit untouched for months on end. But what now? In that moment, we made one of our first big Pakistan decisions. We would start to entertain. We would have the best parties ever. We would meet more people and shore up some of our loneliness. And with that, we filled up our cart.

Soon after this small sojourn, the month of Ramazan arrived. We knew this was on the horizon when we hired our Muslim staff. At that time, they had assured us that the required fasting from dawn to sunset every day for 30 days wouldn't be a problem. Fasting meant no eating, drinking liquids of any kind, or smoking—no indulgences. This was a challenge in itself, but it also led people to stuff themselves after sunset and pray late into the night; then to rise early for breakfast.

After a couple of weeks, many were sleep-deprived as well as starving and thirsty. Sirens went off throughout the city to let everyone know when to begin and end the fast, and tensions ran high. All and sundry still went to work and carried on with their regular schedules. Afternoon traffic became a horror show of cars wandering all over the road—short-tempered drivers raging at each other.

So, of course, Ramazan became a problem for our staff despite all their earlier assurances. It was truly a test of everyone's patience. By late afternoon, the cook was bleary-eyed and staggering around the house, the cleaner was lethargic, and the guard had fallen asleep. From this, we learned another Pakistani lesson, "Nothing is a problem until it's a problem." We needed to escape from the household turmoil.

The four of us piled into the car and directed Nisar to take us for our first family outing, to Murree, a mountain village in the Margalla Hills about an hour out of Islamabad. Murree is a picturesque resort town that was famously used by British troops and families as one of the hill stations established in the foothills of the Himalayas during the colonial period. People had historically retreated here to escape the summer heat of Islamabad/Rawalpindi.

Our drive consisted of breathtaking curves interspersed with glimpses of lush greenery. Jason and Wayne bravely embarked on a chairlift ride that took them over villages and terraced mountain meadows while Julie and I bargained on some Kashmiri shawls. You can see the mountains of Kashmir from Murree.

We all look like sad sacks in the photos we took that day. We were tired, out of sorts, and couldn't eat for fear of offending all the locals who were fasting. Our happiness fizzled into homesickness.

Other trips were more successful. We had started going to the Canadian Club on the grounds of the Canadian High Commission at the weekend. It was a wonderful break from the constant stress of culture shock and the rather restrictive life we, especially Julie and I, were adjusting to. The kids could go swimming while we sat around on the sunny patio slurping ice-cold drinks and exchanging pleasantries with other Canadians.

During my years teaching refugees and immigrants in Canada, I'd observed that, upon arrival in a new country, most people tended to seek out others who shared their nationality and culture. My friends and fellow teachers often questioned why this happened. Why didn't newbies make greater attempts to mingle and assimilate with Canadians? The longer I worked with immigrants the more I understood this need to gravitate to like-minded souls. Now that I was a foreigner in a new land, I had gained an even deeper understanding of this phenomenon. Seeking out others with a similar cultural background helped to alleviate the fear and uncertainty of culture shock. It was soothing to find your home, even for a short time, with others who understood your language, customs, and values.

We were starting to make friends and learn from other expats who had lived in Pakistan for a few years. One day, a welcoming couple from our native Alberta asked if we wanted to accompany them on a trip to Rawalpindi. It would be an opportunity to buy things for the house. Game on!

On a sunny Saturday morning we found ourselves—me in my colourful shalwar kameez and Wayne in his ever-present safari suit—excitedly waiting outside our home as a decrepit black and yellow Suzuki cab pulled up to the curb. Our friends waved for us to climb in and then we could be on our way to a Rawalpindi adventure. Jumping into the taxi provided our first challenge of the day. Where to put our feet? We had never encountered a cab with no floor! We gingerly searched for a couple of strips of metal as we were skyrocketed into the street.

Why were we taking a taxi instead of our own vehicle? Well, "Pindi," as it is known by the locals, is a sprawling city full of hustle and bustle. It is divided into the old city and the newer city established by the British. The shopping area, Bara Bazaar, in the old city was in sharp contrast to the wide streets, lush vegetation/greenery, and precisely designed sectors of Islamabad. Old city Pindi was ancient India—grungy multi-story buildings, narrow streets choked with traffic and pollution, hundreds of people and rickety carts hurrying in every direction—pandemonium in motion. No place to park a vehicle! We were instantly pulled into this vortex of activity even as it frightened us.

Pakistan, particularly Pindi, was our first experience with Asian markets, or bazaars as they were called in this part of the world. A *bazaar* is defined as "a permanently enclosed marketplace or street where goods and services are exchanged or sold. The word originates from the Persian word bāzār. This term is also used to refer to the network of merchants, bankers, or craftsmen who work in a particular area such as "the cloth bazaar." Bara Bazaar was typical of many city markets. Dry goods and general merchandise were found on one side. On the other were shops containing shoes, cloth, vegetables, and fruit. People visited different areas of this market in search of tea and dinner sets, televisions, radios, and cosmetics. The cloth market was of special interest to women.

Fresh from Canada, we were struck by a fundamental difference in eastern and western shopping experiences. In Pakistan, competing businesses were set up side-by-side. All the shops that sold crockery were in one section of the bazaar, the cloth market consisted of rows and rows of shops selling the same types of material, the electronics stores were all grouped together, and so on. This was the opposite of our Canadian shopping experience where the four or five retail clothing stores in one mall were located in separate sections, or at least a respectable distance from each other. After we adjusted to this new kind of shopping, we came to prefer it. It was easier for the customer to find what he or she was looking for and it also made for some energetic bargaining, as shops were always in fierce competition with each other.

We wended our way through a labyrinth of narrow paths until we found several china shops in an area known as Smugglers Market. Yes, everything in these shops had been smuggled in, either along northern routes or through the province of Balochistan. After several obligatory cups of tea and hard bargaining, we walked out with 12 place settings of china, perfect for all future dinner parties.

The next stop was Saad Brass in Satellite Town, a suburb of Pindi. This shop was famous among expats. The owner was a true artisan, fashioning beautiful figures and objects out of brass and copper. You could order almost anything your heart desired—Christmas angels, candle holders, elephants, camels, napkin holders, bases for lamps—the sky was the limit. This was our first of many trips to his shop. We still sit and admire all the gorgeous brass and copper items we purchased from Saad Brass while we lived in Pakistan.

Exhausted from our Pindi shopping trip, on our way home we still somehow managed to summon up enough energy to stop and bargain at a roadside kiosk that was selling Afghan carpets. Thousands of Afghan refugees had settled in Pakistan during this time of turmoil in their country. Post-Russian occupation warlords were battling for territory, creating a dangerous and volatile environment. These refugees had brought their many skills and talents to Pakistan and they were masters of carpet weaving. Wayne and I loved Afghan carpets from the first day we saw them hanging by the side of the road. We eventually found our favourite Afghan carpet shops and became adept at bargaining. On this day we were still acquiring our first treasures. We learned how this game of haggling was an exciting activity for both buyer and seller. Better than a trip to Las Vegas! In the end there was a win for both sides.

Eid al-Fitr[23] arrived right on the heels of our Pindi trip. It is the biggest holiday in Pakistan—like Christmas in Canada—and everyone dresses in their finest clothes and shares elaborate dinners with the family. We gave all our servants some days off and took a little time to enjoy a pleasant outing one Friday, driving up to Daman-e-Koh, a viewing point and hilltop garden north of Islamabad in the Margalla Hills. There was a fine dining restaurant up there, but we had been warned of the intestinal dangers of eating out.

We admired the vista of the city from the gardens and wandered around observing the people in their finery enjoying the flowers and the soft spring air. But we were stunned when we saw several small children run, jump, and teeter at the edge of a concrete wall overlooking a sharp drop. Pakistani families were relaxed and laughing. Our Canadian mentality was rocked by the appalling flirtation with danger. No one around us seemed the least bit bothered.

---

[23] Eid al-Fitr is the feast marking the end of Ramazan.

Median madman, Ramazan surprises, a floorless taxi, Pindi pandemonium, toying with dangerous heights—these encounters that seemed so shocking to us at the time were just glimpses, an adventurous rehearsal, for what was to come.

Chapter 6—Madam Finds Her Voice

May 28, 1991

>*I had to look at the calendar to realize the date today. It seems that I am living in a stupor. Every week one or more of us gets sick with runs or vomiting or fever. It won't stop. Julie is especially susceptible to reinfection and we have had to call the doctor twice. Jason's health is a bit better than the rest of us. But he is angry and sullen.*
>
>*It's been more than two months of unrelenting illness, worries, complications with the domestic staff, shocking observations, outright danger, and aching loneliness. I don't think I can hold on any longer.*

We had only lived in Islamabad a scant three months when I wrote this diary entry. I was a strong woman when I left Canada but, at this juncture, I felt like I had been reduced to a mere husk. So much had happened …

I didn't understand why we were so sick all the time. Life was getting a little easier now that we had a staff and a furnished, decorated house. We even had a small group of friends who helped us to navigate some of the bumps in the road. But one or the other of us had been sick for months. We had blinding headaches, cramps, bloating, diarrhea, fever, weakness, and exhaustion. We got to know a Pakistani doctor who would make house calls, and we gradually learned the names and medications for our bouts of illness:

Giardia was an intestinal parasite best treated with Flagyl. The side effects of this medication were sometimes worse than the illness itself.

Dysentery could be either a parasite or bacteria and was also treated with Flagyl.

Traveler's diarrhea covered a host of bacterial infections and could be treated with antibiotics.

It seemed like these intestinal issues were rotating through our home in a constant cycle. What was causing this? Sometimes we could hardly control ourselves. Wayne and I were out shopping one day and were suddenly hit with such an urgency that we barely made it to the closest hotel bathroom. It was a big problem.

At the same time as we were trying to get to the root of these digestive difficulties, other issues were rearing their heads. Mir Abas, the burly young Pathan that we had hired as our main chowkidar, was having some serious family problems that could affect our safety. But first a little background—because it matters.

Pathans are the second largest ethnic group in Pakistan and the largest in Afghanistan. The majority of the Pathans (also known as Pashtuns) are found in the traditional Pashtun homeland, located in parts of both Afghanistan and Pakistan. This includes part of Pakistan's North-West Frontier Province, western and northern Afghanistan, and northwestern Punjab province in Pakistan. Historically, Pashtuns haven't recognized official borders but rather adhere to cultural and family ties. Living by tribal codes of law or rules of conduct, they are fiercely independent and known to be powerful fighters. Much of their mountainous territory has remained outside of government control. In Pakistan, this part of the country has long been thought of as lawless, the "wild west." The first three principles of the Pathan moral code are hospitality, forgiveness/asylum, and justice/revenge.

46

We'd met Mir Abas at Covered Market where he worked as a carry-boy. He came from a poor Pathan family, many of whom worked at the market as carriers for a few rupees a day. It was especially important to hire guards to protect one's property in Islamabad and, since we weren't assigned anyone by our employer, as many other expats were, we set out on a search of our own. Whenever we entered Covered Market, Mir Abas always greeted us with a smile, and we could see that he was a hard worker. He was beyond happy when we offered him a job as our daytime guard. He was diligent in his work and happy to do any extra chores if needed.

We were familiar with some of his family too. At one point, when I was having trouble holding on to a decent bearer, we interviewed his brother, Mirka, for that position. As soon as that interview was over, Jason came running down the stairs. He had been discreetly watching Mirka from the upstairs balcony. "Don't hire that man, mom. He's crazy." When I asked Jason what had brought him to this conclusion, he told me that he just had a strong feeling. He observed that this guy had a "fanatical glint" in his eyes. We didn't hire him, and shortly after that, Jason's insights were eerily verified. Here is the story as it unfolded:

> Mirka unexpectedly showed up at his home one day for lunch and found his father in bed with his wife. He flew into a rage, smashed their skulls with a concrete block, and cut off their noses (the metaphorical act of a cuckold). He then turned himself in at the local police station and was promptly thrown in jail.

After that, Mir Abas disappeared, and we had no idea when or if he would return. Five days later he reappeared, sullen and restless. We were afraid of outright firing Mir Abas. There was obvious mental instability in his family, and he was brutishly strong. To make matters even more complicated, we heard a rumour that the brother-in-law from the mountains was in town looking to avenge the death of his sister by gunning down Mirka's entire family. Pathans were known for their blood feuds. Every day Jason arrived home from school with the pronouncement, "I see that there hasn't been a drive-by on Mir Abas yet." Could we live like this?

In the end, we didn't fire Mir Abas. We made a deal with him that he could stay on as long as there was no trouble and no one from his family came around our property. He kept his word, but this incident had fundamentally changed him. Bitter and filled with anguish, he eventually left on his own.

Some months later we happened to spot Mirka in the market working at a photo shop. His lips stretched over his teeth in a kind of crazed grin and his eyes were heavily made up with thick black eyeliner. We made a concerted effort to cut a wide swath around that area of the market. Nisar later told us that Mirka had been released from jail after a short time. Honour killings for adultery were generally an accepted practice, particularly if the wife was the guilty party. A couple of months of jail time was considered long enough. Mirka had just been following the Pathan code of justice and revenge.

Meanwhile, we were still searching for the answer to our constant bouts of illness. These frustrations were further exacerbated by the never-ending game of whack-a-mole I was playing trying to deal with staff dilemmas. We had other guards besides Mir Abas—a nighttime guard and a Friday night guard. Their main duty was to open and close the gate. Imagine our surprise when the first guy we hired was on his mat praying every time we went out or arrived home. Of course, we could open the gate but why were we paying him when he wasn't even performing this singular function?

Wayne was adamant that we couldn't fire someone for praying in a Muslim country. I disagreed and we argued this point intensely for weeks. I finally consulted some friends at the Canadian Club, and they informed me that Muslims weren't obligated to pray if they were working. That just wasn't always practically possible. My instincts had been correct. This guy was taking advantage of newbie foreigners. So, I fired him.

Wayne took pity on the next guard and bought him a space heater as the nights were getting chilly. Within a few days, the heater was broken because he was cooking his dinner on it. I fired him. The next in line for this position didn't show up for work for a couple of days. I fired him. When we finally hired someone steady, he found a better job! For a long time, we had a revolving door of nighttime chowkidars. They consistently fell asleep on the job, and I'm sure they would have run for the Margalla Hills if we were ever attacked. The UN eventually decided to provide us with guards but keeping them awake and vigilant continued to be a challenge.

Then there were the cleaners/bearers. I had to fire the first cleaner for laziness and insubordination. My next cleaner was a woman who was constantly being called home for one problem or another. I fired her. Her replacement got "sick" all the time and lied to us about the disappearance of 500 rupees. I fired her. Do you see a pattern here? I was getting good at this.

All those years in Canada I had the impression that Wayne was the hardass in the family, the strong one. When we got to Pakistan, we made a discovery. He couldn't fire anyone. He just couldn't bring himself to do it. But it had to be done. We had to bite the bullet until we got this servant thing right. I stepped up to the plate and found an inner strength I never knew I had. Damn, I was on a roll.

Soon, Peter, a kind, courteous man, and a wonderful cleaner/bearer came to us through friends, and we never looked back. He became part of the family. To this end, staff issues being somewhat stable, I decided to start having dinner parties. I invited Sally and Jim, the Canadian couple who had been the first to invite us into their home and take us under their wings. They'd been working overseas for many years in countries like Nepal and Nigeria and were used to hardship postings like Pakistan. We thoroughly enjoyed our evening together.

Early the next morning the phone rang. It was Sally, "Sharon, Jim and I are dreadfully sick. Your house is the only place we have eaten out in more than a week. I'm certain that your cook isn't following sanitation procedures. It seems that he's carelessly contaminating the food. Get rid of him now!" With that Hamad was out the door.

Looking back, I wonder if Hamad was even a cook. I'd made every effort to supervise in the kitchen and I thought he was doing as I asked. I'd been sorely mistaken. No one we knew in Islamabad had ever been sick for so long. The good news was that our digestive problems disappeared almost immediately after Hamad's exit. We had rare bouts of illness over the next five years, but only when we were adventurous enough to go out to a local restaurant.

I urgently needed a cook and, fortunately, those primeval neighbourhood drums started up again. As a result, one miraculous afternoon Harry walked into our house and changed everything. He blessed us with delicious food and a peaceful home. We loved him instantly. He had a round smiling face, a little potbelly, and a kindness and generosity of spirit that you rarely encounter. He was in his sixties and had been around—working in the *UAE*[24] for many years and then serving as the head cook at the Cuban Embassy.

For our first dinner party, he created an intricate ship out of spun sugar to grace the center of the table. Another night he presented the mashed potatoes in the shape of a bunny rabbit. Jason and Julie were a bit conflicted about eating that!

But we were all so happy to have Harry. He was clean, he knew how to take care of the kitchen and we trusted him. Now that he was at the helm, the entire staff lived and worked in blessed harmony. Harry and Peter were Christian; Rafique, Nisar and the guards were Muslim. There was never an angry word or even the slightest disagreement. We were going to be ok!

---

[24] UAE—United Arab Emirates.

CHAPTER 7—A TRIP BACK IN TIME

Was I dreaming? I was standing in a picturesque mountain meadow filled with brilliant red flowers surrounded by Pakistani men in loose white and beige shalwar kameez. One of them bent over a scarlet bloom, reached in, and scored the seed pod with a curved knife. A thick sap oozed from each cut—raw opium. Although this could be the stuff of a fever dream, it was all too real. Wayne had been hired as an expert in drug demand reduction. Poppy growing was alive and well in the mountainous tribal areas outside of Islamabad.

An official trip had been organized to the Swat Valley, a five-hour drive, nestled in the foothills of the Hindu Kush mountain range—an opportunity for a close-up view of the origins of opium, morphine, and heroin. Did I want to join? Absolutely! I donned my brand new shalwar kameez, threw a dupatta over my head, stuffed several more of these outfits in a suitcase, and off we went.

Historically, poppies have been grown in a narrow 4500 mile stretch of mountains extending across Asia from Turkey through Pakistan and Afghanistan as far as Laos. These days heroin is increasingly becoming an export from Latin America as well, but back in 1991, the Pashtun tribes of Pakistan and Afghanistan were the world leaders in opium production.

Fields of poppies tended by poor, humble farmers in the remote mountains of the lawless North-West Frontier Province generated millions of dollars, as derivatives of raw opium passed through the supply chain. This excursion into a world we had never known turned out to be a defining experience for both of us, creating a tectonic shift in our perspectives.

With Nisar behind the wheel, we started out on wide paved roads that passed through pastoral countryside. After a few hours, we stopped by the side of the road, ate some sandwiches from home, and watched a group of young children slip out of their clothing and dive into the roadside canal. Soon after this, the driving conditions became more challenging as we wound our way up through the steep Malakand Pass then down into the Swat Valley. Exhausted from a full day of travel, we were invited to spend the night at the Mingora home of Mr. Janssen, a regional technical advisor from Holland.

The next day we ascended further into Dir District, closer to the Afghan border and a conservative tribal area that posed a few dangers. There had been kidnappings and they weren't fond of outsiders nosing around the poppy fields. For these reasons, we were provided some protection—a local driver and a couple of Janssen's office staff. One of them, Aftab, knew his way around communal customs.

The Swat Valley and Dir District were truly the Swiss Alps of Pakistan with lush forests and green alpine meadows. The scenery was breathtaking. We were surrounded by rugged mountains, rocky cliffs, and sloping foothills with fields planted in geometrical terracing. We drove through and over babbling streams and rivers as we observed biblical scenes of shepherds tending sheep, goats, and even a few water buffalo. Ancient trees cast shadows over crops of sugar cane and rice. This was Malala country a few years before the birth of the girl who was awarded the Nobel Peace Prize in 2014.

Janssen's staff had decided to take us to an area with large poppy fields. After travelling a few kilometers up a narrow mountain road, we were abruptly confronted with a significant roadblock—trucks, buses, and a large crowd. A couple of men with *Kalashnikov*[25] rifles walked up to our driver and told him that there had been a murder. A community-wide search had been organized to find and punish the perpetrator. All roads to the area were blocked, and we must turn around. Wayne and I were trembling as we scrutinized the menacing

---

[25] The name Kalashnikov refers to a series of rifles designed in Russia, also known as AK-47's. These weapons are exceedingly popular in Pakistan/Afghanistan.

rifles hanging from the men's shoulders and we tried to imagine what punishment they were meting out.

Just then, a throng of people jumped down from the road just above us and surrounded the Land Cruiser, pressing their noses up against the windows. Oh my God! Was this where our lives ended— on a road in a lawless frontier where no one would ever find us? Aftab saw the blood drain from our faces and promptly attempted to calm us, "Don't worry. They are only curious about you." Still, we breathed a sigh of relief as the driver made a hasty U-turn.

As a result of this little snarl in our plans, we changed course to a less-travelled route at a higher altitude. We were on a narrow, rutted road, washed out in places, on the edge of a cutaway that fell hundreds of feet down. We drove for about 20 kilometers like that and sometimes had to stop, reverse, and hug the side of the mountain as another vehicle bore down on us. My nerves were frayed to the last fiber. I was struggling to calm myself when we suddenly caught sight of terraced fields of delicate poppies innocently dancing in the breeze. Their virtuous beauty was belied by the fierce-looking men with AK-47's standing guard over them. Nevertheless, we snapped a few photos while standing amongst the bobbing red petals. The gun-wielding farmers greeted us with smiles, but had they known the nature of Wayne's work, I don't think they would have welcomed photo-ops.

We hopped back into our vehicle—mission accomplished. My satisfied smile instantly turned into a grimace of terror as I realized that our driver was preparing to turn around on the sliver of road carved into the side of the mountain. I swear the tires were partly over the edge of that deadly drop just before the car regained its balance on the road. White knuckles and palpitations seemed to be the order of the day.

Just as my breathing returned to normal, Aftab turned to me and asked, "Would you like to visit a family home up here?"

I immediately let go of my fears and reservations and answered, "Absolutely, yes!"

Aftab offered me his arm and we went slipping and sliding down the mountain until we reached the first house. As we approached, Aftab told me that women in this area lived in *purdah*. In the case of this village, that meant that, after puberty, females were physically segregated from males—except for their husbands or males of their immediate families. Therefore, I would be able to enter this woman's home, but he would not.

We were nearing the first of a series of mud huts built into the side of the mountain. Standing at the entrance between rough-hewn wooden posts was a shy young woman in a worn green shalwar kameez, a soft pink dupatta wrapped around her head and shoulders. Behind her stood six or seven giggling children staring at me in wide-eyed curiosity. She indicated for me to enter and started to speak in a continuous stream of Pashto. At the same time, more women and children were showing up, seemingly out of nowhere.

The only thing I had understood up to that point was the name of my hostess—Fatima. She was fair-skinned, characteristic of Pashtun people, with a round open face, a bashful smile, and striking green eyes. As more and more people entered the tiny space, I realized that they were expecting something from me. But I didn't know what that could be.

Suddenly Aftab appeared at my side. I whispered, "I thought you weren't allowed in here."

He gave me a little smile and said, "They are desperate for an interpreter and I'm the only one available. They have many questions for you."

They indicated for the two of us to sit on the quilt-covered *charpoy*[26] in the corner and Fatima started again with a barrage of Pashto. At the same time, she was touching her head, her stomach, her back. Aftab told me that she was asking what medicine to take for headaches, dizziness, stomach pain, and back pain. I looked at

---

[26] A Charpoy is a traditional bed consisting of a wooden frame strung with light rope.

him in dismay. How could I answer these questions? I wasn't a doctor?

Then he explained, "These women are mostly confined to their village homes. They perform backbreaking tasks beginning at dawn every day, hauling water up the mountain from the river below, washing, cooking, sweeping, and tending to all the children. They bear many children, as you can see, and they're likely beaten by their husbands. They know almost nothing of the outside world and aren't even able to accompany their men to the local bazaar. "Since they have no knowledge of pharmaceutical medicine, just give them the names of pain relievers for headaches, ointments for back pain, and perhaps Pepto Bismol for the stomach. Their husbands can buy these items at the market."

And so, the medical conversation began with Aftab's assistance. The women were hanging on every word. Clearly, they had never seen anyone like me. I'm sure they were all young women but their tired eyes and lined faces bespoke hard lives. I didn't see one clean face among the many children and there was an abundance of snotty noses, but they all seemed happy and content. A kind of magical exchange was taking place in this translated conversation.

I turned to look at the view from the terrace, a sublime mountain landscape for which many Canadians would spend hundreds of thousands of dollars.

"This is beautiful. This place where you live is beautiful."

That provoked much laughter and they countered, "It's only a mountain, nothing more. If you like it so much, then stay with us for one month."

Rattled by this response, I declared, "My husband wouldn't like that. He wants me to be with him."

This prompted a lot of giggles and a quick entreaty, "Bring your husband here!"

Immediately someone was dispatched to bring him into the house. Purdah went out the window that day—a once in a lifetime interaction with foreigners was just too important.

Once Wayne arrived, Fatima bashfully offered us tea in keeping with the first principle of the Pashtun code, hospitality. We diplomatically wriggled out of this obligation as we had already experienced enough diarrhea for a lifetime. Maybe it would have been fine, but we just couldn't take the chance. Instead, we were given a tour of the house.

On the terrace, an area for a cooking fire and a charpoy functioned as the kitchen. Fatima led the way into the dark, unventilated interior. It was like walking into a cave. Bedding, blankets, and charpoys along with a prominently displayed wedding decoration were the sole furnishings of the first room. A second room on the other side housed a couple of goats and some chickens along with some rudimentary cabinets. The family didn't need much as they were either working or sleeping. Plus, most rural Pakistanis ate sitting cross-legged on carpets or blankets laid out on the floor.

Soon, Aftab indicated that it was time to go. We exchanged fond goodbyes and expressed our gratitude for the generous hospitality Fatima had extended to us. Alone with our thoughts, we trudged back up the mountain, settled heavily into the vehicle, and prepared for the long drive back.

I stared out the window at the pastoral scenery and thought about the extraordinary events of the day, especially Fatima and her friends. It was 1991 and I felt like I had just time-travelled to AD 25. It was as if I'd walked into one of those drawings in the Bible stories I was shown at Sunday school as a child.

Aftab had informed me that Fatima and her friends could never imagine the life I lived, the freedoms that I had. She and I had connected for a few brief moments and our lives had again diverged. I still think about her and wonder, *"Is she still alive? Has she found some peace and happiness in her life?"* The memory of that time with her lives in my heart.

As we neared the capital city of Saidu Sharif, we spied a crumbling structure. Aftab explained that this was an ancient *Stupa*[27]. Would we like to stop and look at it? Of course! Back then we had no idea what a Stupa was, nor did we have much knowledge of Buddhism. We were given a quick lesson.

The Swat Valley had a history going back about 2000 years. It was a prominent center of Buddhism up until about the 10th Century BC. This Stupa dating back to 300 BC was one of a few still standing in the Swat Valley in 1991, along with some Buddhas carved into the rocks. We were awed by this haunting ruin devoted to the Buddha. We didn't realize what a golden moment we were having that day. From 2007 to 2009, the Taliban destroyed most of this—the stupas, carvings, sacred and historical monuments from the Buddhist era. This fills me with deep sadness. Fortunately, I still have the photo we took that day to remember this remarkable sight.

The Pakistani men accompanying us wanted to take a break and eat at the "best hotel in the pass," so we stopped for a bit. They bought a tasty-looking stir fry combination of tomato, beef, and veggie curry for a few rupees. Wayne and I politely declined. Our Canadian mentality still couldn't cope with the swarms of flies indiscriminately feasting at every table.

We arrived back in the city of Mingora at Janssen's, exhausted, around 7 p.m. His cook had prepared roast quail stuffed with hard-boiled quail eggs. I was a bit shocked when this tiny bird was set in front of me! But it was considered a special treat, and, after one bite, I found the wild intense flavour quite delicious. It had truly been a day of firsts and directly after dinner, I was content to fall into bed, worn out, my head filled with a swirl of emotions.

---

[27] A Stupa is a dome-shaped structure erected as a Buddhist shrine.

The next morning Janssen informed us that he was going to drive us to Peshawar and then on to Islamabad. He had sent Nisar back home with our vehicle. That sounded good to us—someone who had lived in Pakistan for a few years showing us around. Easy-breezy after our days in the lawless frontier. As it turned out, the two of us weren't even the least bit prepared for the adventures ahead!

After taking in the stunning views of the Malakand Pass and the intricate water tunnels that had been constructed through the mountains during the British Raj, we were on our way. As we passed through countryside villages we took in the sights. We saw an old man waiting on a roadside dentist's chair. He had a filthy rag wrapped around his head to mitigate the swelling from an infected tooth. An unqualified street dentist would soon show up and yank his tooth out with dirty pliers.

For a fleeting moment, we caught sight of some children throwing stones at an old woman sitting on a concrete stoop. We sped past. Janssen had become accustomed to scenes of village cruelty. As a foreigner, he had to gauge how effective his interference would be. Grudges, superstitions, and bullying were ubiquitous and beyond his control.

An official stoning, often a punishment for suspected adultery, would have been a different story. In remote tribal areas, this was sometimes done as a kind of *honour killing.*[28] Stones were thrown until the blunt force trauma resulted in death. Seeing that old woman being abused filled me with sadness and chagrin. At the same time, I was grateful not to have witnessed the ancient, brutal, barbaric practice of capital punishment by stoning. I think I would have jumped, screaming, from the vehicle in that case.

Before we reached Peshawar, we stopped to visit a Pakistani farm. The landowner was a man named Bara Khan, a friend of Janssen's. A dignified man in his seventies, he sported a trim white

---

[28] An honour killing refers to the killing of someone—usually female—perceived to have brought dishonour to the family.

beard and white shalwar kameez with a round white *kufi* skullcap. When he welcomed us to his home, the first thing we noticed was the destruction that had been caused by a recent earthquake. Several of his buildings had been leveled and workers were busy repairing and rebuilding. This was the first time we had seen evidence of the consequences of earthquakes in this part of the world. We'd never experienced this natural phenomenon but were soon to learn that earthquakes were a frequent occurrence in Pakistan, sometimes causing terrible destruction.

Despite his temporary living conditions, Bara Khan invited us to sit on charpoys under some shady trees by a stream. We were served ice-cold glasses of a sweet, spicy ruby-red concoction while peacocks strolled by and servants laundered clothes farther down the banks of the stream. It was a treat to just sit in peace and watch the animals wander around. As we were cautiously taking small sips of our drinks, he asked if we wanted to have a look at his mosque. *What?*

We rounded a corner and, voila, there was the private mosque that he had built for his family on the farm. It came complete with a mullah who bore a striking resemblance to the wild man that had jumped in front of our car outside of Pindi. I was beginning to realize that not all mullahs were created equal. They had varying levels of training. Some of them were scholars of Islam while others resembled religious fanatics with loud voices who spouted vitriol from the minarets on Friday mornings.

Mullahs were supposed to be the wise teachers in the village, but we didn't often see that. Sometimes they whipped people into a fervour—like the mullah at the mosque near the Friday market in Islamabad. We were all told to be careful about going to that area of the bazaar on Friday mornings. Those exiting the mosque might decide to turn on foreigners.

The time spent in Bara Khan's garden was a peaceful interlude. Our next experience proved quite the opposite. We passed a family sitting around what looked like a body in the back of a pick-up truck.

Janssen stopped the car. He told us to sit tight while he checked out the situation. He peered into the truck bed and saw a teenage girl with a large bleeding gunshot wound. She had been caught in a crossfire and her family was preparing to take her to the hospital in Peshawar.

Guns were prevalent in the *Khyber Pakhtunkhwa*, at that time known as the North-West Frontier Province located along the border with Afghanistan, and in Afghanistan where warlords were fighting for control of their fiefdoms. This girl had been an innocent victim of that strife. I had never been so directly confronted with bloody violence. What could I do? If we were in Canada, we would probably have called 911 for emergency help. There would have been a quick police/ambulance response. None of this was possible in tribal Pakistan. Janssen offered assistance. They declined. They would handle this themselves.

How would I feel if this were my child? My heart went out to that family—in the grip of forces beyond their control and fearing the worst. I hated guns. Where I came from this kind of tragedy was unheard of. The worst that might happen was a hunting accident and those were rare. I felt sick and raw and helpless in the face of so much suffering. I hoped and prayed that this child would receive the help she needed.

Hours later we finally reached Peshawar. My first impression was of the wild west featured in old cowboy films. Everywhere we looked, people were brandishing guns, most of all, the omnipresent Kalashnikov. A picture postcard of Peshawar at that time would have been a Suzuki truck with Pakistani/Pashtun/Afghan men sitting along the sides of the open cargo bed holding machine guns. Peshawar sheltered many Afghan refugees at that time, both in the city itself and in the miles of countryside dotted with refugee camps. Warlord mentality pervaded the streets.

I didn't get to see much of everyday Peshawar because Janssen decided to speed right through to the "lawless" part of the city. The farther we progressed into this seedy, dodgy side of town, the more nervous I became. There were no women in sight, just plenty of severe faces and dark shadows skulking around the edges of the street. There had been kidnappings and shootings and I didn't feel at all safe. We had no protection whatsoever.

Here, they sold weapons and drugs openly. Rows of rough wooden shacks displayed sheepskins full of hashish in gaping doorways. You could also pick up a cheap bag of heroin or the automatic weapon of your choice as you cruised along. Wayne and Janssen got out to examine some of the merchandise. I stayed in the vehicle by myself with my dupatta wrapped tightly around my head and shoulders. I had taken up praying on this trip and some of my most fervent prayers were uttered sitting among the drugs and guns of Peshawar.

CHAPTER 8—LONELINESS, LETHARGY, AND LIFE

Wayne and I returned from our mountain trip in a state of numbness that lasted for days. There was a lot to process. Islamabad seemed like the cosmopolitan capital of the world for a while, and the comforts of our home felt like the lap of luxury. Our tailor was working diligently at creating outfits for the four of us—shorts for everyone, trousers and safari suits for Wayne. He made a soft pink silk jumpsuit for me and a black lace and satin dress for Julie from material I had purchased at the cloth market in Pindi.

With the end of the school year rapidly approaching, prom and graduation events were on the horizon. Julie would wear her new dress and Jason was having a silk suit and a shirt with French cuffs made at the tailor shop in Covered Market. Why such fancy outfits? We were beginning to realize that the American International School was the center of the community, and these celebrations were significant and well-attended events.

Benazir Bhutto, at that time the leader of the opposition party, was set to speak at the Graduation ceremony. Jason and Julie had gradually discovered that they were attending a prestigious school with an excellent staff dedicated to ensuring a quality education for everyone. I hoped to begin working there in the fall.

I thought things were getting a bit easier. The excitement of wind-up school year activities was coming to an end and there were no more out-of-town trips for the foreseeable future. Then the long, hot summer set in. We suddenly realized that, as soon as school let out, most of the expat community left for vacation to their countries of origin. It was also the time of year when some international development projects, sponsored by foreign governments or non-governmental organizations, often terminated. That meant other new friends were leaving for good.

We had just begun to enjoy being invited to dinner parties and attending community events and now, most everything involving expat social life would shut down until August. These community events had become an important part of our lives. Local entertainment was almost non-existent—no nightclubs, no movie theaters—not for us anyway. Apparently, the local cinemas were known to be places that Pakistani men gathered to smoke hashish. There were restaurants if you were very judicious in your choices. And, even then, people still got sick.

Because of living in an environment that was almost totally void of local places to go, hang out, be entertained, or socialize, expats created their own soirees in their homes, embassies, or various expat clubs. This filled a need in all of us to shake off the stresses and constraints of what was, at times, a difficult posting. Now, with many of our new-found friends escaping the hot, sticky days of June and July, our family felt like a new and comfortable rug was being yanked from under our feet.

The temperature soared into the 100 plus degrees Fahrenheit range. We could go to the Canadian Club, but all our friends had left and the outdoor swimming pool there bore the consistency of thick warm soup. Even going for a walk was a challenge due to the intense heat. As Noel Coward wrote in 1931, "Mad dogs and Englishmen …"

Nighttime walking was out of the question due to very few streetlights, holes and buckled concrete to trip over, and vicious feral dogs. Daytime or nighttime strolls posed all these challenges but there were also other customs that we found problematic.

There was no smiling. Pakistanis weren't unfriendly but welcoming smiles weren't customary. We'd come from Alberta, arguably the friendliest province in Canada. Strangers always gave each other a smile or a nod wherever they passed. Here, especially as women, we couldn't even make eye contact, let alone say "hi." Once inside a store, place of business, or someone's home, there were warm greetings and some great conversations, but out and about in

Islamabad, I rarely saw smiling faces. Did they lead such grim lives or was this merely a part of their culture? Perhaps I would understand this better as time went by.

Another habit I couldn't get used to was Pakistani men indiscriminately stopping to urinate by the side of the road. A friend of ours told us that there was only one public toilet in the entire *Punjab* province of Pakistan. I never did find out where that was! Maybe this partially explained this "the world is my outhouse" practice, but I'm sure any woman would have been jailed if she had tried this.

The disgusting habit of "hocking a loogie" in the streets didn't impress me either. It struck me as a great way to spread disease. In years to come, after travelling around Asia to countries where men ruled the roost, we came to understand that Pakistan wasn't the only place where these behaviours were commonplace.

Even staying at home wasn't easy. I was still getting accustomed to managing my staff. In some ways, the caste system applied to foreigners as well. When Pakistanis worked in your home, they expected you to project a higher status, to have authority over them and to be neither too friendly nor too severe. The boss, particularly the man of the house, was perceived as a parent. The servants wished to be taken care of, reminded, and reprimanded about their (lack of) attention to detail. If the madam or sir rewarded the workers too much, then she or he was a mark, a softie to be taken advantage of. Servants needed to feel as though their boss was someone to be respected and, above all, obeyed. This was quite different from employer/employee relationships in Canada. It was a fine line for us to walk.

I also had two despondent teenagers on my hands. School was out, their friends were gone, they had no place to go. Their days were spent watching videos and complaining about everything. At that point, our only TV entertainment consisted of Pakistani programming in Urdu and CNN.

When we left Canada, we had an idea that we might fly back in June or July for a quick visit with family and friends. As we got settled in Islamabad, however, some of our new acquaintances, who had many years of experience in overseas postings, suggested that this was an ill-advised arrangement. They said that our children wouldn't adjust to living in Pakistan if we took them back to Canada so soon. They needed to have time to absorb their new life.

The day we sat Jason and Julie down and announced this change of plans, we were demoted to the ranks of the world's worst parents. On international telephone calls, I joked, "I'm surprised that they haven't killed us in our sleep." Joking aside, the atmosphere around our house was pretty tense. So, Wayne and I came up with a new plan, "How about a trip to Thailand?" This picked up the family spirits a bit. Jason and Julie would have preferred Canada, but Thailand would do. I was excited to embark on a new kind of adventure.

Wayne needed to get away as well. He wasn't depressed or homesick or lethargic like the rest of the family. He was swamped with the expectations and goals of setting up a whole new project and overwhelmed by organizational paperwork.

All four of us had been through so much, both before and since our big move. Thailand was a bright spot on the horizon and just a few weeks away. Having something to look forward to renewed the family energy.

Jason had been developing his passion for video and film since he was 13 years old. He used this time before our vacation to grab his video camera and shoot scenes of daily Pakistani life, with Nisar as his driver.

Islamabad was (and I am sure still is) a beautiful city. In the 1960s a location outside of Rawalpindi was selected as a suitable site for a new national capital to replace the more business-oriented Karachi. A Greek firm of architects designed a master plan for this new city based on a triangular-shaped grid with its apex toward the Margalla Hills. Islamabad was divided into zones—administrative, diplomatic, residential, industrial, commercial, parks—and sectors. Each residential sector was delegated a letter of the alphabet (A to I) and a number. These were divided into further subsections. For example, we lived in F8-1. Every residential sector had its own small market of one sort or another. Islamabad became the official capital of Pakistan in 1966; newer, more modern, and richer than any other city in the country. It boasted a large middle and upper-middle-class population, was the center of government administration, and the home of foreign diplomats and international agencies.

When we lived in Islamabad the population was a comfortable 450,000 and you could drive anywhere in about 20 minutes. The Blue Area, which wasn't "blue" in any way, shape, or form—the name was always a mystery—was the commercial hub of the city. Constitution Avenue, one of the multi-laned wide avenues, led to the Secretariat which was the seat of the government. The diplomatic area contained embassies and high commissions including those of Canada and the US. The dominant landmark of Islamabad was Faisal Mosque, sleekly designed as a modern, geometric Bedouin tent.

Located in *Punjab,*[29] Islamabad was known for its parks, forests, and greenery. It had a subtropical climate with five seasons: winter (November to February—highs 65F, lows 45F), spring (March and April—highs 80 to 91F, lows 66F), summer (May and June—highs 99F, lows 75F), monsoon (July and August—highs 93F, lows 75F) and autumn (September and October—highs 85F, lows 60F).

Jason was filming in June, throughout some of the hottest days of the year. Other seasons could bring their own sets of extremes. During the July monsoons, heavy rainfall led to cloudbursts and flash floods. January had the coldest days of the year; the temperature could be as low as 38F. Frost and snowfall, although a common occurrence in the higher elevations of the Margallas, were rare in Islamabad.

---

[29] Punjab is a geopolitical, cultural, and historic region in eastern Pakistan and northern India that is referred to as the "breadbasket."

I loved the weather in Islamabad. It was sunny most of the year. Yes, it was damp and chilly on those December and January mornings when we had to wear sweaters and turn up the gas heaters. The intense soaring temperatures before and during the monsoon season could also be unbearable. But most days we relished the bright, warm sunshine.

During the more temperate months, the red silty soil produced bountiful crops of vegetables, citrus fruits, mangoes, papaya, and pomegranates with the fattest juiciest seeds I had ever seen. In the hot dry months preceding monsoon season, we would be living in high desert conditions, but when the heavy rains fell, all the plants and greenery shot up and wound around themselves creating a dense, humid jungle.

It was fascinating to observe the beauty of each change of season. In May we were surrounded by the luxurious purple blooms of the Jacaranda trees; in September and October, the stunning orange, red, and gold of the falling leaves danced before our eyes. Islamabad was considered an artificial city, not representative of Pakistan, but I always thought of it as a unique place populated by diverse ethnicities from all over the country. Islamabad had a life of its own.

Jason continued to film in the main markets. Covered Market included a food market and various shops all under one roof. But other markets—Jinnah, Supermarket, and Kosar Market—were laid out like Canadian strip malls. There were many makeshift outdoor shops in these markets as well. For instance, in a corner of Supermarket, an entrepreneurial family had set up a rudimentary table and chair plus a basket of tools. Here they made shoes and provided a shave and haircut. Some markets in town specialized in electronics or hardware, others had great video shops, still others had the best jewelry shops.

During this first summer in Islamabad, Wayne and I came to enjoy our Saturday shopping trips in the Islamabad markets. We had a favourite jeweler, a favourite tailor, and favourite carpet shops. The kids had their favourite video shops. There were no North American goods available nor could we have the shopping mall experiences that we'd grown used to in Canada. We began to buy intriguing items that were a fraction of the cost of Canadian goods. We all made an amazing discovery in Pakistani markets. Once vendors in the bazaar got to know you, transactions were often based on trust. If you were shopping for vegetables and were suddenly short of rupees, the shopkeeper would just wave his hands in a gesture that meant "you can pay next time."

Every time we went shopping for carpets, we were always told to take home the one we liked and try it out for a week or two. We could go back and forth with exchanges for as long as it took to make a decision. No deposit or payment of any kind was required until we were satisfied with the product. There was a sacred bond of trust throughout the marketplace.

Of course, Friday Market was popular on the Muslim day of rest. Besides the massive food bazaar, it also included an amazing Afghan market, a large section of which was given over to displays of carpets—hanging, on the ground, rolled up. The Afghan market was also a treasure chest of spectacular bargains if you looked closely. They had all kinds of Russian watches and other Russian paraphernalia. The Russians had occupied Afghanistan for many years. There were also displays of antique glassware. I bought several Iranian vases, some painted with the likeness of the Shah of Iran. Further along, buyers would marvel at all the intricate pieces of silver and beaded Afghan jewelry, downright dangerous knives, and sparkling semi-precious stones. It was a browser's paradise. Much to my chagrin, Jason managed to purchase a butterfly knife. Thankfully, both he and his friends survived this "knife phase" unscathed!

Islamabad also boasted many talented craftsmen. We had purchased some elegant rosewood furniture inlaid with brass as well as other locally crafted pieces. Local bazaars were a great place to buy leather too. Jason and Wayne had leather jackets made for a song and artisans would also make shoes, purses, or sandals in any style you wanted. Our family had never experienced prices like this.

Everything was cheap even though hand-crafted. In the long run, we learned where to go for what we needed.

The best hotel in town was The Holiday Inn, now known as the Marriott. We would walk through there just to marvel at the highly polished marble floors and elegant décor. There was a gorgeous outdoor patio with a swimming pool, the only place in town besides the private clubs where people could don a bathing suit. Foreign dignitaries often stayed here, but for our family, it was the home of the barber that Jason and Wayne used. (In 2008 a bomb was detonated at the entrance to this hotel and many were killed or injured. This jarred us across time and space—remembering that place we had inhabited so long ago.)

Jason went on to film Saidpur Village located on the slopes of the Margalla Hills just outside of Islamabad. This village had a rich cultural and religious heritage, having been influenced in three different eras by Muslims, Hindus, and Sikhs. It was a garden resort in the Mughal era and boasted Hindu temples in later years. Saidpur is one of the oldest villages in Pakistan and has been converted into a quaint tourist attraction in recent years. In 1991 the village contained mud huts with cow dung, to be used for cooking fuel, slapped along the exterior walls. Crude open sewers were running along the middle of the dirt roads. The population included indignant goats, sleepy water buffalos, and curious children. I wonder if becoming a tourist attraction and a "quaint village" has been a benefit or a liability to the inhabitants.

While Jason was busy filming and Julie was catching up on reading and creatively decorating her room, Wayne and I prepared for our Thailand trip. During the preparations, we befriended a travel agent. He wasn't exactly a travel agent in the Canadian sense of the word, but more of "a person with an office that had thick vacation catalogues." We ultimately came to understand that Islamabad was full of people who travelled all the time. Over coffee, at the Canadian or American club or evening dinner parties, we would learn about these travels—how to get there, where to go. We learned how to fashion our own adventures, since it was so inexpensive to travel out of Pakistan and exotic destinations were close at hand. As small-town Albertans, we had never before been afforded these opportunities. Expat life was laying the magic carpet of travel at our feet.

At that moment, however, we were organizing our very first Asian holiday and we had a travel agent who lived on a property with some acreage outside of Islamabad. He invited us out to his place for dinner one evening, which was another new experience for us. Part of the drive there took us along the Grand Trunk Highway, a road we had been warned never to take, especially at night. Wayne commanded the driver's seat and we both gritted our teeth waiting for some kind of apocalyptic event. Thankfully, the trip there and back was uneventful. I'm not sure whether we were foolish or brave or both that night, but we lived to tell the tale.

Qamar's place was surrounded by small villages and Punjabi farms, and his land backed onto a sizeable river. He gave us a whirlwind tour of his outbuildings populated with peacocks, water buffalo, geese, and guinea fowl. His servants prepared *roti*[30] by slapping the dough on the sides of an underground clay oven. It was delicious—soft and buttery—served with a variety of sizzling Afghan kabobs. After dinner, we stood on the flat roof of his house, the typical design of many rural Pakistani homes, and watched the sun go down over the stark countryside. My heart travelled back to the farm of my childhood. I couldn't believe I had come so far!

---

[30] Roti is a round flatbread of the subcontinent also known as chapati.

CHAPTER 9—RENEWAL

The Islamabad of those days had no shopping malls, no coffee shops, no escalators. We didn't even use our basic Canadian computer for the first year or so. The Saudi Pak Tower in the Blue Area was the tallest building in town. We were never sure how they managed. Did they have an elevator? Did they have a generator? Generators were the magical saviours of the rich and powerful in Islamabad. Anyone who had a generator didn't have to do homework or paperwork by candlelight. For them, everything still operated during those long hours of power cuts.

Our little vacation to Thailand would be like stepping back into the future, a time of shopping malls and coffee shops. But first, we had to navigate the local airports and experience our introduction to PIA (Pakistan International Airlines). In the early 1990s, the Islamabad airport, located in Pindi, could best be described as bleak, dirty, rundown, and full of men whose favourite sport was cutting the line. We came to learn that "cutting the line" was the number one sport throughout South Asia. This first experience of it was a shock to us. We would be waiting in line and someone would just walk up to the front and immediately get attention. Most of the time there was no such thing as a queue. People would all just bunch around the counter, shove, and shout. Sometimes we would be talking to a ticket agent and another person would reach in front of us, slap down his ticket, and demand attention. No one was ever told to step back or wait for his turn. The squeakiest wheel definitely got the grease.

Canadians are known to be terminally polite. We were cured of this ailment after a few trips to the airport. We would still be waiting at the Islamabad airport frozen in time if we hadn't learned to join the madding crowd.

After dealing with all the airport confusion, we finally boarded PIA. Here is my diary entry after that first encounter with this airline:

PIA is dirty and smelly; their airplanes are falling apart, and the cabin crew ignores the passengers. We asked if there was any kind of pop to drink and were told 'no.' But when I got up to go to the washroom, I saw the flight attendants hiding around the corner drinking from a large bottle of coke. The washroom was another story—something out of a horror show. Did they ever clean it? The food was even worse. Pakistani curries are delicious, but these offerings had the consistency of garbage slop, the taste of rancid vomit, and the smell of a full, fly-blown outhouse.

I was obviously not enthralled with my PIA experience, and that would never improve in the years to come. PIA had a reputation for terrible delays, rude and inconsiderate cabin crew, incompetent ground staff, flouting of health and safety regulations, poor maintenance of their carriers, and loss of luggage. The list went on. Unfortunately, most of our flights out of Islamabad involved PIA.

We were feeling a bit more optimistic as we approached Karachi Airport (where we would be getting out of this godforsaken plane), until the unnerving announcement, "Inshallah we will soon be landing." Inshallah means "if God wills it." This kind of announcement on any western carrier would have all the passengers on the edge of their seats to put it mildly. But every single flight on PIA starts and ends with this phrase. Thankfully, God willed our landings for all the years we lived in Pakistan.

Karachi airport offered another level of culture shock. I had never seen so many people sleeping everywhere—on the ground, on ledges, on sidewalks, behind the counters. Pakistani men didn't seem bothered about finding a proper bed. You could walk into a hotel or a shop in any city and find employees sleeping behind the counter or even in a public dining room. As I mentioned before, telephone operators were famous for sleeping at the switch. But Karachi airport represented the largest mass sleeping event I had ever seen. It was also a hothouse of teeming flocks of humanity struggling to be the first up to the counters. In short, it was a zoo.

Any stopover of more than five hours, which meant almost every flight we took, required a stay at the Karachi airport Midway hotel. We were shown to sticky, grotty little rooms where we checked for bugs and slept on top of the covers fully clothed. Apart from that, it was fine.

It would be an understatement to say that our family of four breathed a huge sigh of relief when we boarded Thai Air. The cabin crew smiled at us, and all the food and drinks were garnished with orchids. Great start to our vacay!

After a relaxing flight we were refreshed and ready to go. We stepped out of the airport into the tropical steam room that is Bangkok and blithely ordered a taxi to take us to our resort. Within a few minutes, a tiny Peugeot pulled up to the curb. As Wayne sweated it out and grappled with getting the luggage into the trunk, the rest of us squeezed into the car. Jason, at 6'5", had to fold himself in half to fit. Finally, we were on our way. Well, not exactly. We spent what seemed like a lifetime inching through Bangkok traffic. No one had warned us about this. To make matters worse, it was about 95 degrees F with 100% humidity and we quickly discovered that the taxi had no air conditioning.

When we finally reached the highway heading south, we thought, "Ok, now we're finally approaching the resort. Not too much longer in this miniature sweatbox." We did ultimately reach our vacation spot—four hours later. This had seemed like the longest drive of our lives. And maybe one of the most expensive. On the way back we found a comfortable air-conditioned bus for less than a third of the price. Live and learn!

Blessedly, the rest of our holiday was just what the doctor ordered. We'd never experienced a setting like this in our lives. The closest we had come to any kind of exotic holiday was a Christmas spent at an all-inclusive resort in Mexico. But this was exotica plus. Palm trees, tropical flowers, miles of beach, three massive swimming pools, five restaurants, a shopping center, a nightclub, roaming elephants ... Our Cha-Am resort on the South China Sea was everything we could dream of and more. We stayed in cozy cottages with thatched roofs and spent our days sunning, swimming, collecting shells, and gorging on seafood. We loved roaming around the seaside town of Hua Hin, watching skilled masters carve and sculpt fruit into intricate flowers, and receiving the best massages we had ever had. Every day we walked down the beach to watch the fishermen bringing in their catch for the day. In the evening Julie and I went to dinner with frangipani blossoms in our hair.

English wasn't spoken in much of Thailand back then, but service and communication were never a problem. At dinner one evening, Jason and Julie decided to have a contest to see how many times the server would return to replenish their water glasses. I'm sure the Thai waiter won that contest as the water never stopped flowing. The kids must have been up all night using the bathroom.

We knew nothing about Thai food at this point in our lives. We tried their sweet spicy curries and peppery salads—all good but extremely hot for our Canadian palates. The resort offered many types of cuisine, but we weren't adventurous in our food choices just yet. We mostly stuck to what we knew. Jason loved ordering room service. One day he ordered so much food that even he was embarrassed, so he pretended that he was ordering for two. I'm sure the Thai staff neither understood nor cared.

Southern Thailand was a sleepy place back then. The countryside was dotted with fields of rice, hops, and sugar cane, people on the roadside sold fruit and flowers, and after sunset, local eateries attracted potential customers with hundreds of twinkling lights. Regrettably, we could see what was coming. Amidst the Thai stilt houses and floating lotus blossoms, were mile after mile of construction sites. Resorts of the future. It wouldn't be sleepy for long.

We learned a little about Buddhism as we toured temples and viewed Buddha statues and images. The mangy dogs and wild monkeys inhabiting some of the temples made us nervous, but we marvelled at the shaved heads and saffron robes of the meditative monks.

We were typical tourists, visiting the snake farm, the floating market, and the Rose Gardens. This was the first time we slipped through the labyrinth of canals over to the market where everything was sold from floating longtail boats. Bargaining was the order of the day, but we were old hands at that now!

We had mixed feelings about leaving the nurturing comfort of the resort, but Bangkok beckoned, and we loved it! The tuk-tuks, the motorbikes, the street stalls crowding the sidewalks, the constant chaos and excitement. Shopping, shopping, shopping. They made copies of every shoe, purse, and clothing label in the world it seemed.

One day Julie and I bought eight pairs of shoes for $30. How long did they last? I don't remember. I just remember the fun we had that day. The kids stuffed themselves at McDonald's, Pizza Hut, and a few other fast food places. I wish I could go back just for a few minutes to that time—when we were still innocent; before life dealt us one too many blows.

We finished up with all the usual tourist stuff. Wayne and I made a quick trip through Pat Pong, famous for its sex shows, which we didn't attend. The family did have some gorgeous silk clothing made, bought crafts, went to a couple of movies, and viewed crocodile and elephant shows. It was the most comprehensive overview of Thailand we could have had in the time we were there. We filled ourselves with the joy of just being. Then it was time to return.

Back in Karachi at the Midway Hotel, we found ourselves in the middle of a severe heatwave along with a major power cut. We slogged all our luggage up three flights of stairs, tossed and turned in our hothouse rooms, and groggily pulled ourselves together to catch an early PIA flight to Islamabad. As we boarded the plane each of us was possessed of one thought, "I can't wait to be home in a couple of hours." Imagine our dismay as we proceeded to sit on the runway in the penetrating heat for three and a half hours while they hammered and banged on the engine. No coca cola available that day either!

We eventually arrived home, somewhat rumpled, but in one piece. At our cheerful Park Road house, Harry, Peter, and the whole gang welcomed our return. Jason and Julie had their photos taken in front of the blushing pink bougainvillea vine at the entrance to our driveway, brandishing cherished letters from Canada.

We loved getting letters from family and friends. Unfortunately, even something as simple as a letter came with unique complications.

Everyone else we knew in Islamabad received mail from outside the country through a diplomatic pouch or special private service. Of course, we didn't have this option. We had been parachuted in, remember? Mail was delivered to our house via the neighbourhood post office and that posed a problem. Every single letter was opened, read, and re-sealed. How did we know this? Well, we would excitedly open a thick envelope and start reading the news from home only to find some of the pages inadvertently glued together. After finally managing to pry them apart, we would then chance upon a local 'watermark' of sticky yellow curry fingerprints. Who was opening our mail? Why? Did they think we were spies? What were they looking for? We never knew.

We had nothing to hide, but I think some mail that was sent from Canada never reached us. Also, magazines were often censored— pages of swimsuit fashions or ads for underwear had been torn out. This was one of those situations, like the "shared" use of our international telephone line, that we simply had to tolerate.

In later years, we found out that we had been lucky to receive mail of any sort. A friend of ours once had a chance to get a rare glimpse at the inside workings of the local post office. He told us that he saw letters and all sorts of packages scattered high and low— some of them sitting in puddles of water. In the final analysis, our mail delivery was probably nothing short of a miracle.

Chapter 10—Settling In

After our Thailand trip the start of school was still a month away, but the break had done us all good. We were refreshed and felt more settled. It helped a lot that we finally had a satellite dish installed and it delivered Super channel, movie networks, CNN, and BBC. Heaven! Not only that, but we finally had a chance to set up our Canadian speaker system and the echoes of our much-loved tunes soon reverberated off the walls, pillars, and ceiling fans throughout the house.

Our shipment had been sitting in Karachi for months, so it felt like Christmas Day when all this reached us—our precious belongings. It took us a long time to get organized after our small consignment of kitchen stuff, bedding, towels, and some personal items from Canada had finally arrived. The speaker system had been problematic. Not because we didn't know how to assemble it but rather due to electrical challenges. We were so naïve from the start.

In the months before leaving Canada, we went to Radio Shack, and, trusting their expertise, bought adaptors. We understood that the voltage in Canada was 110 as opposed to Pakistan's 220. However, the first couple of days in the Islamabad Guest House revealed our (and Radio Shack's) utter ignorance about the whole voltage thing.

Wayne and I had been deep in conversation about how we might begin to find a family home in Islamabad when we were jolted by a blood-curdling scream from the other room. Julie burst through our door crying in pain. She had almost electrocuted herself using the Canadian hairdryer with our new adaptors. After calming her down and making sure she was okay, we approached the manager of the Guest House about the problem. He pointed out that the adaptors we'd purchased in Canada were for the plugs. They had nothing to do with converting or regulating voltage. Whaaat!? Oh well, Julie was still alive, and we didn't need hairdryers anyway.

Then we moved into the house and eventually received our goods from Canada. We had purchased both large and small appliances in Pakistan so our electrocution problem at the Guest House had been forgotten. One evening, shortly after the Canadian luxuries arrived, we were preparing to watch a movie and joyfully plugged in the beloved popcorn machine that had traversed oceans to get to us and blam! It died in a dramatic show of sparks and smoke.

This time, we had a few friends to ask for advice. And that's how we found out about transformers, those miraculous little boxes that converted voltage and regulated flow during surges that were a necessity for North Americans in Pakistan. Wayne went right out and purchased a few. From then on, our home was a place of electrical peace and happiness. We could watch TV and listen to music without being blown to kingdom come.

Another heart-in-the-mouth incident occurred during the sultry sweltering month of July. A large window at the bottom of the house overlooking the garden patio had cracked during one of Islamabad's earthquakes. Many of these were small tremors that we barely felt, but multiple shakes often created shifts and cracks. Our window had been cracked for a while before the landlord decided to fix it. Then, suddenly, one day, a crew of Pakistani men appeared with a replacement window. Hallelujah!

We peered outside and saw two men in baggy shalwar kameez and flimsy sandals walking along our ten-foot-high concrete wall carrying a seven-by-eight-foot piece of glass with their bare hands. The wall was only about a foot wide. They had to balance on this for about 50 feet until they reached the spot in the garden where they could hand the glass down to two of their friends who were also bare-handed. All four were nonchalant as they carried out this task— not one bit of caution or hesitation. Wayne and I held our breath. We had visions of hands or feet cut in half as shards of glass sliced through bone. Happily, none of these gory imaginings took place. The window was installed and off they went, casually preparing for the next duty on the daily roster.

During this monsoon season, we also learned a little more about inequality—the Canadian variation. After we got settled in Islamabad, we were told that, as Canadian citizens, we had access to the British doctor at the Canadian High Commission. We had been to see her a couple of times and she was in the process of administering a series of Hepatitis B injections to our family. Our second shot was due right around the time we arrived home from Thailand.

We reached the Canadian High Commission on the appointed day only to find out that the British doctor was on vacation and a Pakistani doctor had taken her place. Dismissively, he informed us that he'd used up all the vials of Hepatitis B serum. We were shocked! The High Commission doctor had assured us that the vaccine would be available when we returned.

This doctor clearly had no time for us and rudely turned on his heels, waving us off. I immediately saw red. As a woman, I'd been brushed off one too many times since arriving in Pakistan. At that moment I lost control of my senses and my mouth. I exclaimed, "Screw off!" as we stomped out of the room.

The result of all this? He reported us to the upper echelons at the High Commission and someone from those lofty corridors decided that we would no longer have access to the High Commission doctor. Wayne wasn't a diplomat and neither of us was employed by any Canadian institution. The High Commission officials informed us that they had been doing us a favour by allowing us to use their facilities and their doctor. Of course, I should have been more judicious and controlled my anger but believe me, I wasn't the first expat to express frustrations in Pakistan. Or at the High Commission for that matter.

We had just learned our first lesson regarding the class system at Canadian Embassies and High Commissions. Within Canada, just having Canadian citizenship meant that you had access to all Canadian institutions. Outside of Canada, not so much. High Commission staff, by virtue of having their housing on that compound, felt that everything on that property, including the Canadian club facilities and swimming pool, belonged to them.

All other Canadians were invited there at the discretion of High Commission people. Of course, most of the Canadians in Islamabad went to the Canadian club on the weekends. But there was always a subtle relegation of status. We outsiders needed to be grateful for the opportunities bestowed upon us.

As for our medical situation, we found Pakistani doctors to look after us and we became adept at diagnosing and prescribing medications for ourselves. Pakistani pharmacies were fully stocked; you didn't need a doctor's prescription for anything. We researched the uses of antibiotics and remedies for our ailments and proceeded to purchase whatever was needed. Most medications needed in Pakistan were for intestinal illnesses anyway. The ban from High Commission medical services lasted for close to a year and then it eased off. We were once again "allowed" to see the doctor. By that time, we had learned to keep our heads down and our mouths shut.

Another Islamic holiday was coming up on the calendar, *Eid al-Adha* or sacrificial Eid. This second Eid is celebrated worldwide and considered the holier of the two. It honours Ibrahim's, Abraham in the Christian bible, willingness to sacrifice his son Ishmael (Isaac) to God. At the last moment, God substitutes a ram for the child. In commemoration of this intervention, each Muslim family ritually sacrifices an animal, usually a sheep, and divides it into three parts. One share is for the poor and needy, another is for relatives and the third is for the family. Sometimes, depending on the wealth of the family, more than one animal is sacrificed.

Prior to this event, the live animal markets are remarkably busy as everyone is acquiring sheep, goats, and oxen to fatten up for Eid. Our guards were fattening up a couple of sheep on the median across from our house. On the appointed day, after prayers, the head of the family slits the animal's throat and cuts it up.

Anyone with a delicate stomach would be advised not to walk outside for a few days as the streets run with the blood of ritual sacrifice. After you get beyond your squeamishness, though, you come to realize that this is one time of year that rich and poor alike can dress in their finest clothes and fill their bellies.

The dates for Islamic holidays and celebrations varied from year to year. In 1991, *Muharram* followed soon after Eid al-Adha. Some background is required to understand the significance of Muharram. There are two major denominations in Islam—Sunni and Shia. Sunni Muslims are the majority in Pakistan but there are a number of Shias as well. Sometimes there is a conflict between the two groups due to differing beliefs. This is the historical reason for ongoing tension between Saudis and Iranians. The former are majority Sunni, and the latter are majority Shia.

A primary example of the Sunni and Shia divergence of beliefs is how they mark Muharram. For Sunni Muslims, the month of Muharram is the beginning of the Islamic New Year which symbolizes peace and reflection. For those who follow the Shia branch of Islam this month also represents a solemn commemoration of the death of the Prophet's grandson, Husayn ibn Ali (Husayn son of Ali).

During the days of Muharram, all Muslims will take some time for fasting and prayers. But Shia Muslims grieve the death of Husayn ibn Ali on the Day of Ashura. Sometimes, young men will gather in the street and flagellate themselves with razors attached to ropes. They often fall into a frenzy or a trance.

We were warned that it was dangerous to go anywhere near these demonstrations of self-punishment. One of our friends took surreptitious photos of the blood-drenched bodies of men whipped into a fever pitch of hysteria. They were terrifying. Our family made every effort to avoid these small pockets of madness during our time in Islamabad. Our Canadian teenage children couldn't understand why anyone would want to carry out such barbaric customs. They didn't realize that self-flagellation had once been practiced in the Catholic church. In modern times, the practice of flagellation is widely condemned by the majority of Muslims and Christians.

On a happier note, just before school started Nisar invited us to visit his family home in the mountain holiday town of Nathia Gali in the district of Abbottabad. About a two and a half hour drive out of Islamabad, at an elevation of 8200 feet, the area proudly displays forests of pine, walnut, oak, and maple trees. We were told that monkeys, leopards, and a variety of birds live in these forests, but despite taking a few long walks, we didn't see much wildlife.

The mountains, streams, and forest scenery reminded us of Banff in Alberta, only much more rugged. Villages were terraced all down the mountainsides with bazaars at the top along the main roads. Children sold strawberries and roasted corn along the roadside. We took a photo of Nisar's family home way down in the valley. Our Canadian legs wouldn't take us there, but we did meet his father and some of his family at a new restaurant they had just opened.

We stayed at the best hotel in town, *Greens*, none too clean by our standards but adequate for one night. The next day we stood on the border between Punjab and, what was then known as North-West Frontier Province and bought intricately carved mountain walking canes at the local market. We stopped at St. Mathews—a quaint wooden church built by the British in 1900, Ayubia National Park with its famous chairlift, and then it was back home to Park Road to prepare for the next phase of our lives. We thought we were ready for anything!

CHAPTER 11—A WHOLE NEW WORLD

We still have copies of Jason's videos of Pakistan in 1991. The early ones are fascinating—a teenager's perception of a new world that had been totally beyond his wildest imaginings just a few months previous. One scene in all this footage eternally captivates me:

> There they are, Jason and Julie, in the TV room of our expansive Park Road house. The speaker system from Canada has recently been set up, and they are alone for a while. Jason finds what he's looking for, presses play, and turns up the volume. "Like a Prayer" by Madonna pulsates through the bare rooms. They start dancing around and lip-synching. They are young, beautiful, and spirited. All the mystery of their lives is just out of reach, over the horizon. In their dancing and teenage goofiness, you can palpably feel their loneliness and longing for home, their need to be with friends, their momentary soul connection with the music. They needed roots. We all needed roots.

And the next thing we knew, the world shifted once again. It was the start of a new school year and, with that, another portal opened in our journey.

The American international school in Islamabad was where most of the expats and wealthy locals sent their children to be educated, known as the International School of Islamabad. It was ISI when we lived there but is now referred to as ISOI. The abbreviation for the intelligence service in Pakistan is ISI so I assume that's why they inserted the "O."

A K-8 school was established in Rawalpindi in 1965 for the US Military Advisory Aid Group. In 1970 they decided to move the school to Islamabad and in 1975 the current school was built and located on a 23-acre site on the outskirts of the city. It became the prominent international school in the area, accepting, not only expat American children but students from countries around the world as well as local Pakistanis. ISOI was, and is, a striking architecturally-designed enclosed campus divided into three quadrants or quads— elementary, middle school, and high school. We were told that the site was designed so that the quads looked like the guls (an angular medallion-like design) of an Asian carpet from the air. Also, this design would make it easier for future additions in keeping with the carpet theme.

There were classrooms and outdoor hallways around the perimeter of each quad with peaceful green areas, flowering trees, and ponds in the center. In the early and mid-90s, ISOI boasted a gymnasium, an auditorium with excellent staging capabilities and great acoustics, an open-air theater, playing fields, library, computer room, and cafeteria. In 1994 they added a six-lane swimming pool.

Before we got to Pakistan, we learned that ISOI was one of the best schools in South Asia with excellent academic staff and a history of leadership among international schools. We had completed a long-distance interview with the high school principal who told us that ISOI was a college prep school with an American curriculum and Advanced Placement classes. Class sizes were small, and students received a lot of individual attention. As such, all pupils were closely monitored, and problems and learning difficulties were dealt with promptly. Students and teachers generally wore western-style clothing at the school, but any type of dress was acceptable if it was conservative.

When the kids and I first arrived in Islamabad, it turned out to be the last week of the Gulf War. As I stated earlier, for a short time

Jason and Julie attended school in American Embassy housing because that was considered safer. Before the end of that school year, the students and staff were able to move back to the original campus, but school life still hadn't swung back to normal—too many Americans were still missing, still on evacuation back in the US.

Arriving at ISOI for the new school year in August was a real turning point for our family. Many students and teachers had returned, other newbies had come from various countries as international projects opened once again, and there was an air of excitement and renewal on campus. For returnees, life was merely getting back to normal, but our family was about to experience what the school meant to the entire community. During the five years we lived in Pakistan, ISOI recorded its highest enrolment of more than 600 students.[31]

The best news of 1991 was that I had the opportunity to begin teaching at ISOI. Our house and staff were sorted. The kids and Wayne were focused on school and work. I needed meaningful work in my life, too—a chance to get out, make a difference, and find friends. In retrospect, I don't know how I would have managed in Islamabad without my job. It provided me with independence, freedom, and a sense of self-worth that I otherwise might not have enjoyed as a foreign woman in Islamabad.

Some foreign spouses didn't work outside of their homes. Perhaps they were happy with that and felt fulfilled in other ways. I don't know how they managed. Without a job, I would have been largely confined to the house unless I was accompanied by Wayne or the driver to other, specified, venues. I wouldn't have had an intellectual or creative outlet. What would I have done? Micromanaged my family and the household staff? Spent endless hours playing cards with other ladies? I think I would have lost my mind!

---

[31] Recent years ISOI has seen a decrease in enrolment due to terrorist events and unrest in the region. However, standards of excellence have never fallen. In fact, they are probably higher than ever.

Fortunately, this was never to be my fate. I was hired to teach middle school and high school ESL (English as a second language). My degree said that I was a Drama and English teacher, but I had taught and designed curricula in ESL for five years prior to our move. In a small room tucked away in the corner, I was to be the sole teacher for all upper school students, grades 6 to 12, who needed to garner enough English language skills to survive and graduate from this highly academic school. I would also be responsible for teaching an ESL version of the ninth grade World History class.

This was a tall order as ISOI didn't have a massive enrolment of non-English speakers and, therefore, none of my classes were homogeneous groupings. Every class was made up of students at the same grade level but with widely varying English language skills— beginner to medium to advanced. Students would enter my classroom, and I would then group them according to proficiency and teach individual programs to each group. I was also responsible for testing, placement, and decisions about when students were ready to leave behind the security of their ESL classes. I loved every minute of it!

My boss was Mike, the high school counsellor. He administered the Counselling office, Registrar's office, ESL and Reading programs, Learning Support, School Psychologist, and the School Nurse—a motley crew of Pupil Personnel Services or PPS. Towards the end of my time there we were bequeathed a much simpler name, Student Services.

Mike was new to ISOI that year as well, and was, hands down, the best boss I ever had, always kind and willing to listen or give advice if asked. But mostly, he let me be me. He trusted me to run my program and make decisions as I saw fit. Because I had that kind of autonomy, I flourished as a teacher. I will be forever grateful for those years working with him and my little group of beloved colleagues. Mike is no longer with us, but I always think of him with a warm smile. I get ahead of myself....

There was an influx of new staff at ISOI. I think the interruption of the Gulf War had put things on reset and left room for new blood. During orientation week for teachers, we had some initial sessions in the auditorium. The first morning we were asked to stand up and introduce ourselves. One by one, people rose from their seats and talked about their degrees, their credentials, and their many career accolades and awards. Most of the teachers were American.

I was dumbfounded. I had taught for many years in Canada and never experienced anything like this. I started sweating profusely, trying to think about what I was going to say. In Canada, I had never been encouraged, more like discouraged, to proudly list my accomplishments in a public setting.

When it rolled around to my turn, I gave a bare-bones sketch of my teaching career and quickly sat down. I never did learn how to "blow my own horn," as my grandmother used to say. Maybe it wasn't just a Canadian thing, maybe it was a family thing too—good old Scottish values.

Those early days were also my first lessons about the hierarchy at international schools. There were three kinds of teacher—the overseas hire, the local hire, and the host-country staff.

Overseas hires were teachers employed by recruiting fairs in various cities across the US at specified times of the year. International schools sent superintendents or principals to these events to interview and vet candidates for teaching positions at their schools. It was, and is, a highly competitive environment. Schools often like to hire married couples as they can fill two positions at once. Credentials, overseas experience, and reputation can make all the difference.

I fell into the category of local hire. These teachers had followed their spouses to overseas postings and usually approached the school in search of a position. My colleague, Liz, bright, blond, and cheerful, was the primary/elementary ESL teacher. She hailed from Manchester, England, and was also a local hire. I like to think that both of us did an excellent job of being the ESL resource people for the entire school. I know that Liz did.

The third category was the Pakistani staff, and there were some superb Pakistani teachers at ISOI. Besides that, there was a large population of Pakistani staff who worked as teaching assistants and tech assistants who operated the printer, delivered projectors, etc., cafeteria staff, maintenance workers, security staff, janitorial workers, malis, drivers, auto workers, and business office employees. The teaching assistants were largely educated young women from wealthy open-minded families. For them, working at an international school was considered a great opportunity. I think most of the Pakistani workers enjoyed being at the school.

Overseas hire teachers tended to be a tight-knit group who often exclusively socialized with each other, particularly if they had started in the same school year. There was a subtle underlying message that they were at the top of the staff hierarchy. A handful of teachers from the other two categories were able to straddle the spaces between groups, but sometimes it was complicated.

My friendships on staff tended to be with those I found the most personable and down-to-earth no matter the category. Everyone at ISOI respected those that put in time and energy and excelled at their work. I enjoyed my job and the atmosphere at the school, plus I didn't believe in a hierarchy when it came to teaching. Almost everyone at ISOI was a top-notch employee who worked in a spirit of cooperation. For the time being that was good enough for me.

Jason and Julie were finding their way, making new friends, and taking part in school activities. They had a much better understanding of the courses they were taking as they were now starting at the beginning just like everyone else. Julie, the cute new girl in high school, garnered a lot of male attention. In no time she found her first boyfriend, Brian, whose father worked for USAID. He was in Jason's class and the two of them became good friends as well.

As a result of having more American friends, Jason and Julie were often invited to swim and hang out at the American Club on their extensive embassy grounds. There were abundant gardens around an Olympic-size swimming pool, tennis courts, and restaurant. It was such a pleasure to be able to spend time there. Security was tight as the embassy had been burned and some were killed in a 1979 attack. Upon arrival at the gates, people and vehicles were checked and visitors needed a reason to be there. Other embassies in Islamabad didn't have this kind of security in place in the '90s. Even the entrance to the diplomatic area where most of the embassies were located wasn't secured. The American Embassy grounds also featured a large baseball diamond, and Wayne joined a slow pitch team for weekend games. He was often the pitcher and I worried about accidents. Sometimes they were playing against marines! At one point he thought he had cracked ribs after a ball hit him at some velocity. But he recovered as he always did after these little "baseball mishaps."

Fridays at the American club were an eagerly anticipated treat. After the game, we would often go for dinner at the spacious outdoor restaurant with friends. It was larger and offered more selections than our Canadian counterpart. We loved spending time at both clubs, though, enjoying activities, laughter, and fun after a week of hard work.

Wayne's project work was running much more smoothly as well. He had a well-educated professional staff and first-rate private office space. I always marvelled at the level of care that was afforded a boss in Pakistan. Someone was designated to serve him tea and there was even a person employed to stand at the entrance and carry the boss's briefcase upon arrival and departure.

His driver was responsible for the car and was also sent on errands such as banking and paying bills or anything else that required dealing with bureaucracy and long lines. There were long lines at every public service building in Islamabad due to the mind-numbing, crippling levels of paperwork required for every business transaction. We always wondered if these bloated administrative procedures had been handed down from the British Raj. Whatever it was, we had to be prepared for the inevitable wait, since all official business took an inordinately long time.

As a teacher, I didn't have all of Wayne's privileges, nor did I want them, but I learned an important lesson one day at school. I was in a hurry and I had a lot of binders and bags to cart across campus to a meeting. One of the teaching assistants was hanging around, and I innocently asked her if she could help me by carrying my school bag. She was indignant. How dare I ask her to perform such a menial task! I might as well have asked her to sweep the floor, the lowliest of jobs in the caste system. I apologized profusely. I had momentarily forgotten where I was. I didn't make that mistake again.

CHAPTER 12—LIVING THE EXPAT LIFE: PAKISTAN STYLE

Our days were settling into a rhythm. We all rose early in the morning, and Harry served breakfast at our elegant dining room table complete with a centerpiece of artistically arranged flowers, compliments of Peter. The four of us ate our meals together, never interrupted by television or phone calls. It was our family bonding time and it brought us closer every day.

After breakfast, Jason and Julie caught the school bus at the end of our street—they enjoyed the camaraderie of the ride—while I was driven to school by Nisar. Wayne drove himself to work and most days he went home for lunch. He'd decided that he could manage driving around Islamabad for the most part and that freed Nisar to drive other staff members or attend to errands. Nisar also took me back and forth to school as I stayed on at work long after the kids had gone home. After dinner, we all sat down at the desks in our bedrooms and worked—the kids and I did homework and Wayne forged ahead with never-ending paperwork. Sometimes this was completed by candlelight due to load shedding.

Most days passed in this peaceful routine, but Islamabad was always full of surprises. Big earthquakes were few and far between. However, tremors were a regular occurrence. I would often be sound asleep and suddenly waken thinking, "Why is Wayne tossing and turning so much?" or "Who's moving the bed." Once I finally realized that it was a tremor, I had to decide whether to leap out of bed or just lie there and let it pass. Of course, I should have quickly moved to safety every time. You never know how serious a "little quake" can become. Unfortunately, humans adapt to these shakes and become too lazy to move.

Another recurring phenomenon in Islamabad was random gunfire, mostly at night. Where were all the guns coming from? A town named Darra Adam Khel outside of Peshawar in the Khyber

Pakhtunkhwa was notorious for its bazaars packed with gunsmiths and weapons merchants. They sold everything from anti-aircraft guns and hand grenades to automatic rifles and pen guns. In tiny rooms, men made accurate working copies of every type of gun in the world using primitive tools. Thus, Afghans and Pakistanis had easy access to all kinds of weapons. Many Pashtun men considered guns to be part of their everyday work attire, in the same manner a Wall Street businessman would carry a briefcase.

Nowadays, I'm sure that it's dangerous and downright forbidden for foreigners to venture into Darra. Back then, expat men would organize day trips into that town so they could try out all the different firearms. These trips were nothing but a lark, and as far as I know, no one purchased a gun. But they could have. And they probably could have boarded a local flight with a gun in hand too, as long as it wasn't loaded. After all, some rules had to be observed!

Most of the time, guns were used at celebrations, notably weddings. Those nighttime gunshots that we ultimately learned to sleep through were usually activated by exuberant wedding guests. And, occasionally, we would open the morning newspaper to the headlines *Groom Shot Dead at Wedding*. Of course, no one shot him on purpose. There was truly little thought given to where the bullets might land when a gun was shot into the air. It's a miracle there weren't more "celebration casualties."

Since we were acclimating to living life on the edge, Wayne and I decided that we would venture forth on a few more day trips. First on the agenda was Rohtas Fort. It was built in 1541 by Sher Shah Suri, the emperor who introduced the currency of the rupee to Asia, after he took control of the Mughal Empire in that part of the world and founded the Suri dynasty. He built the fort to protect from an invasion by Humayun. That didn't work for long and the fort soon became part of Humayun's *Mughal* Empire.[32] Later, in the 1700s, it became part of the Sikh Empire—until the British came along.

The fort is a UNESCO World Heritage Site about two and a half hours out of Islamabad between the mountains of Afghanistan and the plains of Punjab. Built on a hillside, it covers about 170 acres with two and a half miles of walls, 68 towers, and 12 gates. Rohtas Fort is an example of the early Muslim military architecture of south and central Asia. It blended the artistic traditions of Turkey and South Asia and, thus, created a model for Mughal architecture and the subsequent adaptations of European colonial architecture. The fort is outstanding for its many sunflower motif carvings, calligraphic inscriptions, and glazed tiles. No architecture from this period is as complete or conserved as well as this fort. It is the precursor to Fatehpur Sikri in India which is a popular tourist destination and well-known for its architectural beauty.

We had a great time that day walking along the wide fortified walls and standing under the intricately carved archways of the gates. Julie's class went on an overnight camping field trip to Rohtas Fort not long after this. This was our first inkling of how special and historically educational our Pakistan posting was going to be for our children.

Wayne took a couple of work trips at this point as well. The first one was to Peshawar and the Khyber Pass. I don't think he saw much more than we did during our first excursion to Peshawar, but the Khyber Pass was a singular experience. Throughout history, it has been an important route of both trade and invasion between central Asia and the Indian subcontinent. It connects Kabul and Peshawar and has always been dangerous, volatile, and unstable. Wayne was flanked by protection and only allowed to go as far as the Afghan border. At that time, some drug warlords had palatial homes up there.

Wayne's next work-related trip was to Bangladesh. His camera was stolen so his first impressions were simply burned into his

---

[32] Humayun's *Mughal* Empire was a 16th and 17th Century Muslim Empire

memory. He talked about the masses of humanity, carts, rickshaws, and motorized tuk-tuks in Dhaka—the merciless poverty. Here are two vivid lingering memories: One is of men sitting in the fields dressed only in *lungis*[33] which were tucked between their legs, threshing wheat by whacking the sheaves against wooden poles. The other lingering memory is of other men squatting by the side of the road making gravel by hammering bricks apart one crumbling bit at a time.

Back at the school, things were moving along. I was making friends and getting into the flow of my work; Jason was raising his grades and doing much better than he had in Canada; and Julie was selected for a major role in the fall school play, *The Odd Couple*.

Almost every expat, as well as many Pakistanis, came out for this entertainment. We were proud of Julie's performance. Both of our kids had belonged to a community musical theatre group back in Canada, but ISOI was expanding their horizons and providing greater opportunities.

Speaking of performance, it didn't take long for the word to get around that I was a drama teacher. Drama wasn't an important course of studies at the school but presenting musicals and plays was a must.

"Would Mrs. Bazant like to direct the February winter musical in her spare time?"

"What spare time?"

"The choir teacher and the band teacher would be willing to get involved."

So, it seemed that I had no choice but to say yes. How hard could it be? I would meet this challenge when it arrived. In the meantime, I had classes to teach and places to see.

---

[33] A lungi is a type of sarong.

My next outing with Wayne took us to historical heaven—Taxila. This was, and remains today, a significant archaeological site on the Indian subcontinent located about 20 miles northwest of Islamabad.

Ancient Taxila sat at the vital junction of the subcontinent and central Asia and the origin of the city goes back to 1000 BC. However, the area around it dates to the Neolithic era, and some ruins from the early Indus Valley civilization of 2900 BC have been found. Taxila has changed hands many times over the centuries due to the importance of trade routes. Ruins have been found from the Achaemenid (Persian) Empire of the 6th century BC, followed by Mauryan (Hindu/Buddhist) Empire, Indo-Greek, Indo-Scythian, and Kushan Empires. It was finally destroyed in the 5th century by nomads, only to have the ruins rediscovered in the mid-19th century. It was declared a UNESCO World Heritage Site in 1980.

Taxila is mentioned in ancient Vedic texts and featured in the Hindu epics, the Mahabharata and the Ramayana, as well as the Buddhist Jatakas which describe it as the capital of the kingdom of Gandhara. According to Greek historians, Taxila came under the control of Alexander the Great in 326 BC. Later, as part of the Mauryan Empire, it became a great seat of Buddhist learning. According to early Christian legend, Thomas the Apostle was said to have visited here. And, for a long time, Taxila was known for its trade links in silk, sandalwood, cotton, pearls, and spices.

The ruins at Taxila reveal an evolution of the subcontinent through more than five centuries. The day we visited we were shown two main sites, the ruins of the city of Sirkap, from the Indo-Greek period which began around 180 BC and lasted until the 10th century BC and the Jaulian monastery and stupa dating from the Kushan period in the 2nd century, during which Taxila was a center of Buddhist learning.

We saw main street Sirkap with the mound of the ancient acropolis in the distance. The double-headed eagle stupa at Sirkap is a Buddhist shrine with Greek designs—a melding of two cultures. There were also several well-preserved Buddha images at the Jaulian site. The ancient history and significance of this site were mind-boggling. Taxila is well-known but I'm not sure how many visitors it gets these days. Pakistan is comprised of many areas that are richly historical and quite unfamiliar to most of the world.

We were becoming acquainted with many traditions in this part of the world as well. I was lucky enough to attend a mehndi party. Pakistanis have arranged marriages and weddings are by far their greatest celebrations. Families, particularly the bride's family, spend their life savings on wedding events that last for days. South Asian wedding traditions were started in the time of the Mughal dynasties in the 16th to 18th centuries and continue to this day. Apart from the cultural and historical significance of South Asian weddings, these lavish parties served a much greater need in Pakistani society. As I have said before, there was very little in the way of social outlets or local entertainment. Weddings were sanctioned events where everyone could feast, gossip, and let their hair down.

One of the festivities in the days leading up to the actual wedding ceremony is the mehndi party, a get-together where the bride has the red-orange mehndi (henna) stain applied to her palms, back of hands, and feet. A teaching assistant at ISOI had invited a few of us teachers to her mehndi party, and we were excited to take part. Female relatives and friends of both the bride and groom arrived on time (one of the rare occasions when being on time is considered important). The bride-to-be was ceremonially led into the room and seated in her special chair. She was wearing a sparkling shalwar kameez and dripping with jewels. Most importantly, her face was covered with a red veil—no one could see her.

As the evening progressed, friends approached the bride, lifted her veil, stuffed her mouth with sweets, and wished her well. She alternately laughed and cried throughout the celebrations. It's customary to cry at the thought of leaving your family.

The primary activity at the party was the application of decorative designs on the bride's hands and feet using a paste made from the henna plant. When first applied, the henna designs are a light orange but with oxidation, they darken to a reddish-brown and last for one to three weeks. Tradition says that the deeper the colour of the bride's mehndi, the happier the marriage will be. The intricate designs symbolize various blessings, luck, joy, and love, and the groom's name is usually hidden somewhere in the patterns. Guests can opt to have henna applied also but it's important to keep it simple and not outdo the bride.

There were many guests that night, so I didn't get a henna design. However, I did enjoy the singing, dancing, and entertainment that went on as the bride and her guests received the henna treatments. The party started with rounds of traditional songs and then moved into "family camps." Those associated with the bride clustered on one side of the room and the groom's friends banded together on the other. Each side was challenged to sing an insulting song about the other. Everyone was obligated to be "a sport" even though the insults got more hard-hitting as the party progressed. Through translation, I found out that some of the name-calling descended into labelling the bride's mother a cow or describing the groom's father as useless.

After this rousing game of put-downs, some of the women got up to do traditional dances in the center of the room. This was one of the few times when it was acceptable for women to dance. I never saw much dancing done in Pakistan. Only men performed conventional dances at get-togethers now and again. Many Pakistanis found dancing women to be too provocative. I remember one of the teaching assistants telling me that Bollywood movies were vulgar— all that vulgar dancing! On this night of female-only guests, everyone revelled in the freedom and joy of the undulating rhythms.

Something that really struck me at this party was how movie-star gorgeous all the women looked. At school and around town, local women dressed conservatively and kept themselves covered. Here, they were all wearing shalwar kameez or *saris*[34] in bright primary colours shot through with sparkling threads of silver. They had

---

[34] A sari is a garment of silk or cotton that is elaborately draped around the body.

obviously raided their jewelry boxes for all the gold and precious stones they could find and then spent a few hours applying glamorous, dramatic makeup. In a room without men, each could flaunt her inner enchantress.

As the festivities went on, the expat teachers were getting hungrier and hungrier. We knew that Pakistani meals were often served later than ours. Most of us thought that meant we would see some goodies around 9 pm. As it turned out, the food wasn't served until close to midnight. By that time, we were past hunger, so we wolfed down a couple of bites and hurried home. It had been a unique and enjoyable experience, but we had to get up early the next day.

CHAPTER 13—COMING UP CHRISTMAS

Despite the adventurous escapades we'd undergone, we were still pretty green towards the end of that first year of living dangerously. With the help of friends, we were beginning to make some savvy choices. Remember that huge allotment we had been given for alcohol? Well, we learned that some of our new American friends had no alcohol allotment whatsoever. But they did have access to the American Commissary, which was off-limits to all other expats. Everyone in town knew that this was the mecca of food and groceries. The American Embassy always got the best of everything shipped into Islamabad. So, what did we do? Of course, we made a deal! Some of our alcohol for some of their pork and peanut butter. This arrangement was mutually satisfying, and no one ever found us out.... Until now.

Since we still had lots of alcohol plus access to all kinds of food and a great cook, I could graduate to hosting something bigger—a Christmas party! As the cooler December days arrived, we started planning our family Christmas events. First, there would be a blow-out party and then ... What about a trip during the school holidays? We wanted to explore some of the well-earned vacation perks that came with our new life. What about Sri Lanka and Singapore? With friends? We were making some lists and checking them twice! There was so much to look forward to.

At that point, we thought Christmas would just be a private Bazant thing. After all, this was a Muslim country—no seasonal festivities here. Consequently, we were unprepared for what was about to happen in the school and community around us at the beginning of December. ISOI, the embassies, and most of the expat families created a Christmas beyond compare, a testament to expat ingenuity when faced with no ornamented shops. Jason, Julie, and I were pleasantly surprised to find decorations fashioned and hung in almost all corners of the school. As well, everyone on staff came to school dressed in red and green, accessorized with Christmas ties and Christmas earrings.

The teachers created every kind of Christmas ensemble imaginable. Christmas music was piped through the sound system; Secret Santa gifts were exchanged. We were invited to a string of Christmas parties and the school choir travelled around town entertaining partygoers with holiday tunes. In this land far away, the community was becoming our extended family for this Yuletide season.

Even as we revelled in all the Christmas preparations, we were still in "discover Pakistan" mode. Someone had told us about the Asian Studies Group in Islamabad. This was a great organization, with a wealth of educational materials. They organized lectures and tours and published an annual calendar of remarkable member photos. After initial inquiries, we signed up for a tour of the Khewra salt mine. My colleague, Liz, decided to join us.

Are you familiar with that pink "Himalayan" salt everyone raves about and pays the big bucks for in North America? Well, we've seen where it comes from and it's fascinating! The Khewra salt mines are about 90 miles from Islamabad, located in a rolling salt range, a remnant of a lagoon that existed 600 million years ago that is hundreds of miles from the Himalayas.

Khewra Salt Mine is the second largest in the world and is famous for its iridescent pink salt. This area was discovered in 320 BC by Alexander the Great, more specifically, by his ailing horses who began licking the stones during a rest stop. Ever since then, this special salt has been mined and traded through many different eras—Mughal, Sikh, British—up to modern times.

These days they say that it takes about two hours to reach the salt range from Islamabad. But, in December of 1991, it took us closer to four hours. The drive was a spectacle of rural Pakistani life—camels, carts filled with farm produce, country markets. We stopped at an animal fair where farmers wrapped in shawls carried big sticks and herded their water buffalo, goats, and cattle to be sold. After partaking in this brief photo opportunity, we hopped back into the vehicle. Many tiring kilometers later, we approached the mountain range, dazzled by its hues of rust, red, and orange.

Once we reached the Khewra mine, about 945 feet above sea level, we boarded a small train of individual carts that took us deep into the bowels of the mountain. The workers shone lights onto the walls of rock salt to spectacular effect, creating glowing prisms of pastel pink. In one corner of the mine, they had built a mosque of multi-shaded pink salt bricks. A flare was sent up to illuminate where they had mined salt for 36 storeys above us over time. (Wikipedia now tells me that there are 19 storeys. I suppose that is a more reliable number.)

We bought chunks of salt and I still have mine displayed on my desk. It has survived all these years, even in climates of high humidity. Now people buy salt lamps and objects carved from this salt. Salt rooms have been created for healing respiratory ailments. I still wonder why the salt from Khewra is being marketed as "Himalayan Salt"? It needs to be re-branded to reflect its true source. Hopefully, that will happen soon.

We stopped to have tea at a roadside restaurant on the way back—china cups and charpoys. Liz and I had to find some thick bushes for our bathroom break. There were certainly no public toilets in this part of Punjab!

A strange incident occurred after we returned to Islamabad. Wayne and I were driving Liz home when she suddenly exclaimed, "There's George from ISOI!" He was one of the high school teachers. In fact, he taught Julie, but Liz and I didn't know him well. He appeared to be hitchhiking at the side of the street. We thought this was odd behaviour for an expat in Pakistan. Liz suggested that we pull over.

She rolled down the window, called his name, and let him know that we would give him a ride home. He walked over to the car, peered in. Suddenly his smile twisted into a look of revulsion. He said, "Oh, it's you." And quickly backed off. Stunned, we slowly drove away. It took us a few minutes to gather our senses and realize that he was exceedingly drunk—in public, in a conservative Muslim country. Liz and I were concerned about his behaviour but decided to let it go, to consider it an aberration.

A year or so later, we arrived at school one morning to find that George had been quietly flown out of Pakistan in the night. There had been trouble, it got dangerous, and he had to go. Rumours abounded. Julie told me that he had been an excellent teacher and she was sad to see him go. I hope he got the help he needed.

Meanwhile, Christmas was coming. In Pakistan, house parties usually involved spectacular lighting and impressive decor. Intricately patterned loops of multi-coloured lights were draped down the sides of the house and along the driveway which was laid with red carpet and dotted with festive potted plants. With one phone call, all of this could be ordered, set up, and taken down for a ridiculously small price. This was going to be a fabulous look for our Christmas party. But there was one not-so-little problem.

Excavation and construction had begun on the lot next door. Pakistani construction sites were a whole new concept for us. Women, as very low-paid labourers, carried hefty stacks of bricks on their heads, donkeys bore back-breaking bags of sand and gravel, struts were made of spindly tree trunks, concrete was mixed by hand. I was never sure if a house was being built or torn down.

Road construction and repair were a similar story. There were never signs or warnings. Stones and bricks were simply placed around the working area and white lines were painted by hand. Holes and detours were often marked off with barbed wire—almost impossible to see, especially at night.

The immediate issue for us was: We were planning to have a beautifully decked-out house for Christmas. How was that going to work with a chaotic construction site next door? In Canada this situation would bring a bad vibe to a party, but this wasn't Canada. We were in Pakistan and what went on next door was of no importance. Garden walls performed the function of sealing people in *and* out. Garbage, poverty—just close your eyes and live in your own world. That's how it was done in Islamabad. While we never ascribed to this philosophy, we soon learned what we could and couldn't control. This first Christmas season in Islamabad was about sharing goodwill with friends, whatever that might look like.

I started working with Harry to plan a menu for 50. Yes, *50* people. We had a massive house. Fifty was nothing. Most cooks in Islamabad were versatile and Harry was no exception. I had a large selection of cookbooks and he used many of my recipes. He also liked to cook Pakistani food. Early bouts of diarrhea, before Harry's time, had rendered our family quite unadventurous about trying new dishes, but Harry introduced us to some delicious appetizers and entrées that became favourites.

Pakistani cuisine is a blend of cooking traditions of the Indian Subcontinent and Central Asia and includes elements of the Mughal legacy. Punjab and Sindh provinces have highly seasoned and spicy dishes whereas the northern regions prefer the milder flavours of Central Asia. The most common spice in the Islamabad area was garam masala, a blend of cumin, coriander, green and black cardamom, cinnamon, nutmeg, cloves, bay leaves, peppercorns, fennel, mace, and dried chilies. Quantities, combinations, and variations were endless. Also common was basmati rice, aromatic long grain rice which, in my opinion, is the best in the world. This was served at our dinner table many evenings.

Harry started making *pakoras* and *samosas* as appetizers for parties. Pakoras are made by choosing two or three main ingredients such as eggplant, potato, or onion and chopping them very finely. Spices (ginger, chilis, coriander, turmeric, chili powder, garam masala) are added to the mixture and all of this is then dipped in gram flour, made from chickpeas, and deep-fried by the spoonful.

The flavourful golden-brown pakoras are usually served with chutney or raita (yogurt seasoned with cumin, mint, and mixed with a vegetable such as cucumber). Pakoras are a delicious, addictive snack. I preferred to dip them in raita which was served with many Pakistani dishes as it was meant to cool down the hotter spices.

Some people favoured samosas which were a bit heavier. They are the South Asian version of a dumpling—triangular pieces of fried or baked pastry with a savoury filling such as spiced potatoes, onion, cheese, or meat. The spices used in the fillings are like those used in pakoras. Samosas can be served on their own or complemented with chutney. I enjoyed them but found that one was often enough. In Islamabad, they were usually deep-fried and could fill you up quickly.

Here are some of the things we enjoyed the most:

- *Chicken Tikka*—Chicken slathered in traditional spices (masala) and grilled to perfection. It was often served with mint dressing.

- *Biryani*—A mixture of yellow rice (coloured by an assortment of herbs and spices—sometimes saffron) with either chicken or beef topped off with lemons, tomatoes, and potatoes.

- *Kabobs* (called *Seekh Kabab*)—Well-seasoned beef grilled to perfect succulence. These were served with herbed rice (sometimes pilau/pilaf) and roti or naan bread. Naan bread is thicker than roti, leavened with yeast, and cooked in a tandoor oven. These kabobs were more often eaten by Pashtuns and Afghans.

- *Lamb and Chicken curries*—Simple delicious recipes where potatoes were blended with meat/chicken.

- *Nihari*—This stew contained meat that was slow-cooked and simmered in spices overnight.

- *Dal*—A soup made of lentils, onions, tomatoes, and spices. It was usually served with roti or rice.

- *Kheer*—A melt-in-the-mouth dessert made of rice, sugar, and milk spiced with cardamom (sometimes saffron) and garnished with nuts such as pistachios or almonds.

- *Lassi*—A drink of yogurt, water, and spices sometimes blended with fruit. Lassi could be salty or sweet. Mango lassis were similar to milkshakes.

Pakistani cuisine, although delicious, was a bit heavy for us. Curries and deep-fried food were cooked with *ghee*.[35] I asked Harry to make healthier choices with frying. We had Pakistani food from time to time, but we consumed a wide range of Western cuisine as well. We were blessed to be able to eat like kings every day.

One refreshing drink, a perennial preference on the entire subcontinent, was *Nimbu Pani* or fresh lime soda. Fresh lime juice was mixed with club soda and a squirt of sweet syrup. Aficionados skipped the syrup. It was wonderful with lots of ice but, as water-borne illnesses were prolific in this part of the world, we had to be careful about that. We drank Nimbu Pani regularly at home, at clubs, and at parties. After leaving Pakistan, we never found a person or place able to replicate this tart, thirst-quenching elixir.

While Harry and I were planning the party, Wayne was spending a week on a work trip just outside of Manila in the Philippines at a drug prevention training conference. He stayed in an elegant, ocean-front room that was part of a villa once used by former Philippine President Marcos to entertain dignitaries. He was not "roughing it." Thankfully, he was able to tear himself away from this luxurious life and join us back in Islamabad.

Our first Christmas party was a smashing success. Jaffrey, the manager and bartender at the Canadian club, and his staff

---

[35] Ghee is a type of clarified butter higher in fat and calories than regular butter.

commanded the bar and served drinks. Harry had cooked up all kinds of goodies, Peter and our friends' bearer served food and cleaned up. At one point, our guests all gathered around the piano and belted out Christmas Carols.

Suddenly, we were counting down the days to 1992. What a year 1991 had been! Every month filled with the unexpected—highs and lows like none we had ever experienced. We were sure no year could ever top this one for jaw-dropping, action-packed adventure. Once again, we were wrong. But first, we had a trip to take. The four of us packed our bags and set off for Sri Lanka and Singapore.

CHAPTER 14—SRI LANKA AND SINGAPORE

Our first Christmas and New Year holiday overseas was everything we could have hoped for. The doors to a world of travel were opening. This was exciting! The four of us, plus another Canadian couple and their son and an American couple with their son, started out on the usual flight to Karachi. We were dreading the seven-hour stopover there, but it turned out to be relaxing and loads of fun. Instead of sticking around the airport or the Midway hotel, we took a taxi to the upscale Avari hotel and dined at their Japanese restaurant. The company and the cuisine were delightful and, most importantly, none of us got sick.

Then it was on to Sri Lanka where we were to spend Christmas at the Mount Lavinia hotel on the west coast, about 25 miles from the Colombo airport. We had left the chilly, sometimes frosty, days of winter in Islamabad and arrived at the ocean in a blast of tropical heat. We had no choice but to remove our layers of clothing and hit the beach.

The Mount Lavinia was an elegant hotel dating back to British Colonial days. Various governors had redesigned it as their residence in French, Italian, and British architecture. Ultimately it became a prestigious hotel connected to the Colombo harbour by the railway line and wings were added. Several scenes from the 1957 film *Bridge Over the River Kwai* were filmed at Mount Lavinia. Historically, famous people had stayed here—King Leopold of Belgium, Somerset Maugham, Vivien Leigh, Kirk Douglas. The hotel boasted old world charm and plenty of character. We had comfortable rooms and access to a gorgeous, sandy private beach complete with swaying palm trees, thatched huts, and body surfing waves. Regrettably, there were some problems with the service and the food.

Our patience was sorely challenged as we sat in the restaurant for hours waiting for our orders. One night, our friend Patrick couldn't stand it any longer and stomped into the kitchen to ask what was going on. Aghast, he turned on his heel and hurried back to our table with the answer. They were cooking food for the entire restaurant on one tiny burner!

We decided the best thing to do was spend most of our time on the beach eating snacks. Among other goodies, beach vendors sold fresh pineapple on a stick along with colourful *batik*[36] wraps. Most of the guys tried body surfing, but the waves could be a little brutal. One of our friends was sure he broke his toe from being tossed around.

One night the boys decided to set off some fireworks, both legal and cheap, on the beach. We all gasped and clapped as they set off little rockets in starbursts of colour. I wonder why we were crazy enough to let them do that. It could have been a disaster, but it wasn't. We are all still here in one piece. Another night a Sri Lankan man walked over burning coals to the moonlit rhythm of the tide—a performance both gripping and mesmerizing.

Just before Christmas, we all decided to take a trip to Colombo and shop for Christmas gifts. Items available for sale were Sri Lankan specialties: cashews, tea, batik work, spices, and some unique ceramic pieces. At Christmas morning breakfast we had an unprecedented gift exchange. Everyone got loads of tea. Jason and Julie gave us Fred and Barney ceramic figures which I still have on our bookshelves. Only Wayne and I understand the significance of these little guys—memories of Christmas morning 1991 at Mount Lavinia.

We discovered that two other families from Islamabad were also vacationing in Sri Lanka, one of them being Julie's boyfriend Brian's family. Our groups decided to join forces and go to the Oberoi hotel in Colombo for Christmas dinner. I will never forget that once-in-a-

---

[36] Batik is a method of creating coloured designs on textiles by applying resistant wax to certain areas, dyeing the cloth, then removing the wax and dyeing again—thereby creating unique patterns.

lifetime event. We sat down to an opulent table set with bone china on a snow-white tablecloth adorned with a lavish Christmas centerpiece. Uniformed, white-gloved waiters served us a multi-course dinner complete with duck and Christmas pudding. There were eighteen people around the table that day. They made up our Christmas family for a fairy tale dinner.

After our elegant Christmas celebration, we hopped into a van and were on our way on an adventurous road trip to Kandy in the central highlands. There were many stops along the way:

- First Stop:
  A batik factory which we toured while snacking on fresh roadside pineapple.

- Second Stop:
  An elephant orphanage where they fed the babies bottles of milk amid towering palm trees.

- Third Stop:
  Spice gardens where they grew every spice imaginable.

- Fourth Stop:
  A rubber factory—if you could manage the deadly smell and the sight of people working slavishly in the heat and humidity, then it was possible to focus on rubber being extracted from the trees and made into squares of crepe for export.

- Final Stop:
  A tea factory where they sorted, mixed, and packaged the famous Sri Lankan (Ceylon) tea. Of course, we bought some.

Our approach to Kandy reminded me of the descriptions I had read of a Tibetan Shangri-La in the misty mountains. It was about 1640 feet above sea level, sat on the shores of an artificial lake, and boasted many Buddhist temples. This was tea country, an historically refreshing escape from the cloying heat of the lowlands. We wandered around, bought some crafts, and visited the city's most famous tourist attraction, the Temple of the Sacred Tooth. It is said to contain the tooth relic of Buddha. Meanwhile, walkways along the lake beckoned for a stroll. There was a snapshot of picturesque scenery in every direction. But we had to hurry back to our hotel.

When we had first arrived at the hotel the desk clerk warned, "Please come back early for dinner. We currently have a group of German tourists staying here. If they get to dinner before you, they will eat everything. You will go to bed hungry!" We took his advice and enjoyed the sumptuous buffet. Sure enough when the Germans arrived the food was gone in minutes. This was our first encounter with the German tourists of Sri Lanka. We would have many more on future trips.

Our stomachs full, exhausted from a day packed with new encounters, we retired to our rooms. There were stunningly beautiful views of the lake from our open windows, but we made sure to shutter them before falling asleep. Signs warned, "Flying monkeys: close windows." Of course, the monkeys couldn't fly, but they could easily glide into the rooms from the many branches and jungle vines outside. No invitation needed.

The following morning, we rose especially early for the next, and most exciting, part of our journey, the train ride back to Colombo. We found seats and then quickly realized that we could just hang onto the steel door handles and lean out into the open air for most of the ride. This remains one of the most joyous rides of my life. Misty jungle, soft morning rays of sun lighting up the dew drops on glistening leaves, silhouetted farmers labouring in the rice fields, rugged mountains in the distance ... It was like watching the world awaken at the beginning of time. I had lived my life halfway around the world from this tropical forest, but I felt an intense and powerful connection to its silent splendour. This memory holds a permanent place in my heart.

Arrival in Colombo jolted us out of our jungle trance. The train was suddenly crawling with young Sri Lankan men and luggage was being passed hand over hand from the doors, windows, and top of the train without rhyme or reason. This all happened so fast that we could only watch open-mouthed and stunned. Just as swiftly we were pulled along with the crowd and led in the direction of a rickshaw that had been haphazardly loaded with what appeared to be our suitcases. Sure enough, our luggage was accounted for. How did they manage this? We never knew. We simply climbed in, indicated our destination to the rickshaw driver, and spent the rest of the day by the pool at the Ramada Renaissance Hotel. Our love of Sri Lanka began with this trip.

In ensuing years, we would visit Sri Lanka several times but that December of 1991 I diarized my first impressions of the country and its capital city, Colombo. My reactions were positive, but we were all aware of the violent civil war being waged in the northeast. It was taking a toll, as evidenced by the begging and poverty all around us.

It seems that Sri Lankans are more open to diverse cultural and religious practices than Pakistanis. Perhaps this is because much of the population is Buddhist. Other religions practiced are Hinduism, Islam, and Christianity. They don't seem to be so strict about how people dress. Most of the women wear saris or western clothing, and the men wear sarongs[37] *or western clothing. Colombo seems to be a mix of old Buddhist temples, a few mosques, vegetarian hotels, and British Colonial architecture.*

And wow! I found out that they make Noritake china here. It's possible to go to a factory and buy a 97-piece set for about $100! They box it for airline travel—guaranteed not to break. I wish I could buy some, but we're headed to Singapore before going home. Too much trouble. Maybe Wayne will have a business trip here in the future and I can get him to buy some for me.

---

[37] A sarong is loose garment wrapped around the body and tucked at the waist.

Reading this makes me smile. I did eventually get my Noritake china from Sri Lanka, three sets in fact. And I still love all three of them. It was at this point in my life that I embraced a new philosophy: "You can never have enough dishes!"

On to Singapore to ring in the New Year. My first impressions of Singapore: clean and lush! It was different from the Asia that we had visited so far. It enjoyed a tropical rainforest climate with parks full of flowers and vegetation, all perfectly manicured. As darkness fell, we were treated to the most elegant, brilliant holiday displays we'd ever seen. Every building seemed set to outdo all the others around it. We stayed at a luxury hotel and were pampered to the max. On New Year's Eve, we stuffed ourselves with a magnificent dinner and walked up and down Orchard Road with the Singaporeans as they broke into song and dance. It was an evening to remember. After that, we got down to the real brass tacks of Singaporean life—shopping. Our eyes reflected the bright lights of modern shopping malls full of products we didn't have access to in Pakistan. The boys were particularly happy with all the electronics. We were learning the lessons of expat living: "Purchase when you have the opportunity. It likely won't present itself again."

Singapore was also a gourmand's paradise. Every cuisine was available from MacDonald's to French fare. But Singapore was most famous for its Chili Crab. Whole crabs were served with a thick tomato-based gravy warm with chili. This required claw crackers, hands, bibs, and napkins. Our meals of Chili Crab were mildly spicy, sweet, savoury, and completely satisfying—as well as downright messy.

Back then, Singapore was most controversial for its ironclad rules and laws. This was a time before automatic toilets so there were toilet flushing monitors in every public bathroom. If you didn't flush the toilet you could be fined $150. While we were there, they also banned chewing gum. Many people had complained that bits of gum were everywhere and causing problems. One day there were packages of gum on the shelves and the next day it was gone from every single store. Fines were instantly levied. It was gum prohibition. Singapore had a large police presence geared toward enforcing these laws. We spoke to people that lived there. Some thought that it was a safe, clean place to raise a family, and that a benevolent police state was necessary. Others said that it was too strict and authoritarian. We had recently been to Bangkok where it seemed that very few rules were enforced; it appeared to be chaotic. Our family concluded that there must be a happy medium somewhere between the two cities.

All too soon, our holiday came to an end. After an exceptionally long wait at the Karachi airport (thank God we were with friends), we finally arrived in Islamabad. It was January and it was cold! We had just spent two weeks in the tropics and our large stone house hadn't been heated in all that time. Even so, Park Road was beginning to feel like our real home, and it was kind of nice to get back. We turned on the heaters, donned some heavy sweaters, and got ready to meet 1992.

Coming up on the anniversary of the Gulf War, I began to reflect on our first year in Pakistan. We thought we were ready to take on the world when we decided to move overseas. Yet we were so innocent, so naïve. We were looking for adventure and we found it. We were looking at having better, more challenging jobs and we found them. We wanted our children to be exposed to a wider world full of diversity and opportunities and they were finding that.

But, in looking for adventure we'd been confronted with far more than we had bargained for. We had traded our comfortable, cocooned Canadian life for one of rough and tumble unpredictability. We had been bombarded with culture shock, illness, and frequent jaw-dropping discoveries. We longed for the old life at the same time as we delighted in new escapades.

Some changes had been challenging. They confronted our deep-rooted values and tugged at our heartstrings. What could we do about the poverty and disparity that we witnessed almost daily? Our little family couldn't possibly fix these massive inequities. After many soul-searching conversations, Wayne and I decided that we should focus on those around us. We could help our staff and the people that came into our lives. Hopefully, we could make life better for a few people in our little corner of Islamabad.

I looked in the mirror and understood that I'd already begun to change. I was no longer the ingenuous Canadian of those first few months. I was stronger, more assertive. I understood the world just a little bit better. I had developed greater compassion and understanding of suffering and deprivation. I'd made major adjustments to cultural practices I had never known. Was I ready for more?

As Told to Me

The following is a small collection of stories told to me by friends who have lived in Pakistan. They are all true expat experiences except for the first story. That one is a true Pakistani Princess story.

From the classical period of Indian history, the subcontinent had been divided into feudal kingdoms. During the British Raj, they were classified as princely states and had a subsidiary alliance with the British. In the 1947 Partition, these states acceded to either India or Pakistan. However, they retained their status, privilege, and autonomy until the late 1950s. A few even retained autonomy until 1969; it wasn't until the early 1970s that princely families were formally derecognized. Royalty did not always consider themselves derecognized, however. Here is one of their stories.

The Princess's Story

My father had a kingdom on the border of India and Pakistan. He had many wives and a harem. I am the youngest of 24 children. From a young age, I can remember living in the women's quarters and having the car covered when we travelled. When I grew up, I married an American and had a son. I'm divorced now so I live alone in Islamabad, but my son is attending university in New York. I'm incredibly happy when he spends time with me.

Some might call me wealthy but, in fact, I was disinherited. When my father died one of my brothers grabbed everything. The rest of us have been trying to get our share for many years. We still hope to have some influence in making this right.

(I'd never met a princess, not to mention had the honour of sitting beside one at dinner as I did during our first few months in Islamabad. As we were leaving, a mutual friend said to me, "I see you were sitting beside the princess. Did you know that there is a large fort on part of her family's princely holdings? It is said that there's a secret treasure buried under that fort that no one has been able to locate." Being a girl who grew up on a farm in western Canada, this was like a tale from the *Arabian Nights*.)

Tom's Shoe Story

Shortly after my family and I arrived in Islamabad for a tour with the American Embassy, I discovered a shoe store which produced "made-to-order" shoes. While admiring the inexpensive, quality leather shoes on display, I had a brainwave. I had to return to Washington for a meeting so, while there, why not buy a top-quality pair of shoes and carry them back to Islamabad. I could have a few pairs copied for pennies on the dollar.

Upon my return to Islamabad, I rushed to the shoe store and presented my new size 13 brown wingtips. The shoemaker agreed to make an exact pair in black for me. "No problem, Sahib."

A week later he proudly placed both pairs of shoes on the counter. The black (copy) pair were identical in every respect except for one detail. They were a full inch shorter. In dismay, I put the heels of the shoes together to display the difference and voiced my concern, "The shoes you've made are too short!" He shook his head and gently replied, "No Sahib. It's your feet. They are too big."

This Pakistani shoemaker never did manage to craft a pair of shoes in my size. He just kept insisting that my feet were too big. However, he did recognize a business opportunity and his window display began to include beautiful wingtips. Over the next few years,

I saw several men sporting smaller versions of what should have been my shoes.

The Story of Norma's Cushions

When we moved to Islamabad, the house the embassy assigned us was sparsely furnished. With our housing allowance, we selected some pieces of elegant, hand-crafted rosewood furniture and hired a tailor to make the curtains and drapes. Every day he would sit on the floor for hours with an old hand-operated Singer sewing machine, turning out beautiful window coverings. When he was nearing the completion of his work, he asked what I would like him to do with the leftover material. I suggested that he make some cushions for the sofas and chairs.

It was then that I got my introduction to giardia, one of Pakistan's most dreaded parasites. For the next few days, I remained in bed, hovering between fear that I was dying and hope that I would. At one point, my husband came into the bedroom and asked, "How many cushions did you want the tailor to make?" I was close to delirious, shivering from chills, and sweating with fever all at once. "I don't care, a few." I answered. "How about 49?" he asked.

When I'd recovered enough to venture downstairs, I saw what my husband was trying to tell me. The tailor had made exactly 49 cushions using every scrap of leftover material. There were round ones about the size of a side plate, rectangular pillows the size of a loaf of bread, square ones that might cover a child's stool, and many triangular-shaped cushions with a base of 20 inches and a height of five inches. Only three or four of them could be used as actual sofa cushions.

My first thought was, "What are we going to do with all these useless things?" But we found a way to use them. In years to come, we regaled guests with our "cushion story" and then presented them with one.

PART 2

THE CALM, THE STORM, THE AFTERMATH

CHAPTER 15—COMMUNITY

Pakistan was considered a hardship posting—a designation given to places where the living conditions are difficult due to climate, crime, health care, pollution, or other factors. All expat salaries were enhanced to reflect the level of hardship. Islamabad had a lovely climate and little pollution, but other issues qualified it for the label of hardship post. There was limited access to western goods, the hospitals were shoddy, driving was scary, and intestinal illnesses could be severe.

But the greatest risk came from the political and religious unrest which gave rise to violence. This was unpredictable—a stirring rant from a mullah, an overseas incident interpreted to be against Islam, sectarian issues—any one of these situations could generate sudden mob mentality. We were all warned to quickly turn around and get to the closest place of safety if we saw a large crowd gathering. There were days when we had to stay home because there was a danger of riots.

In Islamabad, every effort was made to control these occurrences but that wasn't always possible, as exemplified by the 1979 storming of the American Embassy in which four people were killed. This was the reason that we had a guard for our property. In the early 1990s, there wasn't a big problem with home invasion or muggings. Rather, it was the larger scale rage of the herd mindset that was a problem. We went about our daily lives, always aware of the constant pulse of underlying danger. Today Pakistan has become linked to terrorism but, at that time, we just knew that it could be dangerous.

Surprising as it may seem, by 1992 our family had stopped thinking of Pakistan in terms of a hardship posting. Oh, we understood the day-to-day issues and never forgot that there was potential danger around the corner. We just got used to living with that. We also discovered that the expat community was tight-knit and supportive. Our lives were enhanced by deeper and broader strokes as the days and months passed. We were living a life that few get to have. As a family, we considered our days to be rich and fulfilling. The real adversities in hardship postings are lived by the poor and dispossessed citizens of that country. They live with hardships beyond our imaginings.

Back at school, I was incredibly grateful to have acquired a helping hand with the ESL classes. Enrolment kept increasing, and along with that came a greater demand for individual attention within diverse groupings. I was spreading myself very thin. All the other specialty teachers had assistants, so I requested one for my department. A rather jaundiced eye was cast upon my query at first, but eventually, thanks to my boss, Mike, I was granted an assistant, Naila. She made a huge difference to the smooth operation of my department once I trained her and laid out my expectations.

One of the greatest strengths of ISOI was its sense of community and generous staff participation in school events. Sports, plays, musicals, all major undertakings brought out the best in everyone involved. From teachers and assistants to Pakistani maintenance workers, all and sundry volunteered their services to make each performance, game, or festival the best it could be.

I discovered this strength when, in January of that year, I started directing 50 students ranging in age from 11 to 17 in the high school musical *The Sound of Music* to be performed in the spring. This was over and above my full-time job, and, as a result, I was getting up at 5:45 a.m. and arriving home from work at 5:30 p.m. I was tired but I had compelling work, quality family time, and a flourishing social life.

My PPS colleague, Jan, a straightforward Australian, took it upon herself to produce our show. She was brilliant at recruiting people for all the tasks involved as well as masterminding set design and construction, costume design, and 101 details both big and small. Her husband, Eric, the Performing Arts Director and Band teacher did a marvelous job of organizing the music. The Choir teacher was excellent at directing the vocals and the students involved were breathtakingly talented.

Every high school drama teacher dreams of this scenario, willing and enthusiastic support from colleagues and students. As a bonus, Julie acted the part of Liesel and Jason was on the lighting crew. This made for animated dinnertime conversation at home. No one at the school realized that it had been many years since I'd directed a play. I had gone back to university at the age of 40 and become involved in an acting troupe. Directing had fallen by the wayside. For a few years before that, I'd been very much involved with ESL teaching. So, during the first three months of 1992, every emotion, every strategy, and every teaching/directing/acting/people skill I'd learned in my entire life was utilized. I was both exhausted and exhilarated.

There was one fly in the ointment—a teacher named Tildy. Oh my! She was so difficult to work with. She volunteered to help with the play. However, her true colours started to show within a couple of weeks. Some days she wanted a lot of validation for little work; other days she was pushy. Sometimes she sulked because she wasn't getting enough attention, and other times she seemed non-plussed when asked to do a simple task. Tildy loved to gossip and would try to discredit others if given the chance. Manipulation was her game of choice. And I had thought it was difficult to manage my household staff of seven! How could one person be such a handful? I'd never experienced this in my entire Canadian teaching career. What to do? At that moment, the answer was, "Keep going. Focus on bigger things."

We had a couple of other blips during the period leading up to the performance dates. The lead actress sprained her ankle, and for a while, we worried that she wouldn't be able to carry on in the play. Amazingly, she forged ahead despite all the pain and discomfort. The next hurdle proved to be more complicated. As everyone knows, in *The Sound of Music*, the Captain and Maria fall in love. The script called for a kissing scene. Without giving it much thought I rehearsed the lead characters in a sequence leading up to "the kiss." Then, one day, it dawned on me that we were living in a very traditional Muslim country and there was a rule of no PDA (public displays of affection) at school. Hmmm. I made an appointment with the Superintendent. We talked it over and concluded that the actors would just have to indicate strong feelings of love without kissing. Pakistani parents, workers, teachers were all part of the ISOI community and attended school performances. We needed to be careful not to offend them. While my teenage actors weren't so happy with that decision, they did a remarkable job of conveying feelings of love without kissing.

In the end, our play was a rousing success. The acting, singing, and music were outstanding. I was amazed at the level of talent exhibited by both students and staff. Costumes (so many nun costumes!), makeup, and props had been created with rigorous attention to detail. But the most astonishing success came from an unexpected source—the sets. Jan had made drawings of the sets for *The Sound of Music* and shown them to the Pakistani builders and painters who worked for the school.

We soon discovered that these guys had superior skills. They put together set pieces worthy of a Broadway production. Our play was presented on four consecutive evenings. The first night, when the curtain opened to reveal the living room scene featuring an elegant staircase the audience instantly started applauding. The set was receiving an ovation! Never in my life, before or since, have I had the privilege of working with such talented builders and painters.

We all received lots of accolades from the school and the community at large for our production. This was something I hadn't experienced in Canada. Oh sure, people had told me that a performance or presentation was good, but they had never rained down praise like that which I was experiencing for *The Sound of Music*. Was this the norm for all International Schools or was this simply my first American experience? I was feeling new-found respect from my colleagues. That was a significant confidence booster.

Although the play pulled a lot of focus in the family during those first months of 1992, other events were shaping our lives. Wayne's bosses in Vienna and New York both came for a visit that February. We invited them to dinner, and they seemed more than happy with Wayne's work in Pakistan and beyond. Wayne was stable, hard-working, and results oriented. He also had a lot of knowledge and experience to share in the region. They weren't finished with him by a long way.

In one more year, we would have to decide whether to stay with the UN. When we left Canada there had been an agreement that Wayne could return to his Alberta position in two years. We were hurtling toward that crossroads. Should he stay with the UN and rely on one or two-year contracts or return to the security of his Canadian job? This was going to be a tougher decision than we had originally thought. When we left Canada two years had seemed like a long time. But it wasn't. We'd only just started to understand and enjoy overseas life.

Another good bit of family news was that Jason and Julie were both experiencing some success. Jason was doing so much better than he had in his Canadian high school. His grades were improving, he was enrolled in a course to raise his SAT[38] scores and he'd made a promotional video for ISOI which was shown at a school assembly. Julie was raising her grades as well and was inducted into the National Honor Society. The US ambassador spoke at the ceremony which was followed by a reception. It was a big deal. Julie had also resumed piano lessons. The ISOI band teacher agreed to come to our house to teach her.

---

[38] The SAT is an entrance exam for admission to American colleges and universities.

Of course, we were living in Pakistan, a country where life could take a sudden turn any minute. Spring was fast approaching, and one morning, Jason woke up complaining of feeling ill. Tummy trouble was a given in Pakistan and could sometimes be problematic, so I told him to rest in bed for the day. Who knows? Maybe he just had spring fever. With Jason, you could never be sure, and I didn't feel like arguing that day. The hours ticked by. Rafique was busy with the laundry, and Jason was resting in his room. Suddenly the afternoon stillness was broken by a muffled scream and a loud thump. Jason rushed to his window to see what had happened. He looked down and witnessed a cloud of dust rising from the ground, partially obscuring a body. At the same moment, Rafique burst into the house shouting, "Man is dead!" Disturbed and confused, Jason attempted to calm Rafique down and understand what was going on.

Houses were being built on both sides of us that spring. The building site located next to Jason's bedroom was close to our property and they had recently poured the concrete for the floor on the third storey. Workers on these sites wore loose flowing shalwar kameez, flimsy sandals and had no protective gear of any kind—no ropes, no gloves, no hard hats or headgear, nothing to strap them in. That morning, one of the workers had been removing the wooden struts, made from spindly tree trunks, from under the new concrete floor. Unfortunately, the forms supporting the concrete weren't stable, and the worker was standing directly under the third floor as he was removing a strut. Without warning, the forms collapsed, fell on him, and sent him plummeting to the ground to his death.

None of our staff spoke of this episode after that day. It was almost like it had never happened. Life could be cruel on the subcontinent. There was no such thing as compensation for workers' families. Indeed, there was no obligation of any sort on the part of employers to take care of these workers. The young Pakistani who had tragically died that day would be replaced instantly. I hope that there was someone concerned enough to make sure he got a decent burial. This accident was just one example of a grim reality in

Pakistan. Its population suffered a disproportionate number of preventable deaths.

About this time, we started to make plans to fly to Canada for the summer holidays. The UN only paid for home leave every second year, and by the summer of 1992, we wouldn't have been in Pakistan for two years yet. But all four of us were longing for a trip back, so Wayne and I decided to pay for this one ourselves. Jason was thinking of taking his post-secondary education in California, so we tentatively planned a visit to San Francisco on the way. We were coming up to his senior year and some decisions had to be made about the future. Our trip home was planned with great anticipation.

In the meantime, I found Elena, a gentle lady from Argentina who provided healing massages. Once a week Nisar would drop me off at her house and, for an hour or more, she would melt the tension and release all the worries from my body. Her treatments were my personal luxury, my escape. Except for this one time ... I was in a deep meditative state after a particularly relaxing session. Elena had left me to rest when suddenly, I felt movement. The floor was shifting back and forth with increasing intensity. An ear-splitting screech rent the air. What was happening? My heart was racing as I struggled to crawl to the window and peer out. The trees, the ground, the very earth was uncontrollably trembling and tilting in front of my eyes.

An earthquake, a strong one. Where should I go? What should I do? And then, just as suddenly, it stopped. I was dizzy and disoriented. Elena came running in to check on me. I looked around and saw that everything was ok. Her house was still standing, the trees and the garden had set themselves back in place. Whew! So far, we'd had little shakes but nothing like this. I'd survived my first powerful earthquake.

We had no way of knowing the magnitude of this event on the Richter scale, but it was forceful enough to scare a lot of people. I'm sure it did some damage to less stable buildings. Oddly enough, Wayne and Jason didn't feel this quake. They were in the car driving along at a fair clip. I suppose the velocity of the car overrode the shaking of the ground. I never did understand that. Back at Park Road, Julie had been hustled outside by Rafique and Harry. Both said a few prayers in their attempts to protect her. We all paid more attention to sudden wobbles in the night after that.

By the end of March, we had all been working hard and needed a little respite. Thankfully, spring break was on the horizon. Wayne and I planned a trip to India, Julie was going to Belgium for the International Honour Choir Festival, and Jason decided to stay with a friend in Islamabad and spend his time playing tennis at the American club.

Julie thoroughly enjoyed the beauty of springtime Brussels while buying Belgian chocolates for family and friends. The level of choral work was superb as she was working with all the best singers from around Europe. She made loads of new friends and they all stuffed themselves with newly discovered dishes, enjoyed European nightlife, and shopped to their heart's content. It was a truly memorable and educational experience for her. Yet another amazing opportunity that came with our new life.

As I was packing for my spring break adventure in India, I revisited a disturbing little incident that had taken place just before school adjourned for the spring holidays. Remember Tildy, the thorn in my side during play rehearsals? Well, my troubles with her weren't over. During those weeks of rehearsal, I'd needed someone to confide in from time to time—someone who understood my work environment. Things were getting particularly difficult with Tildy so I picked up the phone and called a friend, who also worked at the school, that I could trust with my uncensored feelings.

I was angry and frustrated during this call in a way I would never have allowed myself to be in public. I unloaded. My friend agreed with me and did some unloading of her own—she wasn't a big Tildy fan either. I put down the phone and felt better. I could go back to work smiling and tolerant. Almost immediately, however, there was a disastrous fallout from this one little phone call. If you remember, telephone lines had a habit of connecting and reconnecting in mysterious ways in Islamabad. My friend's house was in the same vicinity as Tildy's house. By some strange sorcery, Tildy had picked up her phone that night and overheard our call. Oh, no! Oh, yes!

The short version of this story—Tildy went straight to the administration and complained. The friend I'd phoned, being an overseas hire, was called in by the admin. and questioned. She summarily sought me out to recount this disastrous chain of events. I was never summoned by the administration, nor did Tildy approach me. Why was my friend called in and not me? I don't know, but I assumed that I wasn't important enough, as a local hire, to consult about the incident. All I know is that there was a permanent shift in two of my relationships. From then on, Tildy decided I was the enemy, someone to be vanquished whenever the opportunity arose. As well, the high school administrative office was just a bit more formal and distant. Why, oh why hadn't Tildy just directly confronted me and my friend instead of causing all this tension and judgment? I still don't know but this became a familiar pattern in the future.

Should I have made that call? Probably not. Should I have spoken so openly on the telephone? Probably not. Most of us have had these momentary fits of frustration that need to be aired. Truly sorry for my lapse in judgment, I was to pay for it many times over.

CHAPTER 16—TRAVELS

India! I'd heard and read so much about it. I'd been wanting to travel to this magical, exotic land for many years—eastern spiritual practices, the maharajas, the harems, the mysterious secrets tucked away in the folds of a sari … Yet, others who had travelled to India complained about the congestion, the filth, the poverty, and the disease. What to believe? Now I would get to see for myself.

Perhaps when you visit a country your impressions are guided by where you're coming from. Had I visited India while living in Canada, my perceptions might have been much different than those I had when travelling from Pakistan. All I know is that the minute I set foot in India I felt like I was home. I was Canadian through and through, but I had a mysterious visceral connection to this place. This is the India I saw in 1992 …

We started out in Delhi. The pavement rippled with heat; the women wore sparkly bangles and vibrant saris that gracefully swayed with each jingling footstep. Everything was intense—the scorching sun, the din of the traffic, the shouts of the vendors. Yes, there was poverty and crippled and deformed beggars—some of them aggressive—and street people living in degraded conditions. But there were also lots of people smiling. My impression was that Indians smiled more than Pakistanis. New Delhi had wide streets, parks with imposing trees, brilliant flower beds, and magnificent colonial buildings. Old Delhi had narrow winding streets, congestion, and ancient structures. We stayed at the Oberoi Hotel which seemed like the lap of luxury and, after getting settled, we went to see the sights.

First on the list was the *Mughal*[39] Emperor Humayun's tomb, built in 1570, the original garden-tomb of the subcontinent. It set a precedent for Mughal architecture and informed future innovations such as the Taj Mahal. The gardens were inspired by the description of paradise in the Holy Quran.

Next, we visited Qutub Minar, a minaret tower standing about 240 feet tall that was built in the 12th century. Some say it was erected as a tower of victory to signify the beginning of Muslim rule in India. It was a majestic tapering tower with intricate relief work, inscriptions, and projecting balconies.

We went on to view the India Gate, a monument built in memorial to WW1 Indian soldiers, and the stunning British colonial architecture of the former Viceroy's residence. The Red Fort, made of red sandstone and marble, was a gorgeous monument built in 1638 by Shah Jahan. It rose 108 feet above old Delhi and spread over 255 acres.

All these architectural wonders provided an important lead-up to our Taj Mahal visit, but for me, the most interesting place in Delhi was the Raj Ghat, a memorial to Mahatma Gandhi. This monument was a stark black marble platform that marked the spot of Gandhi's cremation in January of 1948, the year of my birth. A stone path surrounded by manicured lawns led to the walled enclosure of the memorial. Always adorned with wreaths or petals of jasmine, marigolds, and roses, it was open to the sky and the elements. An eternal flame burned at one end. Everyone had to remove their footwear before entering the enclosure. Even though there were always people walking around the platform to pay respects, a sacred silence prevailed.

Before departing Delhi, we were compelled to stroll through the markets and shops and gaze at silk saris, antique miniature paintings (Mughal era), exotic block printing designs, remarkable oriental

---

[39] The Mughal Dynasty was a Muslim Dynasty, founded by Baber in 1526, which ruled India until 1857.

carpets. It was difficult to drag ourselves away. When it was time to move on, we hopped into an *Ambassador*,[40] enlisted a driver, and were on our way to Agra, home of the Taj Mahal. Along the way we were treated to sleepy countryside scenes—herding of sheep and goats, people working in the fields alongside the proverbial water buffalo, families carrying loads of branches on their heads, laundry day at the riverside.

Our driver pointed to a ruin and informed us that we were viewing the birthplace of Lord Krishna. Then, further down the road, we passed through a village packed with people. This was the home of a famous guru and many had travelled great distances to see him. It was like a scene from a biblical movie as hundreds of people dressed in sackcloth laboured at building a shrine.

When we found ourselves in traffic jams of tuk-tuks and cyclists, we realized that we'd arrived in downtown Agra. We checked into our hotel, complete with intricate carved screens and views of the Taj Mahal through the thick city pollution. We couldn't wait for our first clear, up-close glimpse of the famous wonder of the world.

The Taj Mahal is an ivory-white marble mausoleum built on the banks of the Yamuna River. As we entered the 42-acre complex through the archway gate, the striking domed edifice with its four minarets was framed in perfect symmetry. A long rectangular tree-lined fountain indicated the way forward. The Taj Mahal's gleaming white marble was inlaid with semi-precious stones and it appeared to shimmer, float, and reflect on the water.

Part of the wonder of this amazing feat of architectural beauty is the romantic story of its creation. In 1632, Shah Jahan, the Mughal Emperor, commissioned the construction of this mausoleum to house the tomb of his favourite wife, Mumtaz Mahal. She had died giving birth to her 14th child (I question the romance of this part of the story). It took 10 years to be completed. Shah Jahan's plan, according to what we were told, was to build an identical mausoleum of black

---

[40] An Ambassador is a famous Indian car of British origins.

marble for his tomb and join the two with a silver bridge, but fate was not on his side. His son, Aurangzeb, imprisoned him, and Shah Jahan died before he could build the second mausoleum, his dream project. Thus, he was laid to rest beside Mumtaz at the Taj Mahal. His tomb is the only asymmetrical element of the structure.

At the time of our visit, young artisans still carried on the tradition of inlaying marble with semi-precious stones and we bought a marble box, a circle of elephants, and a plate, all with exquisite inlay designs.

We went on to view Agra Fort, which had been the residence of Mughal Emperors until the capital was moved to Delhi in 1638. The imposing walls were rebuilt in red sandstone during the reign of Akbar, Shah Jahan's grandfather. It was a massive fort, and, at one point in history, was said to have housed about 500 buildings. Most of these were destroyed over time. A poignant story clouds the history of this once great capital. Shah Jahan had been imprisoned here for eight years in a room that faced the Taj Mahal. He died gazing upon the mausoleum he had built for his wife.

We then journeyed on to Fatehpur Sikri—ghostly and melancholy. This famous town was founded as the capital of the Mughal Empire by Akbar in 1571. It was built to honour a Sufi (mystical Islam) saint and was to be a place of religious tolerance. The palaces of Akbar's wives boasted distinct architectural designs— Christian, Muslim, and Hindu. The sculpted marble screens were out of this world. Akbar abandoned the city in 1585 due to a lack of water, but the rich red sandstone walls still glowed in the setting sun.

Driving on, we entered the state of Rajasthan and the Thar Desert. We passed through a rural desert landscape—tufts of grass, low scraggly bushes with cooling ponds of water here and there. The beiges of the desert and omnipresent camel carts stood in sharp contrast to bursts of colour as women in bright orange and red saris regally balanced clay or brass pots full of water from the communal well on their heads.

Rajasthan was the land of Maharajas; a land of once-great kingdoms. The capital city of Jaipur was designed according to an ancient Hindu treatise and divided into nine sectors that symbolized the nine divisions of the universe. Founded in 1727, Jaipur was a well-planned city of wide avenues surrounded by hills dotted with forts (palaces). The Old City was known as the Pink City. It had been painted pink by the Maharaja in 1876 when the Prince of Wales visited, and ever since, all the homes within it had been required by law to maintain their pink façades.

Jaipur was visually stunning, perfect for an afternoon stroll. The bazaar was colourful—filled with arts, crafts, and trinkets, but for us, the icing on the cake was observing all the cheerful people in the marketplace dressed in traditional attire. We bought a silk carpet there—still elegant and prized after all these years. We happily continued to wander around Jaipur, visiting the City Palace and Museum, which, until 1949, was the ceremonial and administrative seat of the Maharaja. It remained the home of the Jaipur royal family who were said to be descendants of Lord Rama from the Indian Epic, *Ramayana*. We viewed several opulent structures in the complex as well as the sterling silver urns. These unique vases were 5.2 feet in height, and each weighed 750 pounds; said to be the world's largest sterling silver vessels. They were commissioned by the Maharaja to carry the water of the Ganges for his trip to England in 1901.

Another amazing Jaipur sight was the Hawa Mahal or Palace of Winds (1799) built from red and pink sandstone. The façade was a splendid honeycomb shape of 953 carved windows that allowed a breeze to blow through the palace. It was one of the most exquisite buildings I'd ever seen.

During our time in Jaipur, we stayed at the Rambagh Palace, the former residence of a Maharaja, which had been converted into a hotel. Built in 1835, it was set in 47 acres of greenery and Mughal gardens. The hotel retained its original splendour due to marble latticework, sandstone bannisters, and domed ceilings. All the rooms were appointed with oriental carpets, Mughal art, vintage furnishings—everything you would expect in a royal palace. Over the years this hotel had hosted Lord Mountbatten, Prince Charles, and Jacqueline Kennedy, to name a few. We'd never stayed in such a place of luxury and distinction. We dined under the crystal chandeliers of the former palace ballroom complete with waiters in traditional white uniforms and red turbans. Our private terrace overlooked lush gardens and the Moti Doongari (Ganesh Temple) atop a hill in the distance.

This still stands as one of my most memorable stays—from the tiny elevators with latticed doors to the massive old-fashioned bathtubs to the wandering peacocks. It was like living in a fairy tale. I would return in a moment!

The next day we visited the Amber Fort high on a cliff overlooking Maota Lake just outside of Jaipur. Amber (town) was once the capital of Jaipur state and the fort/palace was the home of its rulers. The palace was constructed in 1592 on the remains of an 11th-century fort and added to by successive rulers until 1727 when the capital was moved to Jaipur. Made of sandstone and marble, the architecture was a fusion of Rajput (Hindu) and Mughal (Islamic) styles. This opulent palace was laid out on four levels, each with a courtyard. The outer courtyards were for parades and public audiences; the inner courtyards were private quarters in which buildings were separated by ornamental gardens. One of these inner buildings was Sheesh Mahal or Mirror Palace, embellished with inlaid panels and multi-mirrored ceilings using glass imported from Belgium. The mirror mosaics and coloured glass reflected and shattered candlelight into a million jewelled stars—an intoxicating effect.

The Fourth Courtyard was the women's quarters, where the royal family women, as well as concubines and mistresses, lived. There were separate rooms for each of the queens. Secret passageways allowed women on palanquins to be escorted from one part of the palace to another. Exploring this palace was much like reading an intriguing historical romance novel.

Jaigarh Fort overlooked Amber Fort and was similar in structural design, although much more rugged. The two forts were connected by a subterranean passage. Jaigarh fort was considered the defensive fort, to which the royal family could escape if attacked.

We had approached these regal forts perched on a steep hill in a jeep. Coming down, however, we hitched a ride on a painted elephant. Our very first elephant ride! Partway, we encountered a *saddhu*[41] sitting cross-legged on the rocks. He was wrapped in a light-yellow cotton cloth, face painted white, with wildly matted hair and a long beard. He had a begging pot and a staff, so we thought perhaps he was a *fakir*.[42] We later learned that our first saddhu encounter was with a famous one: he sat in that same place for years as tourists filed by.

And so, our Golden Triangle tour—Delhi, Agra, Jaipur—came to an end. We loved every minute of it and were sad to leave. We meant to get back to India soon, but many things got in the way.

---

[41] A saddhu is an ascetic Hindu holy man.

[42] A fakir is a holy man who lives by begging.

CHAPTER 17—TROUBLES

We arrived home, happy to behold the purple, pink and red blooms in Islamabad. Summer months were around the corner and I should have been feeling energetic and ready to go back to work, but I felt like I had the flu.

After a few days, I developed a fever and severe pain in both ears. One by one, I enlisted the help of several doctors including the doctor at the Canadian High Commission. I was told to take pain killers and use hot washcloths or hot compresses. None of this worked. I was going crazy with pain. I had no idea what was wrong.

Eventually, I found a doctor with some understanding of what might be happening. He provided a rather obvious diagnosis—severe ear infection. But by that time, there were boils/abscesses in both of my ears, which were swollen closed. I can honestly say that this was the most excruciating pain I've ever had in my life. I woke in the middle of the night screaming, flirting with the idea of jumping off the roof just to stop the pain. I was a madwoman. Painkillers didn't work. They tried several different medications—none of them worked. My ears were poked, packed, and filled with drops more times than I can remember. Multiple times, the doctor used a long needle-like object to suction and drain my ears of pus. I had one blood test after another and, one day, they administered a narcotic painkiller from which I thought I might never recover.

They wanted to admit me to the hospital and hook me up to intravenous antibiotics, but Wayne said a firm "no" to that. The local hospitals and clinics could only be described as filthy. Used bandages, swabs, cotton balls, and other medical debris were simply thrown on the floor. We had enough challenges just making sure that the clinics used disposable needles for every injection and blood test. Among our expat friends, we discovered a Canadian nurse and she graciously agreed to come to the house and give me antibiotic injections. With that, the infection finally started to clear, and the pain receded. Thank God!

Finally I got the green light to go back to work. Soon after, at a follow-up visit, the doctor told me that I still had granulation in one ear. It would have to be cauterized under general anesthetic at the hospital. The American Embassy doctor, speaking as a friend, advised me not to go under anesthetic at any medical facility in Islamabad. There were some excellent, foreign-trained Pakistani doctors, but the conditions and backup systems in the hospitals were deplorable.

After a few days of pondering our options, Wayne approached the UN representative and got clearance for the two of us to fly to Karachi for an appointment with the top ENT specialist in the country at the Aga Khan hospital, a stunning edifice. This hospital was established in 1985 as a private international hospital and teaching facility. A sleek, open design of modern Islamic architecture, it reminded me of those sandstone palaces in the desert. We found the medical staff to be second to none.

What were the wise words of the ENT specialist? He told me I had a chronic ear condition that had probably been brewing for some time. It was later labelled "swimmer's ear." Any resulting infection could be accompanied by the most excruciating pain known to mankind. I'd already learned that the hard way! As it happened, cauterization wasn't required. I walked out with medication and advice to be careful of water and sugar. In other words, don't get water in my ears and don't eat too much sugar. According to him, those who were glucose intolerant or diabetic were more susceptible to these infections. (It would be a few more years before I was diagnosed with glucose intolerance.)

Intense bouts of ear infections have never visited me again, although I do have to be careful with my chronic swimmer's ear. I think this episode permanently damaged my hearing. Nevertheless, I'm grateful to be pain-free.

I mused on what bacteria might have caused such a serious infection in the first place. We lived in Pakistan. Was it the water from the shower? Or maybe it was from the swimming pool at the Canadian Club? We had just visited India. Lots of questionable microbes there too. Did I scratch my ear and get further infected? I will never know.

Because I wasn't admitted to the hospital, we had some time before our flight home. We decided to celebrate my good health and explore Karachi, capital of Sindh province, a sprawling coastal city populated by varied migrant and ethnic populations. We'd seen little of Karachi at this point—the airport and vicinity, a nighttime drive to a hotel and back. This had left us with a dubious impression of the city. Maybe we needed to cast a wider net. Karachi was the largest city in Pakistan, the business and manufacturing hub. Wealth was generated here. Sections of it, including some that had been developed by the British during the colonial years, were graced with large houses and estates. In stark contrast, a much larger portion of the population faced daily conditions of poverty. Rigid norms around social and political status rendered the poor powerless and consigned them to a never-ending cycle of generational subjugation. It seemed that Pakistan was still largely operating as a feudal system.

Clifton, a posh seaside district, was home to embassies and international schools. We went to Hawke's Bay Beach to catch a glimpse of the Arabian Sea. It wasn't a particularly clean beach area. However, they were offering horse and camel rides and people were running into the sea fully clothed. This was our first encounter with swimmers that frolicked in the water dressed in their street clothes, mostly shalwar kameez in this case. Of course, this was in keeping with covering the body. I would have been afraid my clothes would drag me under. In any case, judging by the screeches of laughter, these swimmers were having a wonderful time.

These posh areas were the exception rather than the rule. Most of Karachi was chaotic and crowded with a hot desert climate only somewhat moderated by proximity to the sea. At that time, despite being the most secular and liberal city in Pakistan, Karachi was riddled with ethnic, sectarian, and political violence. We carefully ventured into an area that was known for race riots, as I wanted to see the *Juna Dhobi Ghats*. This distinctive area about 4 miles along the banks of the Lyari River, was the place where the dhobi caste had been gathering to wash clothes for centuries—a vast ancient outdoor laundromat. Via donkey cart, they collected loads of laundry from homes and lugged them in backbreaking loads to their designated spots in the Ghats. These spots were a series of concrete tubs and cisterns where they boiled, beat, bleached, washed, starched, and wrung many pounds of laundry every day.

The clean clothing was hung to dry on ropes intertwined between bamboo poles that went on for miles. Then it was on to the task of ironing, folding, and re-loading the laundry for home delivery. This grueling work was done seven days a week, only closing for heavy rains. Despite earning very few rupees for this labour, dhobis took great pride in their life's work. The Dhobi Ghats were a sight to behold. I'm so glad we took the time to visit that day. Nowadays, due to ad hoc urbanization and a dramatic increase in population, the Lyari River has become polluted with sewage and industrial waste. In addition, a freeway was recently constructed which further shrunk the area available for laundering, while modernization has brought washing machines into middle-class homes. "Tourists no longer visit here", they say. "These Dhobi Ghats are fading and at risk of disappearing", they say. You might say, "This is a good thing." By western standards, I suppose this might be true. However, the caste system is still very much practiced. If dhobis lose their place in the system and are no longer able to succeed in securing the only work they know, they will be left with no choices. The miles of colourful clothing soaking up the brilliant rays of sunshine heralded the pride of all dhobis that day back in 1992. No pride or dignity will be left once they resort to begging in the streets of Karachi.

We finished off this interlude by doing some shopping for leather items and jewelry and visiting the tomb of the founder of Pakistan, the Mazar-e-Quaid. This mausoleum of Jinnah was a cuboid structure with a white marble dome set on a raised platform located in neo-

Mughal style gardens. There was a four-tier crystal chandelier inside. It was a remarkable structure but, after our trip to India, I was maxed-out on mausoleums and monuments.

School activities were in full swing when we arrived back in Islamabad. ISOI was hosting a regional Fine Arts Festival and *The Sound of Music* had been rehearsed and performed a final time. I'd missed it but the students dedicated their performance to me. I felt humbled and honoured by this.

There had been a little issue though. Because I wasn't there to keep a lid on things, the lead actors had taken it upon themselves to go ahead with "the kiss," not a popular decision with the administration. Despite all this, the play once again received rave reviews. I was pleased for everyone involved. We could be proud of all our hard work. We did manage to attend the final evening of the festival. They had a talent competition and Julie won the best actress award. We were proud parents once again.

In contrast, we were also rather annoyed when we discovered that Jason had organized a party while we were gone. He'd enlisted the help of the servants. The kids had them wrapped around their fingers. Because Wayne and I'd had to leave on the spur of the moment, we trusted our kids to be responsible for the few days we were gone. All their needs were looked after, and they were safe and protected by our staff. We thought everything was under control. However, Jason had decided to push the boundaries with a party. Had the other parents known that their kids were invited to a house with no parental supervision? There was no harm done thankfully. As parents, we wouldn't make this mistake again. From now on the kids would stay with friends when Wayne and I had to travel. Jason was good at convincing us that he could handle things maturely. But he wasn't yet old enough to think about potential consequences.

Once again, we were gearing up for Prom season and the end of the school year. ISOI adjourned at the end of May and would start up again in mid-August. We were looking forward to June and July in Canada. Going back would be familiar and strange all at once. We were acclimating to a new culture. How would our adjustment to Pakistani life affect our experiences at home?

We had learned to live with loudness—the constant honking of horns, shouting, Bollywood music blaring from music stalls, jingly buses (named for the sound of the chains and pendants hanging from the bumpers), roaring and racing trucks, guns, and more guns. Maybe Canada would be too quiet now.

We were also adjusting to life with all sorts of insects. A cute little gecko had taken up residence behind Julie's drapes and he helped control some of the tiny terrorists. As such, we granted Mr. Gecko a safe haven and welcomed him to the family. We knew a little about learning to live in a new, foreign environment.

Unfortunately, Pakistan's sizeable cockroaches were out of his league. They were everywhere, and Peter would regularly pour poison into our household sewage system to get rid of them. These pests were notoriously difficult to kill.

One night I was sound asleep, and I felt something wet slithering across my face. I slapped it away and jumped out of bed. There it was, on my pillow, a king-size cockroach. I grabbed one of the magazines on our bedroom desk and started whacking away at it.

Wayne bolted upright and shouted, "What are you doing?"

Working hard at smashing this repulsive intruder to smithereens, I retorted, "Go back to sleep. I'm just killing a cockroach."

I soon vanquished the enemy, flushed him down the toilet, and went back to sleep. But not before I realized why my nighttime visitor was so slimy. It was covered with Peter's poison. Yuk! In Canada, an incident like this would have kept us up all night. In Pakistan, it was but a slight distraction. From then on, we remembered to keep the master bathroom door closed as we slept.

There were some scary-looking wasps in Islamabad too. The skinny orange and red ones with hanging legs and a protracted sharp stinger could leave people with a massive agonizing swelling that lasted for days. We had a recessed light above our bathroom mirror that was switched on by pulling a chain. One morning, Wayne reached in for the chain and was painfully surprised by the orange wasp making his home in there. Wayne's finger swelled and pulsed with pain for more than a week.

And we just stayed as far away as possible from the big black and violet angry-looking bees. I knew nothing about them except that they looked like they could kill you.

We had two more insect problems at our house—ants and termites. At certain times of year columns and columns of ants would march through any room that they found attractive. Julie's bathroom was one of them. This army of inexorable pests worked hard to defeat Peter in his every attempt to annihilate them. The termites that made their home in Jason's closet persisted as well. In five years of attempts, I don't think we resolved either of these issues effectively.

On the flip side, there were plenty of entertaining events in the Islamabad community that we got used to as well. Just before we left for our summer holiday the Canadian Club held a Fifties Night party. In addition to the outdoor pool, wading pool, playground, and covered patio, the club had a spacious air-conditioned interior with a bar and games room complete with a big-screen TV. There was ample room to set up tables and hold dance parties.

We all donned our rolled-up jeans, t-shirts, flared skirts, and Bobbi socks to jive the night away. Someone had parked a 1958 Chevy in front of the club, and everyone clamoured for photo ops. Vintage cars were never seen in Islamabad. This one must have been a well-kept local secret. So … Much … Fun.

Our social life in Islamabad was ever-expanding. We were taking the opportunity to travel to new, exotic locations, and we were meeting new dynamic people along the way. The life we'd led in Canada before we left had been nothing like this. Did we want to return to that old life anytime soon? I guess our summer holiday back to Alberta would tell the tale.

CHAPTER 18—AROUND THE WORLD

I'm looking at a photo of Jason, Julie, and me. It's Mother's Day 1992 and we will soon be flying back to Canada. What is remarkable about this photo is how tired we look. We're happy but all three of us are completely spent. It was time to relax and recharge. The four of us were beginning to understand that there was a rhythm to the life we were living. We could work hard; we could play hard. But then we had to find some time away from it all. This gig was intense. We needed to breathe. It was "Canada here we come."

Some friends of ours had advised us that if we travelled via India, we could fly around the world for a nominal price. Hmmm, around the world! We would probably never have a chance to make this trip again, and the price was right! It sounded like a plan. So, we were on our way ...

We landed in Delhi and this time the airport was crazy. It was just a tumultuous mess of people on top of people, on top of people. We literally fought our way through a surge of humanity to get to the agent providing boarding passes. Then, Jason got stalled in a bureaucratic nightmare of explaining why he had a video camera. He had to provide information to an old guy hunched over a desk spitting streams of betel juice into a bucket (and mostly missing). Our near-sighted Indian agent was punching keys on an outdated computer at the rate of one letter every five minutes it seemed.

We finally made it beyond customs only to find that the crowds were so thick, and the lines so disordered we couldn't make it through security to the boarding gate. People were in a frenzy, worried that they would never get on an airplane. Sweat was streaming down our faces as we clutched our betel-stained boarding passes and prayed we would somehow make this flight. Then came the announcements of flight delays—again and again. We stood rooted to the floor for two and a half hours.

Even through all the pandemonium of sweat and swearing I registered the sights around me. Every race, colour, and creed of humanity had converged at the Delhi airport that night. A teenage British traveller directly behind me had a large bone pierced through his nose; two young European women in filthy floor-length dresses made out as if this were their last day on earth (pretty shocking in 1992); snotty-nosed children screamed with impatience; a group of glassy-eyed Swedes in dreadlocks were high as a kite. All families— Indian, European, North American, Australian—were beginning to crack under the strain of the chaos and uncertainty.

Finally, we heard an authoritative voice at the front of the crowd. He announced our flight number and stated that all those with boarding passes must follow him now. Did we knock people over getting to him? Did we walk over the limp bodies of the Swedes? I have no idea. All I remember is that the next thing we knew, we were on the plane. Inshallah, we would eventually be landing somewhere else!

It was a long journey indeed. We must have had to transfer in Bangkok; I don't remember. All I remember is that, when we reached San Francisco, we had been travelling for more than 30 hours. We registered at a quaint boutique hotel and fell into our beds—the best beds ever. The four of us slept and slept and slept.

Then it was time for some serious shopping, soaking up California culture and taking the famous cable cars going "halfway to the stars." We rented a car for a day and drove around the city and into the countryside, floating through the lush, forested hills edged with panoramic vistas of the ocean. One of the best tourist highlights was our half-day visit to Alcatraz. This island federal penitentiary operated from 1934 to 1963 and had housed many famous inmates including Al Capone. Correctional officers claimed that no one had ever successfully escaped from Alcatraz. We took the full tour and heard all the infamous stories about long-term prisoners. Jason wore his black and white striped t-shirt that day, so he fit right in. We caught the cool breezes of a bracing boat ride on the way back. Our smiles returned. We were refreshed.

Living in Islamabad meant no clothes shopping opportunities. Even when we visited Bangkok and Singapore we couldn't shop for clothing because nothing fit our larger Canadian bodies. We had clothing made for us in several places, but this was mostly limited to outfits for special events. As a result, we became familiar with yet another expat rule of thumb. Shopping for family necessities had to be done during home leave or summer holidays.

Thus, we'd landed in the US ready to buy! Not only that, but I also wanted to outfit Jason and Julie for the coming school year. We went to The Gap store. After all, San Francisco was where The Gap had started. Jason and Julie were in their element trying on clothes, and after some time, we were finally ready to make our purchases. As we left the store, big bags in both hands, the clerk came and opened the door for us.

He put up his hand and smiled, "The next time you decide to shop here please phone ahead. We will have someone waiting for you."

I guess we'd made an impression. What a day! This was the only time in our lives when we felt a little bit like Julia Roberts on her shopping spree in the movie *Pretty Woman*.

The next day, Julie and I went shopping on our own. She wanted a unique dress to wear to the prom as Jason would be graduating the following spring. We had a fun girls' day trying on all sorts of classic gowns and finally found the perfect dress. We headed back to the hotel room to find the boys glued to an American TV series, after having spent a day at the movies. They were surprised to realize just how much they'd missed these rather ordinary pastimes.

Wayne and Jason managed to take their eyes off the TV long enough to ask how we'd managed with our day. Julie produced the elegant white party dress and announced how much we had spent. I honestly think that Wayne came close to passing out. It was a once-in-a-lifetime purchase!

Some of our over-spending was a consequence of not being able to inhabit western clothing stores for a long, long time. Shopping sprees, movies, favourite foods, rejoicing in all the things we missed so much! It felt so good to experience these familiar pursuits. We were beginning to understand that this was part and parcel of being an expat. You could simultaneously enjoy an intriguing new environment as well as long for the familiar comforts of your home continent. We learned to temper our appetites in later years.

All too soon we said our goodbyes to San Francisco and headed for Alberta, Canada—first to Calgary where our families lived, and then on to Edmonton and St. Albert which had been home for many years before we ventured overseas.

Our hearts overflowed with gladness as we hugged family and friends. My mother decided to have a big party to welcome us back. She rented a hall, served food—the whole package. I recall that we donned our 'Pakistani clothing' and stood on the stage to be viewed by everyone in the room. One by one, my mom handed each of us a microphone and asked us to talk about our time in Pakistan.

Even though I'm a teacher and actress, and I've done a great deal of public speaking, I found this exercise excruciatingly embarrassing. I'm not sure how Wayne, Jason, and Julie handled it, but they must have felt the same. How could we boil down all that we had been through into a sound bite for an audience? It was impossible. In the year and a half since we'd left Canada, we had fundamentally changed, both individually and as a family.

Our physical appearance was virtually the same as when we'd left, we still spoke with the same accent, but there were profound inner shifts that no one could see, and few could understand. It was perplexing. We'd become aliens in our own land. But no one knew we were aliens. Our family kept telling us how much Canada had changed since we had been gone. We observed just the opposite. Nothing had changed at home. Everyone was still living the same lives, keeping the same daily schedule. We were the different ones. Our lives had moved on in another universe far removed. But we couldn't say this. Over the microphone, we talked about the weather, the school, our house, the food—bits and pieces of a puzzle that were never the complete picture.

We also began to perceive our old habitat from a new angle. Canada seemed so rule-bound—speed limits, traffic lights, so many safety rules. Why did we have to keep the speed limit if there were few people on the road? Why did we need to sit through a red light late at night with no one else at the intersection? This seemed superfluous. We were accustomed to a life without these limitations. Crazy? Maybe. But change is a process.

Even more disconcerting were our interactions with the healthcare system. We were no longer Canadian residents; our insurance coverage was provided through the UN. That was no problem for us. We'd been instructed to pay upfront and then submit forms for reimbursement. But doctor's offices and laboratories in Alberta didn't know what to make of us. We looked Canadian so why didn't we have a card like everyone else? Receptionists eyed us suspiciously and briskly ordered us to pay immediately—no further conversation until they saw the money. Once they received the cash, they didn't seem to know what to do with it. And a receipt? They weren't in the habit of giving receipts. How and why would they do that?

We maintained our patience, let them know that we were average, trustworthy citizens, and led them through the billing process. We all needed proper check-ups, so this scene played out a few times. In the end, the biggest surprise for us was the cost of everything. Of course, we were reimbursed, but in the meantime, we realized the charges connected to doctor's visits, lab tests, and procedures. We'd never had to think about this through all those years of universal coverage when we presented our magical healthcare card. What an eye-opener! We wondered if our fellow Canadians understood how lucky they were to receive these costly tests for free.

All things considered; we had a wonderful Canadian break. There were long visits with friends we treasured, meals comprised of all the foods we loved and missed, evenings at the movies, trips to our favourite shopping malls. Jason and Julie observed that they now had more friends than ever—some in Canada, some overseas. Julie's boyfriend and Jason's best friend, Brian travelled from his upstate New York home to spend some time with them.

Before we knew it, we were once again boarding a plane bound for South Asia. This was our round-the-world trip. We had entered Canada via Delhi, Bangkok, San Francisco and we were returning to Pakistan via Toronto, London, and Delhi. As a result, we were able to observe the differences between eastern and western airports. Indian and Pakistani airports could be somewhat chaotic but there were always people standing by to help. You never, ever, lugged around your own bags. In Canada, the land of independence and equality, we "lugged" a lot. And our bags were heavy!

We were typical expats who stuffed our cases with everything we missed and needed to take back with us—mostly food items. We had friends in Islamabad who purchased large hard-shell luggage just so that they could transport frozen pork roasts and ham, in the hope that this precious cargo would still retain some chill when they reached the hotter climate of Pakistan.

Heavy bags and all, the three of us—Jason, Julie, and me— touched down in London. Wayne had gone ahead. He was never on the same schedule as we were. I don't think the four of us were ever in London as a family. At any rate, this time we knew our way around. We located double-decker bus stops and toured around London on an all-day ticket. We took photos of ourselves at the Buckingham Palace changing of the guard, London Bridge, the Tower of London, Big Ben—most of the tourist haunts.

Jason and Julie wanted to go to HMV music and the Hard Rock Café. And, of course, we had to go back to our favourite Italian restaurant, *Sale y Pepe*. But the best night of all was that spent at the Palace Theatre where we saw *Les Misérables*. This show had an impact on all of us—especially Julie. That night she decided she wanted to be an actress. She had come under the spell of the theatre.

Then it was on to Delhi and the hot, wet monsoon season. We immediately hit the Janpath market for some afternoon shopping. Julie and I loved those brightly-coloured bohemian skirts hanging in the windows, and we each bought several. Unfortunately, it started to rain, and we were soon up to our ankles in water. We beat a soggy retreat to our hotel. We also spent some time in a favourite Delhi restaurant. The Bukhara had the charming rustic vibe of stone walls, wooden pillars, and rough-hewn furniture. The chef created succulent kabobs, bread, and vegetable dishes from tandoor ovens—recipes from the western frontier. Apparently, many famous people and heads of state had eaten here. We didn't know that then; we just knew we loved it!

Before long, it was time to board the plane for the last leg of our journey. At this time in history, most people weren't accustomed to having bodies and bags searched at airports. But in Pakistan this was the norm, particularly if you were returning from India, the archenemy. At the Lahore airport, we endured the usual full-body pat-downs and then they went through our cases. It often appeared as if they were taking their time mulling over all our stuff with a kind of cynical curiosity. That day, the security guy was painstakingly pawing each item in my carry-on when his eyes suddenly narrowed with suspicion. He held up one of my tampons.

"What is this"? he demanded.

I was dumbfounded. I'm sure he wouldn't have wanted an explanation. I just gave him a hostile stare. He finally relented, dropped the tampon like a hot potato, and we were on our way. I shook my head in amazement. Real life is often stranger than fiction.

CHAPTER 19—A SEASON OF REGRET

Hot, sticky monsoon breezes greeted our return to Islamabad, and another year of exciting school activity was on the horizon. Jason and Julie were happy to rejoin their friends and we all found a renewed happiness in returning to what was now familiar turf. It was going to be the best, most memorable school year ever—Jason was a senior, and Julie was a junior. And it did turn out to be memorable, just not in any way we had expected.

We had a couple of good months before the dark times arrived.

After careful deliberation, Wayne and I had made one of the most pivotal decisions of our lives that summer before returning to Islamabad. The end of January 1993 would mark two years in Pakistan for Wayne. If we didn't return to Alberta, his government employer would no longer hold his former position for him. We were at a proverbial fork in the road. Would it be adventurous contractual work with the UN or the familiar fixed stability of the Canadian job? The UN won hands down. We were beginning to relish the journey of "destination unknown." This decision was to rechart the course of our lives, and we never looked back.

I was also beginning to see a shift in Jason and Julie's attitudes about Pakistan that fall.

Wayne had been to Peshawar while we were still in Canada. During that trip, he'd picked up a striking *kilim.*[43] Wayne and I were thoroughly enjoying exploring the world of oriental carpets. We spent many weekends bargaining in carpet shops, and Wayne had

---

[43] A kilim is a flat-tapestry woven carpet of bold colours and geometric designs traditionally produced in the geographical area that includes parts of Turkey, North Africa, the Balkans, the Caucasus, Iran, Afghanistan, Pakistan, Central Asia, and China.

developed a hobby of collecting these exquisite works of art whenever possible.

Up to this point, Jason and Julie had laughed at our new obsession. They didn't understand what we saw in what they viewed as "a bunch of rugs." But when we returned from Canada and they spied the kilim from Peshawar, it was a different story. They wanted their photo taken with it, and Julie declared, "I'd like to inherit this one." Perhaps they were beginning to come under the spell of the subcontinent after all.

We were heading into cooler, dryer, almost perfect weather as the school season got underway, with lots of community and at-home activities. I hosted a dinner party for 13, including Wayne's staff. The annual charity bazaar at ISOI was a fun event full of local crafts and handmade sweaters. And, just for fun, Wayne and I decided to become Islamabad tourists one weekend and visit an architectural wonder—the Faisal Mosque—tucked into the base of the Margalla Hills not far from our house. Construction had begun on the mosque in 1976 with money donated from King Faisal in Saudi Arabia; it took 10 years to complete. Although this is no longer the case, in 1992 it was the largest mosque in the world. To date, it is by far the most beautiful mosque that we have ever seen. The modern geometric design resembled a Bedouin tent, and its four minarets were each 260 feet high. They were in a perfect one-to-one ratio with the base creating an invisible cube that alluded to the Kaaba, the holiest site in Mecca.

The mosque and the courtyard were said to hold up to 300,000 worshippers. The main hall was covered in white marble and decorated with mosaics and calligraphy. We perused the fountains and porticoes and even managed to go to the top of the minarets for a spectacular view of Islamabad. I have an eerie photo of myself there, wrapped in a dupatta, peering out from behind the carved marble screen of the women's section. It was to be my last peaceful moment for a long time.

The beginning of September brought the first tragedy. Our Harry had a heart attack and died. I remember that day so well … It was a Thursday evening and Harry was cleaning the kitchen after dinner, getting ready for his day off. Friday was the day of rest. I walked into the kitchen to thank him for the great meal and wish him a good night. He appeared to be in pain and complained of not feeling well.

I knew Harry wasn't in particularly good health. He was overweight and smoked heavily. He always said that he didn't eat, and he was perplexed by his protruding belly. But he was a master grazer, constantly eating as he prepared and cooked our food. Also, he was in his sixties, had worked long and hard most of his life, and endured several bouts of malaria. Poorer Pakistanis didn't have the luxury of longevity.

That night I didn't consider his distress to be a sign of anything serious. Digestive illnesses were common in both Pakistanis and foreigners, something we all encountered. I told him to go right home and rest. Hopefully, he would feel better in the morning. I've never forgiven myself for not paying closer attention to Harry that night. Why didn't we immediately take him to the hospital? I've been told repeatedly that it probably wouldn't have made any difference. But I've never been able to take comfort in those words.

The following night there was a knock on the kitchen door—an unusual occurrence. It was Nisar. He wanted us to know that Harry had suffered a serious heart attack late Thursday night and was now in the hospital intensive care. We rushed to the hospital to see him. Sweating and anxious, we traversed a dingy, grimy hallway and approached the front desk only to be told that Harry had just died. I walked away defeated, full of grief and remorse.

On Saturday, we found Harry's family home in Pindi just as the priest was finishing his prayers. The body had been prepared by the family, wrapped in white cotton, and placed in a cloth casket over ice. People were buried as soon as possible in this part of the world. It was hot and decomposition followed swiftly.

Our funeral procession marched through several neighbourhoods until we came to a magnificent old graveyard. Many of the mourners were dressed in white, the colour of purity and grieving in this part of the world. We all stood around the gravesite as the priest delivered more prayers.

Most of the people around us were Christian Pakistanis—ragged, poor, untouchable. Without a doubt, they had led lives of poverty, misery, and injustice. That day they put aside their hardships and came together as a loving, caring community united in their grief of losing a great friend. I will never forget standing there in the heat and humidity encircled by ancient stones, monuments, and gigantic gnarled trees. Sweat ran down my back and large bugs crawled over my feet. They lowered the casket into the ground and piled heavy stones over it. Family and friends, impervious to the oppressive weather, laboured at shoveling dirt into the excavation, eventually creating a significant mound overtop the grave. A handmade wreath of roses was placed on the mound as candles and incense were lit around the edges.

The outpouring of grief was raw and real that day. Family and friends had crowded around the body and wept loudly and openly. They let their feelings flow freely, circle the air, and bounce back once again. I'd never seen anything like it. Their sorrow was an open wound. I remembered how my mother had admonished my sister and me not to shed a tear at our father's funeral. Had this show of stoicism mitigated our loss? I began to wonder.

That day I observed the collective heartache of these people halfway around the world from my father's gravesite. They weren't holding the pain inside to fester and grow. Rather, they held each other up with their humanity. This lesson pierced my soul. I would never again stop myself from grieving freely and naturally. I loved Harry. We all loved Harry. Every morning when I left for work, he would turn and say, "Goodbye Madam, and God Bless You." We missed him so much. Today, after all these years, I still think of you, Harry, with a smile and a tear.

Heartbroken and burdened with grief, I set about the task of finding a new cook. Our family had to eat. I had a full-time job but, apart from that, I wasn't even remotely capable of undertaking all the tasks required of a cook in Pakistan, so the neighbourhood drums beat anew, but this time the rhythm was sorely off. We went through such a parade of incompetents that it would have been comical if it weren't so unpleasant and sad.

The first cook we hired sweat profusely, especially when he served food. As if this wasn't enough to thwart our appetites, he created the strangest of recipes. We finally fired him after a dinner of steak topped with mustard, soy sauce, ketchup, and cinnamon. He insisted that his former employers had loved this dish. We begged to differ.

The next cook left as soon as he realized that one of us was going to accompany him to the market, an obvious sign that he was planning to skim from the grocery money, so we hurriedly hired another one and thought we might be able to relax. The following day, while I was enjoying a leisurely lunch in the ISOI staff room, I mentioned the name of our latest cook. A substitute teacher across the room heard me and piped up, "Oh no! I know that guy. We hired him and he stole from us. Get rid of him before he robs you blind."

I called Wayne, whose office wasn't far from our house, and asked him to hurry home and fire the new cook. Wayne succeeded in getting this cook/thief to leave but not before he managed to steal a towel off Rafique's clothesline. I guess he just had to steal something!

We finally hired and settled on Simon, who was halfway competent. We missed Harry every day, in every way. Simon stayed for a while though. We were suddenly faced with far greater issues, and staffing problems faded into the background.

CHAPTER 20—THE IMPACT

It was October 11, 1992. Julie was staying overnight at her friend's house, and Jason was hanging out with other friends. Wayne and I had gone to bed early that night. The sharp, insistent ringing of the bedroom phone jolted us awake. Wayne jumped up to answer it as I lay there in a stupor trying to grasp what was happening. I looked at the clock—10:30 p.m. Wayne's voice was becoming increasingly terse, strained. Was something wrong? I sat up. Wayne was deathly pale.

"Who is it? What's going on?" I implored. My heart was beginning to beat faster.

Wayne shakily lowered the phone and sank into the chair as if his legs could no longer hold him. For a moment he just stared blankly into space. Then, with a Herculean effort, he drew his hands over his face and pulled himself together, "Oh Sharon, Jason has been in an accident. That was his friend, Lorraine. She was calling from the local hospital. We need to get over there right away. She's already called the American Embassy. Jason and his friends are in the hospital receiving treatment. Lorraine survived the accident with few injuries and has been telephoning and watching over her friends until someone from the Embassy gets there. She assured me that everyone is alive and okay, but we must get to the hospital as soon as possible."

I threw on some clothes helter-skelter while my mind worked at putting together the scant pieces of information we'd been given. Earlier that day, we'd allowed Jason to take the car to get together with his friends. We'd wrestled with this decision, but he'd had a few disappointments upon returning to school that fall. He hadn't been able to join the annual mountain trek with some of his classmates among other things, and he'd begged us for permission to drive the car. Jason was a good driver, better than many. So, despite our strong misgivings, we relented. But I'd been plagued with a niggling regret all day. Now this! What kind of shape was he in? What were they doing to him in the hospital? I tried not to imagine the nightmare scenario that could be taking place at that very moment. Dirty needles? Forced surgeries?

The Toyota from Wayne's project was conveniently parked in our driveway. We leapt in and raced across town. Before we reached the hospital, we passed what we slowly comprehended was the scene of the accident. There was glass all over the road, and a large blue van was overturned. We couldn't see our car but what we did see was a horror show of various car parts and belongings scattered far and wide. Someone had to have died in this catastrophe.

With that, I lost all reason. I forgot about Lorraine's assurances. I felt certain that I would find Jason seriously injured or dead. As we turned into the hospital parking lot, I began to feel sick. It hadn't been long since we'd entered a hospital much the same as this one and found out that Harry was dead.

Wayne pulled open the heavy hospital door and we started down the hall. My brain registered blood on the floor, stretchers with bodies. Were they dead bodies? Men in grimy shalwar kameez were hurrying past. I couldn't go on. I started crying hysterically.

The American doctor and his wife had arrived just before we did, and they immediately registered what was happening to me. They'd brought a whole crew of people with them; someone took me by the arm, gently sat me on the floor, and put my head between my legs.

Dr. Penner and his Embassy recruits had one central goal—get the kids out of that hospital as quickly as possible. Jason was wheeled out into the hallway on a stretcher, badly cut up and bleeding. I broke down. I was elated to see Jason alive but distraught by his injuries. I stood and reached for his hand.

He opened his eyes, "I'm ok Mom. I'm ok. I promise I'm ok."

I whispered, "I love you" through a curtain of tears.

There had been five teenagers in the vehicle. They were all in the hospital, but three of them were ambulatory and could be transported to the American Health unit in private cars. Jason and his friend Michael had the most serious injuries and were to be transferred by an Embassy ambulance. I was told to accompany them, so I hopped in.

Just as we were about to leave, a Pakistani policeman scrabbled onto the ambulance. He demanded information about the kids— names, ages, citizenship, a run-down of how the accident had happened, etc. The ambulance driver was a US Marine. He politely told the policeman that these kids had serious injuries and needed to get medical help at the Embassy immediately. Embassy security would look after providing him with details.

But this Pakistani cop wouldn't leave. He kept pushing and pushing for information. Finally, our Marine driver got fed up, told him in some very harsh language to "Get the hell out" and pulled away. Ultimately, this cop got his revenge. The consequences reverberated through our family for some time to come.

However, that night we only had one focus. Get these kids to safety and look after their injuries. Of all occupants in the car that night—three boys and two girls—Jason had suffered the worst damage. He had a deep cut on his arm as well as serious cuts on one side of his face, some close to his eye. Further investigation revealed that his jaw was broken.

His friend Michael had some bad cuts on his face, and one of the girls, Marilyn, had taken a severe blow to her head. The third boy, Rob, had slashed his forehead. Lorraine had a few lacerations and bruises, and I'm sure that they were all in shock. At the American Embassy Clinic, they were cared for and placed under observation. Dr. Penner spent most of the night sewing up Jason's face and arm, along with tending to Michael's injuries.

One by one, the parents of each of the kids arrived at the clinic. During our all-night vigil, Lorraine attempted to fill in the story of the accident:

A bunch of school buddies had gathered at their friend's house for a few hours. When it came time to leave Jason volunteered to drive some of them home. They all lived in the same American expat neighbourhood which was on the way to his house, so they piled into the Honda Accord. Lorraine assured us that Jason was driving safely and cautiously. He was well aware of the dangers inherent in the streets of Islamabad.

As they slowly approached an intersection, Jason checked to make sure that no cars were coming from the opposite direction before he proceeded through the green light. And then, out of nowhere, something hit them with an explosive impact. The next few moments were a blur. When Lorraine opened her eyes, she realized that she was at the center of a nightmare scenario.

As she attempted to crawl out of the twisted wreckage of Jason's car, she became aware that everyone around her was unconscious. The thing that had hit them was upside down in the road. It seemed to be a van of some sort. Pakistani men were lying in the street. Were they dead? Were her friends just unconscious, or were they dead too? There was so much glass everywhere; everything was shattered. She was shattered.

Almost immediately a crowd started to gather in multiplying numbers, appearing from nowhere. They were closing in. Then she heard a siren, saw a flashing light. It was the ambulance from the local hospital. Oh no! She couldn't let them take her friends there. She started shouting, "No, no!" She was running, frantic, as the hospital workers began to put the accident victims on stretchers and carry them to the ambulance. She was helpless. Finally, they took her by the arms and lifted her into the vehicle as well.

Once in the hospital, they began to transfer her friends to different rooms and attend to their wounds. The stone of worry that she'd been carrying in her chest lifted as she soon realized that her friends were alive. Then a new panic arose.

Lorraine ran between rooms begging them at the top of her lungs not to give any injections. Pakistani hospitals and clinics had an injection for everything. It was their first line of defense. Lorraine wanted to make sure that no one got some unidentified substance shot into their veins especially with an unsterilized needle.

At the same time, she realized that she had to call the Embassy. Her parents had always told her, "If you ever get into serious trouble here, your first call must be the American Embassy. Never forget the number." She ran to the front desk and pleaded to use the phone. Her emotions soared when she heard, "Hello, American Embassy Pakistan" on the other end of the line.

After completing that call, she had a moment of relief. The Embassy staff understood the emergency and the danger. They would get there fast. They would notify all the parents. But then she realized, "Jason isn't American. Who's going to notify his parents?"

She ran to the room where they'd taken Jason and Michael. To her immense relief, the boys were groggily conscious. She asked Jason for his home telephone number and, thankfully, he had enough presence of mind to give it to her. Another mission accomplished. And, so far, it looked like the hospital staff had listened to her admonishments regarding no injections. Everyone's wounds just seemed to have been treated with massive amounts of iodine. Soon after that, Dr. Penner and his crew arrived.

I don't think of myself as a religious person but that night I thanked God for so many things ... Thank God for Lorraine. She acted with a swiftness and a presence of mind that few adults could have managed, let alone a junior in high school. Thank God that all these innocent young souls had lived. Thank God their injuries weren't more serious. Thank God for Dr. Penner and his staff. They didn't have to take Jason to their Embassy clinic. And it wasn't this doctor's responsibility to look after Jason, much less spend all night stitching him up. We owed him a huge debt of gratitude. I don't know what we would have done without him. Thank you, God, for watching over all of us that fateful night.

In the morning, we called Julie at her friend's house so she could join us at the clinic. Her eyes filled with tears when she saw Jason. It had been impossible to prepare her for this sight. He was bloody, bruised, swollen, with multiple stitches on his face and arm. But he was alive, and he was going to be okay!

Finally, we were told that we could take our kids home. There was still much healing to be done, but our clinic vigil was over. Marilyn was from a military family, and they sent her to Germany for a week for observation due to her head injury. Thankfully, she was alright. Her head had collided with Jason's jaw. She'd received a concussion, and the impact had broken his jaw.

That was our next obstacle to overcome. An excellent British-Pakistani doctor informed us that Jason needed to have his jaw wired shut—an essential procedure if the jaw were to heal.

What a catch 22! Jason needed to have this operation but, with that, came all the risks of admission to a local hospital. We were exceedingly grateful when, once again, our friend the Canadian nurse stepped up to help. She volunteered to supervise in the operating room while Jason was having his jaw wired. She would make sure that everything was scrupulously clean and that all proper precautions were taken. I was also more than relieved to know that no surgical cutting would be required. In the end, everything went smoothly, and Jason was sent home to convalesce.

But our problems were far from over.

Chapter 21—The Aftermath

Jason had been told to stay home and rest. Due to his tightly wired jaw, he could only get nutrition by drinking fluids through a straw. Along with this came a choking risk; we always had to have wire cutters on hand. We lived in fear. Would we be able to cut the wires and save Jason if he inadvertently choked? I worried all the time and stayed home from work to help him out. Wayne and Julie went back to work and school.

Then it all started. We knew the police had taken our car. American Embassy Security had been able to retrieve most of the belongings of Jason's American friends from the local police. With this in mind, Wayne went down to the station where they were holding our car and asked for it to be returned. They flatly refused, saying it was part of an ongoing investigation.

Wayne was very rattled that day because he had just seen the wreckage of our car for the first time, and he understood just how lucky we were to have Jason at home on the couch. What he didn't understand was why there was an investigation. Investigating what? He snapped some photos of the car and headed home. A few days later, we were still trying to figure out how to get our car when the phone rang. Wayne answered.

"Hello."

"Hello. Mr. Bazant?"

"Yes."

"I am Mr. Hussein speaking, Chief of Police. I'm telephoning to tell you that we are putting formal charges on your son regarding to the accident on the night of October 11."

"What? What kind of charges? What are you talking about?" Alarmed by Wayne's reaction, I picked up the phone across the room to listen in.

"Your son was so much speeding and carelessly driving when he crashed with a van. One Pakistani man is dead. We will be charging your son with homicide."

"What!" All of the colour drained from Wayne's face. I was sure he was about to collapse. "That accident wasn't my son's fault. Are you telling me that you're charging him with murder?"

"Yes. The officer on the duty that night made a report. It informs that your son was at fault and drinking alcohol. He was too much reckless, and a man is dead."

"This is crazy! I saw no police at the scene of the accident, and no one from the police has questioned us or anyone involved in the accident as far as I know. You have no substantiated information about this incident."

"Mr. Bazant, police report is made. Your son is having homicide charges. We will call again very soon. Allah Hafiz."

This Urdu goodbye signalled the end of the conversation and left Wayne staring down into the hollow echo of the telephone. We were simply paralyzed by these revelations. What were we going to do? If they had charged Jason would they come to arrest him?

How could we protect him? Was this a real threat or were the police just trying to intimidate us? Was it true that someone had died in that accident? The foiled Pakistani policeman who had been outside the hospital that night had certainly exacted revenge. He'd written a false report about Jason. But to what end? Were we being set up? We needed help. Now!

We didn't have diplomatic immunity like those who worked for embassies. Only high-status UN people were blessed with that designation. Wayne wasn't on that list. And we couldn't possibly conceive of the notion that Jason might go to a Pakistani jail. We'd read enough to know that prison conditions in Pakistan could be cruel and horrific. Our beautiful son would be lost. He would never return!

We had to act as quickly as possible so, while I stayed home with Jason, Wayne spent most of his workdays talking to the UN Resident Representative about how to navigate this dark passage. The Res. Rep. wrote an official letter for Jason to carry with him that might give him some immunity from going to jail. The operative word was "might."

Wayne had reiterated the story of the accident in detail to the Res. Rep. and they set up a meeting with the Chief Inspector of Police. Prior to that meeting, Wayne asked each of Jason's friends who'd been with him that night to write a letter attesting to the facts of the accident from their point of view.

Every one of them said the same thing Jason had told us: Jason was driving carefully. The intersection was clear when they proceeded through the green light. No one, including Jason, had been drinking alcohol.

I knew that this "alcohol thing" was a police fabrication because I'd been close to Jason in the hospital that night. I had the nose of a bloodhound. If he'd been drinking, I would have smelled it. Also, I had excellent "mom radar." I would have observed any alcohol-induced strangeness in his behaviour.

Wayne took all the letters to the meeting with the Inspector General and laid out the facts of what had happened that fateful night. He also brought the photos he'd taken of our vehicle. The driver's side of the car was badly smashed in. It was obvious from the photos that someone had ploughed into our vehicle, not the other way around. Presented with this evidence, the Inspector-General agreed that the accident hadn't been Jason's fault.

I wish I could say that this made a difference. It didn't. Perhaps this head honcho policeman was just humouring us in front of the top UN official. Or maybe he knew the game. Whatever the case, the police were in no way hindered from harassing us. One part of their story was true though. A Pakistani man had been killed in the accident.

In addition to jingly buses, Pakistani cities had other privately-owned transportation—vans. For a cheap price, they would pick people up anywhere on the street, cram them inside, and rush them to their destinations. There were often one or two men hanging off the outside of these vans to spot potential customers and pocket the fare money. The omnipresent vans were known to be some of the most dangerous vehicles on the road. They travelled at high speeds and famously ignored all rules of the road—even the informal ones that most Pakistani drivers understood. We are talking about a country where almost everyone disregarded standard traffic laws and appalling accidents were reported every day. We all got used to the newspapers describing scenes of absolute carnage when a bus "turned turtle." But these vans were the worst of the worst, flouting any cultural norms that might be associated with driving in a halfway decent manner. Those guys hanging on the sides of the vans were playing a game of Russian roulette with their lives every day.

This was the type of van that had collided with Jason and his friends that night. And the guy hanging on the outside had lost his life. Wayne and I hadn't realized this until that police call, which had caused us to investigate further. But I think Jason may have suspected it. He told us that he had no memory of the accident itself. His first conscious memories were of waking up in the hospital, looking to one side, and seeing Michael lying there with open cuts on his face. As he was trying to process what had happened, he turned the other way and saw a Pakistani man lying there. Jason instinctively knew that this person was dead. I don't know whether he connected that body to the accident or just registered that there was a deceased person in the room. He was in shock. We put all the pieces together later.

There we were, devastated that a man had died and faced with murder charges against our son. The only good that had come out of that meeting with the Police Inspector General was that we finally retrieved our car, after being treated with considerable contempt by the local cops. What a sad state of affairs! Of course, the car had been wrecked, but the police had stripped it of everything they could put their hands on as well—personal belongings, mirrors, chrome, various usable parts. No one cared. They were the police. They could do as they pleased.

About this time, an article came out in the leading Pakistani newspaper detailing the car accident of October 11 and stating that it was Jason's fault. They got his name wrong—thank God. The news story went on to say that two people had been killed, and Jason had been arrested. Of course, he was sitting in our living room, not in a Pakistani jail. It hadn't been his fault and there was one person killed not two. There was just so much lying going on—the police, the newspaper. The entire Pakistani and expat community would be reading this story. Of course, our close friends knew better than to believe all the trumped-up nonsense. But it was another tightening of the noose for Jason and our family. Who could we trust to help us out of this mess?

An officer of the Canadian High Commission who met with Wayne only told him, "We're sorry that this happened to you." They wanted nothing to do with the situation. We were Canadian, but we weren't their responsibility. We weren't American, so we had no traction there either. Good friends of mine from school had come over to the house to comfort and support us. It was wonderful to know that we had caring friends, but they couldn't deliver us from our dilemma.

We were becoming more and more afraid that the police would soon try to arrest Jason. Wayne once again approached the UN offices to see if they could help. This time they made it clear that they had exhausted their influence. They were done. They referred us to a Pakistani lawyer.

The afternoon we spent in that lawyer's office was one of the worst of my life. He informed us that we had to attend a hearing, give up Jason's passport, state his case, and hope that he wouldn't go to jail. We all walked out of there holding hands, in tears. We were so defeated. So powerless.

Could it get any worse? Oh yes! The police began to threaten us. They claimed to have bloodwork from the hospital that proved Jason was under the influence of alcohol that night. They said that the family of the man who had died was demanding money—thousands and thousands of dollars. Money we didn't have. The noose was getting tighter.

As if all this wasn't enough, we were now the fodder of expat community gossip. My boss, Mike, called and told me that he was concerned about me and my family. There were too many damaging stories spiraling out of control. The religious right, Tildy, the just plain righteous—all of them were in judging mode.

One big problem for them, aside from the fact that they considered us to be terrible parents for allowing Jason to use the car, was that Jason was driving without a Pakistani driver's license. Of course, he had a Canadian driver's license, and he was mere months away from being able to get a proper Pakistani license.

The irony here was that absolutely no Pakistanis cared about that—not the police, not the courts, no one. The reason? A good many Pakistani drivers didn't have a proper driver's license. And those that did have a license usually got it by way of baksheesh. All you had to do was observe everyday traffic for five minutes to understand that most drivers didn't know or care about the rules of the road.

This driver's license thing was just an excuse for some expat gossip. Gossip that I chose to ignore. I found solace in my close friendships and let go of the rest. I appreciated Mike's concern, but words couldn't hurt us. The police and the corrupt Pakistani legal system could.

Then, just when we were losing all hope, the universe handed us a full-blown miracle. An ISOI colleague phoned me. I didn't know her well, but she reached out. Her husband had been involved in an accident in Islamabad, and they'd hired an excellent lawyer who had worked for the Bhutto family to help them out. Did we want the number? Yes! Yes, we did! I am forever indebted to this woman for calling me. She truly saved us.

The day we visited our new Pakistani lawyer was a turning point. He listened compassionately as we told our story. When we had finished emptying our souls onto his desk, he gave us a rare gift—the truth. He started by declaring that what the other lawyer had recommended didn't serve our needs. It wasn't in Jason's best interest to have a hearing. The Pakistani courts and justice system were rife with corruption. And Jason certainly shouldn't give up his passport.

Our lawyer went on to clarify the issue at hand. The family of the Pakistani man who had died in the accident was asking for Diya, which means blood money. In Islamic law, this financial compensation is paid to a victim or heirs of a victim in cases of homicide (intentional or unintentional), bodily harm, or property damage.

It is an alternative punishment to Qisas which means equal retaliation—an eye for an eye. Instead of Diya or Qisas, the victim's family can also choose to forgive the murder as an act of religious charity.

A "Qisas and Diya" ordinance had been introduced in Pakistan in 1990 by amending sections of the Penal Code. This had replaced British era criminal laws regarding murder. In short, we were dealing with Sharia Law, law according to the interpretation of the Holy Quran. Legal scholars have criticized the adoption of these laws as they "privatize" crimes and their consequences. Individuals get to assume the responsibility of determining whether other citizens should be punished, forgiven, or bargained over. The state takes a more passive role.

In our case, the family of the deceased hadn't gone down the path of forgiveness nor had they decided on "An eye for an eye." They wanted blood money. I had a strong feeling that they were highly influenced by the police, who I was starting to realize had been setting us up for a shakedown from the beginning.

There were a couple of glaring problems with this extortion, a far better word to describe what was happening. First, the family/police were asking for an exorbitant amount of blood money. Second, their expectations assumed that Jason was guilty. Our hands were tied. We couldn't have a hearing because the system was corrupt, and Jason would likely be found guilty. But in the absence of a hearing, guilt was assumed.

I kept wondering, "What happened to the driver of the van?" and "What happened to the passengers in the van?" and "How had everyone suddenly disappeared except for the spectre of the deceased?" and finally, "Shouldn't they be investigating the driver of the van?" As far as I could see the driver of the van was the real "murderer." But we were foreigners with money. There was no proper investigation of this case or "due process." Monetary compensation was simply determined by how much the parties involved thought they could squeeze out of us.

The truth is, we are compassionate people. We felt great sympathy for the family of the deceased; we would have been happy to give them some money to help them out in their time of grief. But we wouldn't deal in "blood money." Jason wasn't guilty of anything. Extortion blocked any acts of kindness.

Our lawyer went on to explain that the police were likely looking to get a large chunk of that money, and, as a result, they would exert more and more pressure on us. They were closing in, and it was just a matter of time before they showed up at our house. Therefore, the best way to protect Jason was to send him away. Not permanently, just temporarily, while the lawyer and his associates went to work negotiating and resolving the demands.

I couldn't hold back my tears. This lawyer, this caring man, turned and looked straight at me. He said, "Leave this with us. You will have to pay something, but it won't be anything like what they are asking of you. You don't have to worry anymore. Trust us. We will take care of this, and then we will call you."

And they did.

CHAPTER 22—THE SCARS

The next few months went by in a painful blur. We took our lawyer's advice and prepared to send Jason back to Canada. We knew this was the right decision in terms of protecting him, but it was still a tough one. He was in his senior year of high school, one of the most important years of his life. He was now being educated in the American International system, which prided itself on using approaches to education quite different from traditional American and Canadian systems. Jason was doing well in this new environment.

Sending him back to Canada would mean enrolling him in similar subjects (Math, English, etc.) within a vastly different curriculum. A course had been set for Jason when we moved to Islamabad. Now he was being asked to abruptly change direction midstream and still successfully attain the same goal, graduation.

We'd been so pleased, and so had Jason, with the improvement he was showing at the international school. What was going to happen now? Where would he be graduating? Canada or Pakistan? Even more important, would he be able to graduate at all?

We tried to make it as easy as possible for him. Luckily, we knew a Canadian couple, Betty and Lloyd, who were from our hometown and had lived in Pakistan before us. Their daughter was a graduate of ISOI, so they knew and understood both school systems. We asked if Jason could stay with them for a few months and go back to his old high school. They were more than happy to accommodate our request.

We'd met Betty and Lloyd prior to leaving Canada for our Pakistan posting. In 1990, it had been difficult to find any information about Pakistan. This was before the ease of finding information on the internet and there were scant library resources on this topic. Through friends and an old newspaper article, we discovered Betty and Lloyd and were able to discuss their time in Pakistan over afternoon tea. Lloyd retained some consulting connections in Pakistan after his return to Canada, so we saw him periodically after we moved to Islamabad.

Initially, we had thought to ask some of our old friends in Canada if Jason could stay with them for a while, but we didn't want to impose on them once again. They had kept Jason for a few weeks already when the kids and I were waiting for the Gulf War to end. Besides that, Betty and Lloyd had already experienced an expat life which revolved around taking in house guests whenever necessary. All Islamabad expats hosted students, teachers, and others who came from out-of-town. It was a given.

So, with mixed feelings, we put Jason on a plane armed with wire cutters. I was a mess. Our son was under threat of arrest and we were sending him away with a wired jaw, a potential choking hazard. His physical health was a significant concern, but I also worried about his emotional health. Would he get the love and support he needed in Canada? How long would he be gone? I prayed that he would be okay.

Due to Jason's broken jaw, hotel stays were out of the question. Upon arrival in England, Wayne had arranged for him to be picked up by a colleague he'd met while working in Bangladesh. Wayne had great respect for this guy, a Scotland Yard policeman, and he and his family generously welcomed Jason to an overnight stay. It felt like there was a worldwide village supporting us and lending a hand.

I was overjoyed to get the call that Jason had arrived safely in Canada. When he'd left Pakistan, he was so thin. Those wires had to go as soon as possible. Initially, my wishes for him were granted. He was re-enrolled at his former alma mater, and within two weeks of returning to Canada, he had the wires cut and removed. Now he could eat real food! He even managed to travel to the Calgary area and visit his grandparents for a few days.

In Islamabad, we were attempting to return to "normal." Both Wayne and I were back at work, and Julie was doing her best at school as always. The lawyer kept in touch with us to let us know how negotiations were progressing. Yet the police continued to be threatening, and one day, as we'd feared, a couple of them showed up at the house. Thank God Jason was in Canada!

Our guard wouldn't allow them past the gate, so Wayne was called out to speak with them. These two cops, more aptly called thugs, were working hard at being intimidating. Finally, Wayne couldn't take it anymore. He shouted at them to get off our property and never come back. He went off like a time bomb. All the pent-up frustrations poured out. He told them never to bother us again—we had a lawyer, and we were done with this police harassment.

It was amazing how things changed when we were no longer afraid. We had some protection, and they couldn't touch Jason now. When Wayne stood up to their bullying, we were finally free. They walked away, and we never saw them again. At least, not in the context of this matter. The demand for money didn't vanish, but everything from that moment on was done through our lawyer. He protected us from further threats.

There were some positive highlights during those temperate months of autumn. Julie was cast in the role of Marian the Librarian for the school musical, *The Music Man,* presented by the band and choir teachers. It opened to rave Islamabad reviews in November. We were once again very proud of her. She was developing a beautiful singing voice, both in the choir and the school musicals. I'm sure that this, plus a heavy academic workload, helped distract her from some of the ongoing troubles at home—an absent brother and parents who were overwrought and edgy much of the time.

The events of October 11 and the ensuing battle with the police and the corrupt justice system had weighed on us. Shock, stress, whirling gossip, family separation—all of this was taking a mental and emotional toll. Wayne was often withdrawn and depressed. Julie buried herself in schoolwork. Jason was troubled and adrift in a distant land.

And me? As the mom, I was trying to bolster the family spirits. The burden was dragging me down more than I wanted to admit. I felt a burgeoning hatred toward the Pakistani police. Also, I couldn't shake the terrible guilt and remorse I felt for granting Jason permission to drive the car that day. Would I ever forgive myself?

Wayne and I had long been proponents of extended walks on warm weekend afternoons. We were now taking advantage of this routine as much as possible. It helped to heal our minds, bodies, and spirits.

There was a large neighbourhood of military homes close to our house which was an ideal place for walking and talking. This sector was precisely laid out with manicured gardens boasting fragrant flowerbeds. The sidewalks were smooth and straight, and there were fewer stray dogs to beware of. We still took our walking sticks, just in case.

These strolls were therapeutic for both of us. Wayne was having trouble shaking his overwhelming sadness. He would retreat into silence at the dinner table while Julie and I filled the void with chatter. Many evenings he submerged himself in office paperwork for hours on end. I could see that he felt stuck in bottled up emotions. I wanted to support him despite my own jumble of thoughts and feelings.

Some days it was difficult to control my seething anger toward the police and the corrupt Pakistani legal system. We had come close to losing our son. A Pakistani man had died. I was still reeling from profound shock when all the menacing harassment began. The grueling months of negotiations ground on and on. We knew that our family was the subject of dinner party gossip. Most of the time we felt like we could trust no one. Other days we just felt hopeless. So,

Wayne and I walked and talked and laughed and cried. We allowed each other to rant and rave and let it all out. We held each other up and created some space to let go of our misery and let it float up into the ether. These were our mutual therapy sessions.

We also worked at keeping the spirit of Jason's humour and wit alive at the dinner table every night for Julie's sake. We were slowly healing, but we had scars. Jason's were visible. Yet all four of us would bear the intangible scars of October 1992 for the rest of our lives. This ill-fated collision had changed us in ways that we would revisit long into the future.

Suddenly, December was upon us. Our lawyer was still negotiating, but nothing had been settled. We needed to know when we could bring our son back to Islamabad. What about a Christmas homecoming? We were delighted when the answer was a firm and definite "Yes!" Our lawyer assured us that he had the situation in hand, and there were no more concerns for Jason's safety.

So, hearts brimming with joy, we arranged Jason's ticket back to Islamabad. Now we could be together for the holidays, and Jason could finish out his senior year. This was the best news we'd had in a long time. We started decorating for the season. I went ahead and planned a Christmas party for 90 people, including Jason and Julie's friends.

Once again, we lit up the house, threw down the red carpet, and prepared delicious food. I even managed to book the school choir, a fabulous group of singers, to perform Christmas Carols for our guests. It was a spectacular welcome back to Islamabad. There were tears and hugs for days.

Our son was home!

CHAPTER 23—THE HEALING

We'd planned a quiet family holiday in Thailand, some away time to regroup and reflect together. We chose a peaceful seaside resort in Pattaya which claimed to offer up stunning ocean sunsets.

As we were packing our bags, a letter arrived. It was from the couple that Jason had stayed with back in Canada. More precisely, it was from Betty. She'd put pen to paper to inform us that Jason hadn't followed their rules. He'd brought alcohol into their teetotaling household. She went on to say that Lloyd had just done what he had to do.

I was both taken aback and puzzled by this. Jason was a typical 17-year-old boy, and he could be strong-willed. I wasn't completely surprised that Jason hadn't followed all the rules. After all, he'd organized a party without our permission not that long ago. But I was somewhat astonished that Betty had gone to all the trouble of writing to me, especially when Jason's time with them was finished. What was the motivation behind this? I was even more puzzled by her reference to Lloyd "doing what he had to do." What was that all about? I had a lot of questions, so I knocked on Jason's bedroom door.

"Can I come in?"

Jason was searching his closet for beach clothes, "Sure. What's up mom?"

"I just received this letter from Betty."

"Oh, yeah? What does she have to say?"

"Well, first, she's saying that you broke the rules and brought alcohol into their home. What's that all about?"

Jason busied himself throwing t-shirts and shorts into a suitcase, "Well, yeah. I invited three of my friends over and the four of us shared six beers. It was very chill. Nothing got out of hand. No one had too much to drink."

"Ok. But you won't be 18 until January, so you were about a month and a half underage. Plus, you shouldn't have brought alcohol into their house if it was against their rules."

"You're right about the age thing mom, but I'm pretty close to 18, and they didn't give me any house rules. There was no mention of a 'no liquor under any circumstances' rule."

"Alright. We'll get back to that part in a minute. But first, I want to ask you about something else. She says that Lloyd did what he had to do. What does that mean?"

Jason slumped down on his bed and emitted a deep sigh, "Okay, Mom. Here's the entire story. I was hoping to spare you the details because you have enough on your mind. But here it is:

> Lloyd got a contract to do some work in the Middle East, so he and Betty were gone for a few weeks. Their daughter, Cassey, came over to check on me occasionally. I was a good houseguest, mom. I went to school, cleaned up after myself, hung out with my friends sometimes. No problems.

> Just a few days before I had to leave for Islamabad, I asked my friends over to have a "goodbye" get-together. We had some beer, like I told you. While they were there, Cassey dropped in. She seemed totally fine with my friends being there and with us having a beer. She even stayed and talked to us for a while. Then, about two days before I left, Betty and Lloyd returned. Everything was fine—all good. The time came for me to head to the airport, and my friends arrived to drive me there. They were waiting in the car, so I ran downstairs to grab my suitcase. Lloyd followed me.

At first, he was very calm. He asked me if I'd invited my friends over to drink beer while he and Betty were gone. I told him "yes." I added that Cassey had dropped in that day, and she'd seemed fine with it. Then I asked him if there was a problem.

He told me that, yes, this was a problem because no alcohol was allowed in their house under any circumstances. Then, without warning, he went from zero to one hundred. His face turned bright red. He grabbed me, threw me up against the wall, and put his hand around my neck. I don't want to repeat what he said to me, Mom. It would just really upset you. He was livid, out of his mind, threatening. I was stunned. He was so much stronger than me. I didn't know what might be coming next. Then, just as abruptly, he released me. I picked up my suitcase and barreled up the stairs out to the car as fast as my legs would carry me.

"And that's the whole story," Jason said.

I was both dumbfounded and angry. This was a lot to process. My mind was reeling with conflicting emotions. Betty and Lloyd had left a 17-year-old boy to fend for himself while they went overseas for several weeks. The waters were further muddied by the fact that they hadn't specified any important house rules.

When Wayne and I'd had to take an emergency trip to Karachi we made the mistake of leaving Jason and Julie on their own for a brief time with full house staff supervision and that hadn't worked out so well, so I was rather shocked to learn that Betty and Lloyd had abandoned their role as caretakers of a teenage boy who had been through a traumatic experience and separated from his family, all while attempting to navigate a different school system in his senior year. He was alone in the house. Sharing a couple of beers with friends was hardly the worst thing that could have happened under those circumstances.

At the same time, Jason had overstepped. He wasn't 18 yet and this wasn't his home, but why didn't Cassey talk to him about it? She must have known that simply reporting this to her strictly teetotalling parents would create a problem. Why didn't she confront Jason and deal with the boys right then and there?

Also, why did Lloyd confront Jason just as he was about to leave? What purpose did that serve? But, most of all, why did Lloyd threaten my son? He'd been abusive. Now I understood Betty's motivation in writing the letter. She was trying to get ahead of the narrative—protecting Lloyd. What should I do? What could I do?

Jason's Canadian sojourn was over. He'd done the wrong thing. It had been dealt with in a crazy dysfunctional fashion. He'd been through enough. We'd been through enough. There was nothing I could do about Lloyd's vitriolic outburst. We lived half a world away, and there was no evidence that he'd done physical harm to Jason.

Should I mete out some kind of punishment to Jason? What would that be? Hadn't there been plenty of punishment in the last few months?

I left Jason to his packing, went down to the kitchen, and made myself a cup of tea. How much more heartache could our family take? I was so tired of living in turmoil, fear, and uncertainty. The four of us needed to heal, recover, find some normalcy.   •

Lying in the sun listening to the heartbeat of ocean waves would be a good start. Jason and I could spend more time in productive conversation. Maybe we could all begin to forgive and forget. I got up, threw Betty's letter in the garbage, slowly climbed the stairs, and finished packing. My mind and my heart focused on one thought: "Thailand here we come!"

And once again, the Kingdom was all we needed it to be. This time we stayed at an elegant resort hotel in Pattaya. Ocean breezes, intense blood-orange sunsets, swaying palms, swimming, and snorkelling all provided the desired healing. Pattaya itself was far from our favourite place, mostly due to its massive skin industry—sex workers, bar girls, pedophiles—a perversion for everyone. So, we stuck to our resort, a world away from all of that. We had everything we needed with lounging, swimming, eating, and reading daily.

There were some day trips out to coral islands set in crystal-clear waters for the best snorkelling, an activity enjoyed by Jason, Julie, and Wayne. I still didn't have the courage to swim in the ocean depths. We sampled a variety of cuisines—Mexican, Thai, Chinese. Christmas Dinner was a sumptuous ocean-side buffet complete with dripping ice sculptures, intricate fruit carving, and dainty, graceful Thai dancers.

Another outing provided quite a different experience. One of our good friends in Islamabad was Thai. She recommended that we go to a transvestite show while in Pattaya. (The word transsexual wasn't in our vocabulary back then.) She gave us the names of some well-known shows and assured us that they were part of the fabric of Thai culture. We took her advice.

The costumes, make-up, and musical performances were second to none. And the Kathoey (transgender) performers were exotically beautiful. However, our soon-to-be 18-year-old son professed that he found all of this very confusing. Jason and Wayne went to the shooting range in the same building afterward. Perhaps this was a more uncomplicated pursuit!

Just before we were set to travel on to Bangkok for a couple of days of shopping for silks and souvenirs, I had a little mishap. Wayne and I were walking down a ramp that had been temporarily set up over the top of some stairs. Many people were waiting for a performance to start and we were trying to avoid the crowds. I inadvertently stepped to the side and lost my footing. Unbeknownst to me, the ramp had ended. My foot twisted painfully, and I fell backward.

Even though I was hurting, my face flushed with embarrassment as a crowd gathered. A wheelchair appeared out of nowhere and I was quickly bundled off to the nurse's office. The diagnosis: Probably a sprain; I would need to have it checked in Bangkok. I should have followed this advice, but I didn't want to spoil the family holiday. No one wanted to spend precious vacation time in a doctor's office.

All too soon it was time to return to Islamabad. As I limped into 1993, I wondered what the universe might throw at the four of us on this trip around the sun. Discoveries were looming just over the horizon.

CHAPTER 24—WE START AGAIN

We flipped the calendar to a fresh new year back in our Park Road home, our familiar surroundings. Somehow, it felt like we were beginning all over again. Did we see Islamabad through a new lens? We had been and still were, going through some tough times. Pakistan had dealt us a few blows. We couldn't wind back the clock and return to who we were before October 11, 1992. Hopefully, the future would see us dusting ourselves off, acquiring an expanded perspective. There was no crystal ball.

It was glorious to have Jason home. Nonetheless, I worried about how life at ISOI would be for him now. Would his grades drop in this crucial final semester? I couldn't be sure how much the effect of the upheaval of changing schools would have on his academic performance. He didn't have a solid relationship with studying and homework at the best of times.

Even more important was the state of his emotional health. Jason had always been private and reserved when it came to sharing feelings. I think he genuinely didn't want to burden others with his issues. He seemed okay. He had good friends and an enviable social life. I had no idea what might be going on under the surface. Did he have nightmares? Did he have flashbacks about the night of the accident? Whatever the case, he didn't want outside professional help and there wasn't a lot of that available to us at any rate. I needed to remain watchful.

At the end of the previous school year, which seemed like centuries ago, I'd agreed to direct the 1993 winter play at ISOI. During our Canadian summer holiday, I'd chosen *The Foreigner* by Larry Shue. I'd never heard of this play, recommended by the specialty bookshop owner. When I sat down to give it a trial read, I found myself laughing out loud, which was highly unusual, especially from an initial reading. I felt like I was holding a secret gem. I couldn't wait to hone it, present it to the community, and let it shine.

But so much had happened since that light-hearted day in the bookshop. Could I still go through with this? I already had a challenging, fulfilling job teaching ESL. Things were a little fragile at home. Extortion negotiations were ongoing. Moreover, we were attempting to organize ourselves around family transport since we no longer had a personal vehicle.

In Canada, the Honda would have been written off. It was totally smashed in on the driver's side. It was a wreck. But the frame had remained intact, and the mechanic at the Pakistani garage assured Wayne that he could rebuild our car. We'd never heard of such a thing but decided to give it a shot. What did we have to lose?

In the meantime, we shared Wayne's project vehicle, and I limped around at school. My foot was becoming increasingly painful and swollen. Nevertheless, I felt that I just didn't have time to attend to that. Busy, busy, busy.

Jan and I auditioned students for the play, and Jason got the lead role. I was over-the-moon happy for him. This was a boost that he sorely needed. Also, I knew that he would do a superb job of bringing the character to life. He was talented, but this had remained a closely guarded secret. ISOI had yet to see this side of him.

Julie asked if she could be my assistant director, and with Jan's help, I put together a full cast and crew. It was so much fun directing this play! Jason, Julie, and I were all together for long hours of rehearsals after school. Then we would come home and discuss the fine points of acting and directing through dinner. Poor Wayne! He had no choice but to listen to theatre talk day and night. I don't think he minded too much. This activity was pulling our family together and providing a laid-back, lively focus.

Alas, my foot problems were becoming unbearable. I was finally forced to capitulate and make an appointment with a Pakistani doctor. He informed me that I had some broken bones and would need a cast. Damn! I didn't have time to painstakingly hop around on crutches, so I asked him to make a walking cast.

This turned into a minor disaster since he had no idea how to forge such a thing. He didn't have the proper materials and I ended up in a makeshift cast with a lopsided heel. I must have looked a sight shambling around the ISOI campus.

By a strange coincidence, Jan tripped and broke her ankle right around this same time. She had a cast as well—a proper one done at the American Clinic. We thought of calling ourselves "Broken Leg Productions." Fortunately, I only had to wear my cast for about three weeks. Unfortunately, it was a good two years before I walked properly again.

There was a bright spot during these busy times. We finally hired an excellent, responsible cook. After our Christmas party, I'd had enough of so-so Simon and began to cast around for a replacement. Khan wondrously appeared at the house one day, and he was there to stay. He didn't have the warm loving personality of Harry, but he had cooking skills that would rival those of many celebrity chefs. Khan made spring rolls from scratch and baked all our bread. This was such a godsend, as loaves of bread sold in the markets of Islamabad tasted like cardboard. Of course, Pakistanis could be forgiven for not having good western bread-making skills as they were largely consumers of roti and naan. But Khan could do all this and more. He'd worked for several expat families and loved to cook. For him, the culinary arts were both a skill and a passion.

The only caveat was that I had to provide him with a daily menu. So, every week I sat down and wrote out specifics for seven days of breakfast, lunch, and dinner. Sometimes I complained about having to do this, but the time spent was well worth it. I had a ton of cookbooks with recipes from almost every type of cuisine the world offered. Anything I proposed he could make, sometimes better than the original. The kid's friends loved the food at our house. Khan had a knack for baking sweet dishes like my recipe for Apple Crumble.

One of Julie's friends made a special request for this whenever she stayed over.

We had to get used to Khan though. He was much more circumspect than Harry and he could be petulant and fussy at times. He was a devout Muslim and, as such, prepared and cooked all his own food. Luckily, even though he was a strict vegetarian and, according to his religious beliefs, would never eat pork products, he was happy to cook whatever we wished to eat, even bacon and pork chops.

Periodically, he would do up large batches of deliciously spiced stews and freeze enough portions for a month or so. This would be his daily breakfast, lunch, and dinner. He never veered from this regime nor did he eat between meals. As opposed to Harry, Khan was slim, well-groomed, and disciplined. He exercised regularly and he was meticulously clean about himself and his surroundings. As a result, our kitchen was spotless and everything we ate had been safely cleaned, stored, and prepared.

His wish was to work every day and then take all his accumulated days off at the end of the month to visit family in his mountain village. This was fine with us. As the months passed, we gradually warmed up to Khan and began to understand his ways. By the time we left Pakistan we had become quite attached to him and he to us. I even got accustomed to him asking me detailed recipe questions just as I was leaving for work!

January ended with a birthday celebration—Jason's 18th. We had a delicious lobster dinner courtesy of our American Commissary exchange complete with a champagne toast. Every community we've ever lived in has had "that lady who makes the fancy cakes," and Islamabad was no exception. Jason's cake was decorated with a realistic-looking video camera, reflecting his long passion for video and film. Our singular birthday wish was that 1993 be a successful year for our son.

Toward the end of February, newspaper headlines around the world announced that a bomb had exploded in the parking garage of the World Trade Center in New York City. This was an early indication that terrorism wasn't just a regional problem outside of the US but was becoming a transnational occurrence. The group of Middle Eastern radicals responsible for the attack was quickly identified and most of those involved were arrested before they could escape the country. However, one managed to flee—Ramzi Yousef, the driver of the van containing the explosives. There was suspicion that he was hiding in Pakistan. However, it would be another two years before they apprehended him.

The expat as well as the local Islamabad community took great interest in this chilling story. Americans formed a sizeable part of the expat community in Pakistan and they were troubled by this event. Was this an indication that there could be future attacks? Everyone wondered if and where this fugitive might be in Pakistan. Also, these kinds of attacks often had a polarizing effect. Islamic fundamentalism was steadily on the rise in Pakistan and soon to reveal itself on a more global platform. But none of us knew that this was the beginning of a chain of events that would culminate in a world-shattering tragedy.

In the meantime, our everyday life continued with many community events. At the Winter Ball Thai silks and tuxes once again dominated another of ISOI's traditional socials. The Winter Carnival at ISOI was unique. Camel rides were offered, as well as rides on a small haphazardly assembled Ferris wheel, hand-operated by one of the Pakistani staff positioned at the top of a tall step ladder. Photo opportunities abounded. The National Honor Society evening was one of formal capes, banners, a specialty cake, and newly inducted members.

After long days of rehearsals, opening night of *The Foreigner* finally arrived. Our play was met with great enthusiasm by the ISOI community—sold-out performances, ovations, everything we could have hoped for. Jason still proudly displays the poster signed by all his fellow actors and crew members the night of the cast party at our house.

Khan and Peter outdid themselves with food and décor. Peter had a natural talent for flower arranging and had begun to create amazing centerpieces. That night he'd put together gladiolas, mixed wildflowers, and miniature tangerines. I think he walked all over town searching for materials for his creations. People may have been wondering why flowers mysteriously went missing from their gardens.

The cast and crew were all smiles posing around their *Foreigner*-themed cake. Everyone had done brilliant work. We had much to be proud of. Our play had been a comedy, but it spoke more deeply about communication and how humans relate to each other. I think many in the ISOI community could relate to the themes underlying the laugh-out-loud situational misunderstandings. After all, the audience was largely composed of foreigners!

Jason, Julie, and I had poured ourselves into this project. It became a true landmark in our lives, signalling the way forward, a light at the end of a long, dark tunnel. We hoped that it would help to erase some of the negativity that was still surreptitiously hanging at the edges of our lives.

Some of this negativity could be observed in sudden dissension between the Pakistani boys and the American boys at ISOI. This had come as a surprise to teachers and students alike as everyone had been getting along fine, and then, there was an abrupt shift in attitudes and behaviour.

Was the growing Fundamentalism in Pakistan and Afghanistan affecting Islamabad families? How serious were the tensions between nations, perhaps even trickling down to the local level, due to the explosion at the World Trade Center in New York? Did some of the American boys display negative attitudes about Pakistanis?

I didn't know the answers to those questions, but I worried that there might be threats against Jason because of his accident. We were Canadian, not American, but many people, worldwide, couldn't differentiate. The rumours about the car crash could easily be used as fuel in this fiery conflict.

I had a niggling feeling that Jason was being targeted some days. If he experienced anguish over this, he didn't share it with me. Thankfully, this testosterone-fueled rivalry wore itself out and blew over within a couple of months. I breathed a sigh of relief.

I had more imminent worries. Jason wasn't applying himself to his schoolwork since his return for the final semester. I'd feared that this might become a problem. All the trauma of the accident plus changing school systems twice was bound to have an adverse effect. Jason was letting things slide. I felt like I was constantly nagging him to get some schoolwork done.

Julie was worrying me as well. Sometimes I would hear her crying in her room after school. Then, one day, my boss, Mike, approached me to say that he'd seen Julie sitting by herself in the far corner of the quad. He described her as looking "about as sad as a person could be." It was time for a talk.

The house was quiet as the evening was drawing to a close. I knocked on Julie's bedroom door. She was sitting cross-legged on her bed amid textbooks and papers.

"Hey, Julie. How are things going these days?"

"Fine, Mom. Just doing my homework. What's up?"

"You seem a little sad. Is everything ok at school?"

"I guess things are ok. I feel like I should be doing better. I work half the night on homework. I would like to raise my grades but that doesn't seem to be happening."

"Julie, you are achieving high honours in most of your subjects! I don't think anyone could do better than that. I wish you wouldn't be so hard on yourself."

"I know, I know. Sometimes I just don't believe I'm 'good enough.' I don't exactly know why. It's just a feeling that comes over me. I guess it might also have something to do with Brian."

"What do you mean?"

"We've been arguing a lot lately. Sometimes things are great and other times we feel jealous or like the other person isn't paying enough attention. I don't know what's happening. It feels like we might break up."

With that, she burst into tears and I folded her in my arms. I couldn't predict what would happen to her relationship. Still, I understood the pain of a broken heart when "first love" comes to an end. Brian would be graduating soon and beginning university in the US. Their paths were destined to diverge no matter what.

I was troubled by Julie's defeatist mindset. She was doing well in school yet still felt undeserving. I suspected that this was a fallout from the ordeal of the last six months. All I could do was provide support and a compassionate, listening ear. I would have given anything for a magic wand to wave all these problems away.

Despite our worries and concerns, life went on as usual. Wayne had another work trip to take. This time Sindh province and the city of Hyderabad on the banks of the Indus River. Travels in Pakistan revealed fascinating historical landmarks. Wayne took some time out from his work schedule to learn about bygone eras in this once strategically located city.

In the 1700s a fort had been built on one of Hyderabad's surrounding hills for defense purposes. It was made of clay bricks and, astonishingly, still stood as a strong mud fort. However, one of the most notable historic inventions displayed there was the windcatcher. It was thought that the windcatchers of Hyderabad houses dated back 500 years. These triangular rooftop projections caught the wind and channeled it into the house, providing cooling air circulation. The Aga Khan Maternity Hospital incorporated this feature into its modern design.

Wayne was shown relics from the British era as well as examples of the city's long association with *Sufism.*[44] Hyderabad was once a great trading center, but many of its historic structures had been badly neglected. This was the woeful story of many incredible places in Pakistan.

Our family was still experiencing ups and downs but, at the same time, we were developing a deeper appreciation of our South Asian home with all of its contradictions.

---

[44] Sufism is the name of the religion that Sufis practice. Sufism is a mystical variation of Islam by which Sufis seek to have a close, personal experience of God.

CHAPTER 25—AN UNEVEN EVOLUTION

Spring break was upon us, and what a well-deserved break it was. Jason and Brian were seniors, and since there hadn't been a designated trip for all those graduating together, the boys decided to take a vacation by themselves—destination Sri Lanka. They didn't divulge many details of this visit. They told a couple of vague stories about meeting some Russian flight attendants and sitting around the pool much of the time. I decided that I didn't need to know more.

Julie stayed with friends while Wayne and I travelled south to discover Lahore, known as the "City of Gardens" because of its many parks. It was also thought of as the cultural heart of Pakistan thanks to Lollywood, the center of the Urdu film industry. But I considered it to be the educational seat of Pakistan based on its prestigious universities and colleges. However one chose to think of this intriguing city, it was rich in history and architectural design.

Lahore was the capital of the Punjab province. According to legend, it was founded thousands of years ago and served as the central capital during several Hindu dynasties, under some Mughal Emperors, and throughout the Sikh empire of the 19th century. The city reached its zenith during the Mughal period. At the time of Mughal Emperor Jahangir (father to Shah Jahan, builder of the Taj Mahal), Lahore was considered to be the most beautiful city in the world. The ancient "Walled City" reflects much of this history whereas the newer areas and suburbs are from the time of the British Raj.

We loved Lahore, a place of cultural and religious tolerance. Because of the influence of the many Sufi saints that had inhabited the area in the past, there was little religious extremism. Unfortunately, during Partition, this tolerance was lost for a while. In that dark time, some of the worst rioting had occurred here. By the 1990s, this had been long forgotten. We felt comfortable and relatively safe compared with our experiences in other Pakistani cities. It was a welcoming place.

Most of the monuments we visited were built during the Mughal period and revealed the intricate geometric art and architecture of the time. First up was the Badshahi Mosque constructed by Emperor Aurangzeb in 1674. It exhibited an intense beauty—made of red sandstone and highlighted with spherical domes of white marble. Standing majestically in front of the mosque was Lahore Fort. It had been rebuilt by Akbar in 1566 and added onto by all his successors. The Audience Halls, Mirror Palace, and Pearl Mosque enhanced its grandeur.

We went on to visit Jahangir's tomb, built by his son Shah Jahan. You could see some similarities to the Taj Mahal, especially in the design of the fountains and gardens. The interior mosaics were spectacular. After traversing the winding streets of the old city, we stopped by the Royal Bath, and Wayne had his photo taken seated in the Royal chair under an enormous, hammered copper plate. He pretended to smoke shisha from an ornate hookah pipe. The ceiling above him boasted a mesmerizing Islamic geometric design.

A trip to Lahore would have been meaningless if we'd missed viewing the Shalimar Garden, also created by the prolific Shah Jahan. Shalimar means "Abode of Love." This triple-terraced garden with marble pavilions, ornamental ponds, waterfalls, and fountains was built for the pleasure of the royal family.

We were noticing a "water" theme in all Mughal architecture. Since their cities and forts were built in semi-arid or exceedingly hot climates, the fountains and ponds served the function of cooling the air circulating throughout the gardens and buildings—ancient air conditioning.

Next on our tour was Wazir Khan Mosque (1634), considered the jewel of the old city, the most ornately decorated mosque of the era. We were bowled over by the lavish motifs of the original frescoes.

The most amazing stop on this visit was the Lahore Museum made famous in Rudyard Kipling's novel, *Kim*. The author's father had been one of the museum's earliest curators. The majestic red brick building, a blend of Mughal design with British era architecture, opened in 1894 during the British Colonial period.

The Lahore Museum housed Pakistan's largest and oldest collection of historical, cultural, and artistic objects and was one of the most unique and intriguing museums I had ever explored. We viewed archaeological material from prehistoric times up to the Hindu Shahi period.

In the '90s, it was too dangerous for foreigners to visit the site of the Indus Valley civilizations, dating back to 3000 BC, in Sindh province. Harappa and Mohenjo-Daro were some of the earliest settlements in the world. It was a huge disappointment that we lived so close to some of the world's first civilizations and were unable to travel there. For this reason, I was excited and overjoyed to be able to view artifacts from these ancient cities.

We observed relics from the Gandhara and Greco-Bactrian periods, as well as Mughal and Sikh carved woodwork. There was a large collection of paintings dating back to the British period. *The Fasting Buddha* from the Gandhara period was one of the museum's most prized objects. I could have spent a full two days exploring these treasures of the past.

All too soon it was time to wing our way back to Islamabad. Lahore had fleetingly delivered us from the burdens and sorrows of the past months. We'd been transported back in time. I toyed with the fantasy of staying there. Ahh yes, fantasies were enchanting, but I had a real family and real responsibilities waiting for me. Time to get back to Park Road.

We had arrived at the final quarter of the school year, for Jason, the final months of Grade 12. I hit the ground running as I was charged with coordination of all the drama workshops for the upcoming Fine Arts Festival. International schools from the region—Pakistan, India, Nepal, Bangladesh—came to participate in this five-day celebration of art, music, and drama. Concerts and plays were performed throughout the festival and, of course, ISOI presented *The Foreigner*. I was giving a half-day workshop of my own as well.

The final night of the festival included the improvisation competition known as *Instant Rapport*. The participants prepared a general script for a scene in advance but were given an acting partner at the last moment. In 1992 Julie had won the best actress. But Jason won the best actor competition that night in 1993. I was proud of him and secretly hoped that this would provide him with much-needed encouragement and inspiration to focus on his academic courses for the remainder of the year.

To keep adult spirits up, this season of hard work was interspersed with lots and lots of parties. How our lives had changed from all those years living in a sleepy Canadian suburb! The vibrant social life in Islamabad was relished by expats and Pakistanis alike.

As I've said before, the rather restricted environment and absence of local entertainment venues made it necessary for people to create their own entertainment. These social experiences were so much better than a night out at the local bar or restaurant back in Canada.

I loved it. It gave all of us a strong sense of community. I was reminded of my years growing up on a Canadian prairie farm. The long dark winter evenings would be brightened by neighbourhood dinner parties and the community hall would be buzzing with events in every season of the year. It had been years since I'd felt this sense of belonging, of being part of a cohesive identity.

That said, there was a wide variety of social affairs in Islamabad which varied from formal to informal, structured to intimate, political to homespun ... Some parties in Islamabad were lavish affairs where everyone dressed in their finest attire and stood around drinking cocktails. Many of these gatherings were of a business or political nature. Because Wayne worked for the UN, we attended our fair share of these soirees full of small talk; designed to impress. They were attended by ambassadors, heads of state, and other prominent figures. From time to time, we exchanged greetings with the Prime Minister of Pakistan.

I learned two things from these get-togethers. First, I hated small talk. Because I was often thought of as "the wife" people would speak to me out of obligation while actively eyeing their next quarry. I much preferred authentic conversations. The second thing I learned early on was that I needed strong legs. There was absolutely no place to sit—ever. It was like being in a prison that mandated standing room only. There should have been a sign at the entrance to Islamabad: "You need strong legs to live here."

Then there were dinner parties. Sometimes these were composed of close friends and an evening of laid-back fun and conversation. Others were more formal and involved meeting "important" people. Invitations to these dinners included a dress code so we had some idea of what to expect—casual for a relaxed evening or semi-formal for something more starched. However, we never knew who to expect as the distinguished guest(s).

Islamabad dinner parties, ours included, were carried on in the tradition of the British Raj. Tables were elegantly decorated with formal place settings and we were served each course by the household staff (as in *Downton Abbey*). People borrowed each other's cooks and bearers to assist depending on the number of guests attending.

Customarily, there was a seating arrangement. The hostess would go to great pains to make sure that people were strategically placed around the table according to status, temperament, alliances, etc. But these seating arrangements didn't always work out as planned.

One evening we were invited to dinner at the home of a UN colleague. The guests were a diverse mix of people who worked for various embassies. The distinguished guest of honour was the European Union Ambassador, an older, stern-faced German man.

Regrettably, I was seated next to him. He waxed on and on regarding his political views as the dinner guests hung on his every word. He was the very definition of a "stuffed shirt" who enjoyed the sound of his own voice. There had been recent news out of Iran regarding attitudes and policies toward women, so Mr. EU Ambassador decided to bless us with his staunch observations on women's rights. In my mind, some of his dogma bordered on misogyny, but everyone around him was nodding and smiling in approval. I instinctively understood that they were agreeing with him because of his status. I believe the more vulgar term is "sucking up to him."

I pressed my lips tightly together in an attempt to block my inner monologue from escaping my mouth. Finally, I couldn't take it any longer. I caught his eye, straightened up in my chair, and declared that I had the opposite view. I added that I was sure many women would choose to disagree with his stance. The Ambassador was non-plussed by my remarks and everyone's eyebrows shot up. Men of importance were often shocked when I was assertive. My remarks certainly weren't the stuff of revolution, but this kind of confrontation was frowned upon. There was an unwritten code that high ranking folks weren't to be contradicted. I had never been a proponent of this philosophy. If I thought something was unfair, unjust, or plainly wrong I couldn't sit quietly.

In the end, there was no real dustup over this. The conversation around the table was awkward for a minute or two, and then new topics were introduced. Wayne often held his breath during these dinners. My inner feminist would never allow me to be a "good girl" and sit quietly. There was no international incident that night, but the hostess might need to give extra thought to my seat placement for the next dinner party.

On the home front, I was becoming increasingly concerned about Jason's academic performance. His grades were slipping. He wasn't focusing on his studies—math in particular. He and his math teacher had a personality clash that wouldn't be resolved. They couldn't seem to make allowances for each other. Both of them had complained to me. Jason was floundering in a few other subjects at school as well as a correspondence course from Canada. This situation needed to turn around dramatically for him to be accepted into post-secondary institutions. I kept urging him to work harder and organize his studies. I felt like I was pushing a boulder uphill.

I wasn't sure if Jason's issues were a domino effect owing to the accident or if he was just more absorbed with girls than schoolwork. Sometimes I worried about teacher attitudes as well. One day I happened to be chatting with two high school teachers. Suddenly the conversation turned to Jason and they started making snide remarks.

I was very hurt by this. Didn't they realize that Jason was my child? Even though he was a tall teenager he was still my little boy? One of them had a young child and the other hadn't had children yet. I guess they just weren't thinking. Jason wasn't perfect but he was a good kid.

Other apprehensions were stacking up as we headed into Prom season. Jason had a custom-made tuxedo and a new high school girlfriend. Julie had the stunning white cocktail dress we'd purchased in San Francisco. At the time of that purchase, we'd all assumed that she would be going to the Prom with Brian. But high school relationships rarely last forever and, sadly, they had broken up just before spring break. So, who would escort her to the Prom, arguably the most notable affair of the school year?

No one could have predicted that her date would show up in the form of a 23-year-old marine. Wayne and I were not impressed. Julie assured us that he was just a friend and had simply volunteered to accompany her for the evening. We acquiesced on the condition that this "friendship" was not to continue past Prom night.

The Prom itself was a huge success. Some friends of ours hosted the after-party and we provided breakfast to all the kids who were still awake. Soon after, much to our relief, due to a couple of heated conversations at home, Julie ended her friendship with the marine.

The next hurdle we faced was the frustrating experience of filling out college admission forms for Jason. Phone calls revealed that papers were missing, and deadlines were approaching. We were in a mad rush to fulfill all the regulations and get college submissions delivered on time. The good news was that Jason was finally raising his grades. It was looking like he would have enough credits to graduate. Now we just had to get him into college!

Once again, May was the month of goodbyes. End-of-the-year school events provided our celebrations. At the Concert in the Park, families packed their picnic lunches and enjoyed musical performances in the school's outdoor Amphitheatre. The weather was always warm and sunny at this time of year. Soft breezes caressed our smiling faces in the lingering sunset as we shared the bittersweet camaraderie of yet another school year coming to an end.

Hot on the heels of this event was the Athletic and Performing Arts Awards night. I gave out special Thespian awards to deserving students. Jason and Julie were among the recipients, and Julie won a singing award as well. She'd most recently performed *At the Ballet* from *Chorus Line* at the outdoor concert. ISOI had a wonderful knack for nurturing the students' talents.

Before we knew it, we were facing final exams and graduation. We gave Jason some lapis lazuli cuff links and a tie pin as a graduation gift. Although precious and expensive in North America this stone was readily available in Central Asia. Afghanistan had many mines.

I jokingly told Jason that he should probably give me a gift as well. I'd stayed the course, sweating by his side all the way. That night, the graduation ceremonies engendered ear-to-ear smiles for both parents and students. Another milestone realized.

Then goodbye parties were required for our departing friends. Many USAID (US Agency for International Development) families were moving on to other postings. There had been a rather fraught relationship between Pakistan and the USA since the enactment of the 1980s *Pressler Amendment,* which banned economic and military aid to Pakistan unless its government certified on an annual basis that it didn't possess a nuclear explosive device.

In the early 1990s, the United States had begun to suspend the flow of aid to Pakistan due to its emerging nuclear programme. The US was getting tired of hearing what they viewed as blatant lies. Pakistan regularly declared that they had no nuclear capability but there was lots of evidence to the contrary. As a result, we were seeing a gradual exodus of American expats who worked for aid agencies.

Some of our best friends were relocating to exotic locations such as Bangkok, Cairo, and Argentina. We were discovering one of the thorny consequences of living overseas. Fast friendships were formed in a close, small-town environment. But these strong connections were doomed to end in tearful goodbyes. Families inevitably moved on. We made solemn promises to visit each other. Would we do it? Could we do it? Time would tell.

CHAPTER 26—ON THE ROAD AGAIN

It was time to pack our bags for the summer holidays. But before we did that, our lawyer called. He'd reached an agreement with the police and the family of the deceased man regarding blood money. We held our breath. Months of hard-won negotiations had resulted in good news. The final settlement was no small figure, but it was something we could handle. All parties were satisfied. The police, the family, and our lawyer would each take a cut. We never knew how the money was divided. I hoped that the family got the larger share of the loot, although I was no longer naïve enough to assume that was the case. For our family, the nightmare was over. We breathed a collective sigh of relief and walked forward into a better future—we hoped.

In less positive news, our Honda was still at the Islamabad garage. Whenever Wayne went to check on the car there were mechanics crawling all over it. This situation didn't look too promising, but we were assured that it would be finished and as good as new when we returned from vacation.

The head mechanic gave us his word. Strangely enough, in this country rife with corruption, one's word was considered one's honour. Handshakes and verbal commitments were almost always fulfilled. We were willing to wait and see.

We had a big summer ahead of us—part holiday, part work, part family obligations. The first leg of our trip was from Pakistan to Greece. Our Islamabad friends had shared stories of wonderful weeks on Greek islands, and we couldn't wait. First, we had to get through an eight-hour PIA flight from Karachi to Athens.

Our airplane had "smoking" and "non-smoking" sections. We were in the latter. Wayne and I quickly became the smoking monitors as Pakistani men kept lighting up and visiting with their friends all around us. Of course, they didn't care about rules or health. They were accustomed to behaving as they pleased. I was ready to get aggressive with one smoker who was exceptionally rude to me, but Wayne calmed me down. No sense in causing an international incident! We were headed for holidays. It was time to look for some serenity.

Greece was everything we hoped for and more. Jason and Julie were teenagers and could be hard to please, but they loved these islands as much as we did. It was impossible not to fall in love with all things Greek, best described in poetic highlights.

Santorini,
Breathtaking volcanic beauty.
Whitewash and turquoise against black cliffs.
Wine tasting, archaeological digs, dazzling sunsets.
Walking the cliffs, old cobblestone streets of Thira
Dodging donkeys, biting into dripping sweet citrus,
Sleepy-eyed at the taverna, potent crimson cocktails.
Blue Note Café Oia—calamari, ouzo shots,
The sun sets over cave houses.
We are in a movie, a stunning lucid dream.
May we never wake from this.

Afloat on the ferry to…

Paros,
Fishing boats, octopus hanging on the line for lunch.
Whitewash glints in the noonday sun as potted plants
Nod their heads in deep blue window wells.
Warm clear water laps onto sandy beaches.
Countryside of stone walls, villages, windmills, a butterfly valley.
Sit back, stretch, relax.
The island beckons us to stay forever.

A tiny airport, the size of a village garage.
Soaring over the clouds to…

Athens,
Home of the Acropolis
High on a limestone hill,
Citadel of temples, Parthenon,
Homage to Athena, Symbol of wealth.
Ancient Greek theatre, Olympic stadium.
Plaka district, historical neighbourhood,
Labyrinth of streets, art galleries, boutiques,
Cozy restaurants, barrels of take-out olives.
Museum of Archaeology, bronze statues,
Miles of urns, gold jewelry, bust of Zeus colossus.
Smooth, cool drinks on our hotel rooftop,
Mesmerized by the twinkling nighttime Acropolis.

Ruins of Temple of Delphi,
Burial vases, Paros marble statues,
Climbing, climbing to the treasury,
Greece as the center of the world.
Regal temple of Poseidon,
By the sea, breezes and goodbyes.

It took all our willpower to tear ourselves away from Greece. The four of us still remember it as a picturesque, sepia-tinged daydream. It was a unique cultural experience, so different from both North America and South Asia. Santorini held a special kind of magic for all four of us. We vowed to return one day to this volcanic island of soaring cliffs and whitewashed villages. Someday …

Most of our holidays came with some specific memories. Stories we told for many years. Our Greek vacation was no different.

Each place we visited in Greece required plenty of walking. The Acropolis was a particularly strenuous adventure in uphill climbing. We were all close to exhaustion at the end of our last day of visiting this historical wonder. As we proceeded to trek back to our hotel, we were desperately seeking a taxi. With relief, we finally hailed one along a rather deserted stretch of road. Wayne bent close to the driver's window and told him we wanted to go to the nearest McDonald's.

The taxi driver's face clouded over. He refused to allow us into his cab. He shouted, "You are tourists in Athens, city of the world's finest food. And you want to go to McDonald's. You are crazy, stupid Americans!"

With that, he spun out and drove off. There wasn't another taxi in sight. He'd sentenced us to the punishment of walking several kilometres back to our hotel. The kids were disturbed and upset by this, as they loved Greece and Greek food. This cabbie didn't realize that these two teenagers had been living in Pakistan. They just wanted a taste of McDonald's for the first time in many months. Cab drivers in Athens were the least favourite part of our Greek vacation.

Another memory that stands out during this time turned out to be the beginning of a different kind of journey. Something was happening to Julie. At first, she complained of feeling a bit more tired than usual after a day of touring and walking. By the time we were coming to the end of our tour of Greece, travelling to visit the Delphi and Poseidon temples, she had to lie down and sleep all the way there and back. This exhaustion was out of character, but we put it down to a year of stress at home and hard work at school.

The next stop of our summer of '93 four-country tour was Vienna. A check-in at headquarters for Wayne, another new holiday discovery for the rest of us. Vienna boasted a superb mix of classical architecture—everything from the Gothic St. Stephan's Cathedral (1300s) to the Baroque Schonbrunn Palace (1740), Belvedere Gardens (the 1700s), and The Hofburg (1552). The Ringstrasse, once considered the most beautiful boulevard in the world, was lined with over three miles of neo-Gothic and neo-Baroque buildings including the Museum of Fine Arts and the Vienna Opera House. Although there were gorgeous examples of modern architecture and Art Nouveau as well, we were more interested in classical styles.

Like most of the world's population, we still thought of Vienna as the home of Strauss and Freud. Now we were beginning to realize that the city was so much more. After touring the UN buildings, we wandered around central Vienna, lit candles in St. Stephan's Cathedral, and had our photos taken in front of the ornate Baroque Era buildings. Jason and Julie wanted to go shopping, but it was mostly the "window" variety as prices were very steep.

One evening we enjoyed the rides at the permanent amusement park not far from our hotel. The Wurstelprater dated back to the time of the Austrian Empire under Joseph II when it opened to the public in 1766. It accommodated many rides, a wax museum, and some restaurants. But the best-known attraction was the 212-foot-tall Ferris wheel constructed in 1897. Riding this was a blast and one for the memory books. This landmark had come to symbolize the city itself.

Julie and I ventured out on our own and took a whirlwind tour of the Schonbrunn Palace, otherwise known as the Hapsburg Summer Palace. With 1400 of the most ornately decorated rooms imaginable and massive manicured gardens, it was almost impossible to absorb the scope and magnitude of this royal residence. Picture Versailles on steroids.

Wayne wanted to surprise us with a treat, so he took us to the oldest building in Vienna, home of a famous schnitzel restaurant. Eating schnitzel in Vienna was a rite of passage; it was melt-in-the-mouth delectable. Running a close second as a "must-have" experience was an afternoon visit to one of the many coffee houses. There, we were served the famous Viennese espresso, topped with mounds of whipped cream. It was a requirement to partner this with at least two slices of rich Vienna-style chocolate cake layered with apricot jam and decorated with a shimmering glaze of chocolate icing. Counting calories was forbidden!

As we sat in these coffee houses, we were struck by a Viennese cultural curiosity. Most restaurants and cafés strongly disapproved of children. It was a "leave the kids at home" society. But dogs were welcome everywhere and treated like royalty. They sat up at the tables and ate cakes with their masters. They were pampered and doted upon. We didn't see many children on the streets of Vienna. However, we stepped over doggie doo-doo frequently.

As much fun as we were having, our worries were beginning to build concerning Julie's condition. Besides having extreme fatigue, her eyes were becoming very swollen. We managed to schedule some time with a Viennese eye doctor who diagnosed her condition as a type of allergy. We were sent away with eye drops. I had a niggling feeling that this wasn't the answer. I didn't have much time to ponder this diagnosis as it was time to board a plane once again for the next leg of our journey, New York City.

Wayne had spent a week or so there when he first began with the UN. June 1993 was the first time in "the Big Apple" for Jason, Julie, and me, and we all made an important discovery: New York pulled you in, never to let go. Our biggest regret was not having longer to explore this fascinating city.

The first family outing involved whizzing to the top of the World Trade Center. I had always been afraid of heights and was reluctant to join in this dizzying quest. Years later I was grateful that I'd taken the opportunity.

Next, a visit to the Metropolitan Museum of Art took our collective breath away. We'd never imagined that we would one day stand and view original paintings from the Impressionist era or behold such a unique collection of striking masks from diverse cultures.

Jason and Julie wanted to go to the Hard Rock Café, Planet Hollywood, and Times Square. We ate at Lindy's restaurant, once famous for its cheesecake and celebrity clientele, after a night at *The Phantom of the Opera.*

New York is a city of walkers and subway riders, and we joined the herd. We walked and took a buggy ride through Central Park. We walked through Greenwich Village and Soho. We walked and shopped. Because of my childhood fascination with *Miracle on 34th Street*, I just had to shop at Macy's.

We were having the time of our lives, but our main reason for stopping in New York was to visit New York University. It was Julie's top pick for post-secondary studies as she wanted to obtain a BFA (Bachelor of Fine Arts) in Theatre.

We sat through an information session, took a tour, and Julie had an interview with the theatre department. We were duly impressed. The cost of attendance blew us away, however. Wayne and I weren't sure if we could manage that.

Prior to this, Julie had stayed in the hotel room during many of our outings. She was feeling worse with each passing day— dizziness, headaches, more swelling, profuse sweating. I was becoming especially worried and didn't know where to turn in a strange city.

The day we went for her NYU interview Julie's face and eyes were very swollen. She apologized to the interviewer for her unusual appearance. This caring lady took one look at her and gave her the name of an excellent doctor on the Upper West Side. She urged Julie to make an appointment as soon as possible.

We were grateful to be steered in the right direction and managed to get in to see the doctor right away. He examined Julie and took some blood samples. Then he sat us down and explained, "Julie is very ill. I've submitted blood tests and it will take a few hours for the results to come in.

"Based on this physical check-up, I believe she either has leukemia or mononucleosis. Go for lunch and come back in a couple of hours. By that time, I'll be sure of the diagnosis. Then I'll let you know how to proceed, depending on which it is."

Wow! Those two hours were right up there with the worst in our lives. We felt like we had just fought our way through one long grim situation only to be confronted by another. Wayne and I had never in our lives envisaged that we would pray for a diagnosis of mono.

By the time we got back to the doctor's office, we were dazed, picturing a bleak future. We sat before him wide-eyed and waiting. He quietly gave us the diagnosis—mononucleosis. We didn't know whether to cheer or cry. He was quick to inform us that this would be no cakewalk. Julie's liver and spleen were swollen, and her urine had turned an ugly shade of brown. What could we do? Take her to Canada and put her to bed. The only cure was complete rest.

It had been a tough school year for her—Jason's accident, the tensions of the months that followed, working day and night on academic studies, feeling sick and depressed, not eating properly, breaking up with her high school sweetheart. She was the only person in the world I had ever urged to stay home from school and rest occasionally.

The combination of personal sacrifice for the sake of high honours and family/relationship stress had taken a toll. No wonder she had mono! I had a new summer goal: help Julie achieve optimum health by the time we returned to Islamabad.

CHAPTER 27—SUMMER IN CANADA AND BEYOND

We touched down in Edmonton, Alberta, Canada, and it was cold! We'd come from the baking heat of Pakistan and travelled through three very sunny, warm countries. Shivering, we made a beeline from the airport to the closest shopping mall to purchase warmer attire. Canadian weather during that summer visit could only be described as cloudy and cold with a chance of rain. But then, maybe our bodies had simply adjusted to balmier climates.

At first, our prospects didn't look good. The house-sitting arrangement that we'd made while still in Pakistan fell through. We needed a home base—not easy to find even though we were "home." Also, after months of back and forth with several colleges and universities, Jason had finally settled on De Anza College in Cupertino, California, just outside of San Jose. After two years at this prestigious institution, he could transfer to one of the state universities. At that time, it was difficult to get into California universities, so the best way to gain acceptance was as a transfer student. It was an ideal arrangement for Jason. He would also have an opportunity to pursue future film studies, his dream. We'd assumed that we could make submission arrangements for De Anza once we reached Canada. I phoned them as soon as we arrived, only to be told that we'd missed the deadline. Not only that, but they had stringent rules about accepting international students which we hadn't realized.

This wasn't a great welcome back. We were chilled to the bone, had no place to stay, and further schooling for Jason was in jeopardy. Thankfully, things soon began to turn around. We found out that they were renting out married students' quarters at the university, and we got the last one available! It was small but clean and furnished. Plus, it provided all the basics, including kitchenware, for a good price. We moved in.

Jason opted to stay with friends for a few weeks, so we gave Julie the biggest bedroom and ordered her to stay there for the summer. I was looking forward to feeding her nutritious food and letting her be as lazy as possible.

More good news! De Anza finally relented and agreed to mail us application forms. If we submitted them right away, they would determine whether Jason was a good fit. What a relief! We gave my mother's country postal address as we would soon be travelling to the Calgary area. If the college sent the papers by courier, we could coordinate the time of arrival with our visit.

After more whirlwind shopping, we loaded up our rental car for a four-day visit to Calgary. This segment of the summer vacation turned out to be tense, strained, and filled with uncertainty. Ah, family! What more can I say? By this time, we'd been living overseas for almost two and a half years. The novelty of hearing about our exotic encounters had worn off among our families and some friends. We were beginning to experience something that long-time expats had warned us about. People back "home" in Canada were uninterested in our stories or our point of view. This didn't apply to everyone. Friends, and a few family members, that we'd known and trusted for years still wished to be a part of our new, evolving lives, but some close family members were a big challenge.

My mother was sensitive to any remarks that she perceived to be criticisms of Canada. For example, I had new perspectives regarding education now that I was teaching at an international school. I could see that my children were thriving in the overseas education environment, and some aspects of this could be applied in Canada. Also, discipline was never a problem at the international school. That created an ideal learning atmosphere. I felt Canadian schools could take a few lessons from that model as well.

Of course, I understood that international schools had advantages that North American public schools did not. Due to high tuition fees, there was more money available for resources and staffing. Also, class sizes were smaller which afforded students greater individual attention. Nevertheless, from experience, I saw that some programs could be implemented on the North American side of the pond.

But my mother, despite having been a teacher before she got married, shut these conversations down. She perceived me as a know-it-all. Meanwhile, my thoughts and opinions, as well as my knowledge, had evolved into a broader world view. Now I see that I was attempting to expose my mother to ideas that were well out of her comfort zone.

And there was the rub! In a nutshell, our families had no frame of reference for what they were hearing when we talked about our Islamabad lives. As a result, they assumed that we were being arrogant or boasting. Someone would ask how we liked it in Pakistan, a vague question in any case, and we would share funny stories and adventures.

Before long, eyes would glaze over. We didn't know what to do. This was how we lived now. What were we supposed to say? After this trip "home," we learned to smile and say as little as possible about our South Asian life. It was better that way. We were beginning to be seen as outsiders.

The four of us had changed and would continue to change. Our ongoing metamorphosis ensured that we could never go back to the life we once had or return to our former selves. We had grown, expanded. It was as if we had sprouted invisible extensions. We were now star-shaped pegs and those around us were trying to fit us into the same old round holes. The result—frustration and confusion!

On the other hand, family and friends didn't hold back when expressing their opinions about Canadian life. They complained about the economy, unemployment, government debt, the healthcare system, cuts in social services, greedy politicians, and immigration.

After living in Pakistan and observing so many that were eking out a living under harsh conditions, it seemed to us that Canadians were doing fine. We didn't see anyone having to sit on a street corner and wait to have his or her teeth pulled with a crude pair of pliers.

My mother had a combination welcome back/anniversary party for us and a few of my relatives put me on the hot seat regarding immigration. It was the old "They are taking our jobs" refrain. I was so tired of this. If only the haves of the world could trade places with the have-nots for a month or so, these tunes might change very quickly.

There were a couple of other misunderstandings and miscommunications that ramped up hard feelings. We had a small window of time to receive that De Anza application. Unfortunately, mom had given the wrong directions to the courier. We were beside ourselves with worry as this was our only chance to get those papers submitted for Jason. When we approached the local postmaster with this dilemma, he was unwilling to help us out. In fact, he was downright rude and dismissive. For some reason, my mother decided we were to blame for this fiasco, that we were making unreasonable demands. So frustrating! You can imagine our immense relief when, at the last minute, the courier managed to deliver the papers. This was truly a summer of living on the edge, Canadian style.

The final issue with my family was the most disconcerting. I wanted, and needed, to talk about the harrowing months of fear and grief we'd gone through after Jason's accident. At that point in my life, I was full of anger and hate toward the police officials that had blackmailed us.

I remember all of us sitting around the dining room table at my mother's farmhouse. We pushed back our chairs, relaxed, full of homemade chocolate cake. Wayne smiled, took a deep breath, and emitted a soft sigh. "What a year we've had. Probably the most difficult of our lives so far."

I chimed in. "Yes, it's been a long hard climb…. The corruption, the intimidation. I reached a point where I just couldn't take it anymore. The police were the worst of the worst. Scumbags!"

My mother instantly admonished me. "Sharon, calm down. I don't like to hear you talking like that!"

"Mom, you don't understand. The police were so threatening. I was at the end of my rope. That day they showed up at our house … if I'd had a gun, I would have shot both of them."

"Surely you don't mean that Sharon. Would you really have done that?"

At this point, Jason jumped in. "No Grandma, she doesn't really mean that. She's just upset. Right, mom?!" If anyone understood how I felt it was Jason, but he also knew that his grandma couldn't even begin to fathom this depth of feeling. He was instinctively trying to protect me from some serious fallout.

Of course, I never would have shot anyone. I hated guns. Even if I had one, which would be highly unlikely, I would have had no idea how to use it. I was simply expressing some very wrathful, passionate feelings. My mom and most of my Canadian family couldn't handle that. They balked when I confessed to having violent thoughts of revenge after all the harassment we had endured.

Wayne tried to tell me that most Canadians probably couldn't even begin to comprehend what we'd been through. They didn't understand that police could be dishonest and menacing or that the law, in some countries, didn't always protect the innocent. I felt so sad. Suddenly there was a chasm between me and my Canadian family that I could never traverse. It took many years for me to appreciate that very few family or friends would ever understand what the four of us had gone through that fateful year. It was something we would keep locked in our hearts for the rest of our lives.

When we finally arrived back in Edmonton, we were able to stop holding our breath and relax, sort of. We went through a flurry of business and medical appointments and did our best to touch base with old friends. In the meantime, we received the excellent news that Jason had been accepted into De Anza College. I felt like setting off rockets in celebration. But we had zero time for rejoicing. Wayne was ready to return to Islamabad, and I had to get Jason set up in California.

I'd given some thought to taking Julie along to California as well. She was interested in applying to Stanford, and it would have been nice to have a look at their campus and facilities. However, we all decided that the best thing for her was to stay put and rest. Hence, the four of us headed in different directions—Wayne travelled east to Islamabad, Jason and I went south to California, and Julie stayed in the north and reinvigorated.

Jason and I enjoyed some quality time together in Cupertino, San Jose, and San Francisco. Today we recognize Cupertino as Apple headquarters, but in 1993, that wasn't on our radar. This mother/son trip would become a special kind of California caper. We steered out of the rental car parking lot and squinted into the bright, colour-drenched landscape before us. Sunglasses were a must as we drove alongside gleaming red, green, and yellow convertibles. The sun was hot on our shoulders, the sky an endless brilliant blue, and car radios played strains of old *Beach Boys* songs. We passed diners and fast-food joints heralding '50s architecture. Shorts, sandals, and soft, swirly ice cream cones appeared to be the fabric of everyday life. My first thought was, "Jason is going to love it here."

We toured the easily navigated, welcoming campus of De Anza, opened a bank account, filled out forms and schedules, and got Jason a place to stay. De Anza had a department devoted to procuring housing for international students, and they found him a cozy home with room and board near the school. Done and done.

Jason even had extra time to spend with friends. Some of his good friends and classmates from ISOI lived in San Francisco, and a couple of others were attending California universities. I was grateful that he would have someone to reach out to as he settled into a new environment.

Jason and I have often fondly reminisced about this short, jam-packed trip to California. One of our most amusing memories is of the final afternoon, driving in downtown San Francisco on our way to his friends' house. According to the directions we needed to turn left. We kept driving through one intersection after another—no left turn! We had visions of ending up in the ocean but thankfully, after what seemed like endless miles of "no left turn" we finally achieved our objective. They should put up a sign at the entrance to the city "San Francisco, Right Hand Turns Only!"

Back in Edmonton, I had seven days to prepare for our return to Islamabad. For the first time, there would be just two of us, Julie and me. Jason would go back to California in a few weeks to start college.

I was still having trouble with the foot I'd broken, so I managed to squeeze in a couple of physio appointments before leaving. Why wouldn't this heal? All that walking in Greece certainly hadn't helped. Oh well! I didn't have time to focus on my aches and pains. My attention was demanded elsewhere.

Déjà vu. We had been here before—Jason, Julie, and I at the airport crying. The tears were different this time. We were leaving Jason behind. There would only be three of us in Pakistan now. How was that going to work? How did we get here so soon? Wasn't Jason just a baby yesterday? Was he going to be ok without us? Were we going to be ok without him? He waved goodbye for as long as he could until Julie and I disappeared into airport security.

After hours of smooth flying and soft reminiscence, our plane touched down in London where Julie and I would spend a couple of nights before journeying home. We had booked a small hotel room close to the theatre district. Since we both loved going to the theatre, we picked two shows that were a must-see—*Grease* and *Miss Saigon*. What a disappointment to find out that *Grease* was sold out for months in advance! But the concierge gave us some good advice. We could stand in line when the box office opened and see if we might be able to get into a performance. We took this recommendation, and by a twist of fate, we managed to get tickets that someone had turned in at the last minute. Not only that, but we also ended up sitting dead center. We had the best seats in the house. Julie and I had a rollicking good time singing and dancing along to the show. And we had an equally good time crying along with *Miss Saigon*. We did a bit of shopping and I spent a few hours at French's Theatre Shop in Soho. I hadn't had time to pick a play for the coming school year. This was my only chance.

Our favourite restaurant, *Sale y Pepe*, was as welcoming as ever. We missed Jason that night. We missed Jason most nights. However, as two females on our own, we got the royal treatment. The food was delicious and, predictably, the waiters burst into short arias as they served dinner. This time one of the servers tricked Julie into kissing him. We decided not to tell him that she might be contagious. She was feeling much better, but we weren't sure if she was finished with mononucleosis.

Just before leaving for Gatwick airport, we took a stroll down Tottenham Court Road and bumped into one of Julie's teachers, which was a pleasant surprise. Then, we boarded the plane only to find that Julie's best friend and her family were on the same flight back to Islamabad. Eventually, we got accustomed to suddenly running into friends in airports and cities around the globe. The world was getting smaller every year.

CHAPTER 28—WHAT NEXT?

We arrived on Park Road about 10 days before ISOI began ESL testing. Just about enough time to get over a massive case of jet lag. Because our family travelled so much, one might assume that we could recover more easily from this time-travel ailment. On the contrary, it seemed to get worse with every trip. That was the price we paid for living halfway around the world from where we started.

As a teacher, the new year for me was always the start of the school year, rather than the traditional January 1. I made a private resolution. We'd initially arrived in Pakistan as fresh-faced Canadians looking for adventure. We'd lost our innocence in a flash. Joy, grief, shock, disgust, exhilaration, fear, anger, happiness, pride, anxiety—this roller-coaster of emotions had lifted us up and knocked us to the ground in the past two and a half years. There had been no need to search out adventure. It found us. I took a deep breath and resolved to keep my family safe. The best I could do was keep us all tightly strapped in for the duration of the ride.

So it began … Julie had some time to relax and hang out with friends before the hectic days of her senior year. And Wayne and I spent some time running errands and sprucing up the house, as it always needed some TLC after we'd been gone.

There was one fantastic welcome home surprise—our Honda was sitting in the driveway, as good as new. Seriously, as good as new! I don't know how the Pakistani mechanics performed this sleight of hand, or even how they managed to get all the parts. Unless they bought some of them back from the police!! That car shone like new and purred along perfectly. Wonders never ceased. For every negative it seemed there was a startling positive.

I began my preliminary ESL testing, and soon it was the first day of school for all the teachers. We were off to a jolting start. That night Islamabad residents were confronted with a frightening rolling earthquake followed by severe storms that uprooted trees and flooded many homes. All were accounted for at school the next day albeit bleary-eyed and exhausted.

This natural phenomenon was no match for the series of political quakes that dominated the ISOI landscape that fall. There had been some issues in the previous winter term, conflicts between some Pakistani and American students, incidents of theft, and of inappropriate dress. The administration had decided to confront these problems by clamping down and reinforcing some of the rules. PDA would be closely monitored, and there would be a stringent dress code duly enforced—no skirts above the knee, no sleeveless blouses, etc. There would also be tighter control of movement around campus and restrictions concerning student socialization.

These rules were laid down with good intentions. The school wished to facilitate greater unity between the Pakistani students and staff and those from other countries. However, people had grown accustomed to some relaxation of host country norms at the American school. Parents and students greeted these new rules with surprise, confusion, and some resentment. In their observation, most of the previous school term problems had disappeared with May graduation, people moving away and new people arriving.

Thankfully, these quakes of misunderstanding rumbled on for a few months and then gradually dissipated. Trust was restored, controls were relaxed, and students adhered to the rules. For the most part, students at international schools were a good bunch.

Julie and I did have a few go-rounds about how she dressed for school. Dress restrictions in Pakistan mostly pertained to females. I felt conflicted about reprimanding her because I believed that women should be able to dress as they saw fit. However, Julie took the bus to and from school, and we lived 4 houses up from the corner stop. Even walking that short distance put her in danger. A foreign female in a short skirt was a target, and there would be no redress should anything happen. My worries had multiplied now that Jason and Brian were no longer there to protect her.

If Julie had been in her senior year of school in Canada, she would have enjoyed the freedom of going out on her own even if she were just taking a trip to the local shopping mall. In Islamabad, she required protection, specifically male protection. Wayne and Nisar needed to be available to escort her. Otherwise, she was confined to home or school. This created a brand-new parent/child tug-of-war. Julie had gone everywhere with Jason and Brian. Now she was more vulnerable but, at the same time, she wanted to spread her wings, and as a result, tensions were building at home. For the first time, Julie was flouting a few rules.

At the same time, in a land far away, Jason was going through some jitters. He telephoned us one night at 12:30 a.m. wondering about some receipts. Wayne asked him if he was anxious, and he replied, "No, I'm just nervous." My heart went out to him—so far away from family, starting school in yet another new country, still haunted by memories of the previous fall's disaster.

On top of these personal worries, I was challenged with very pressing issues at work. My middle school ESL classes were overloaded. Students were jammed into the classroom like sardines, and resources were limited. Naila and I couldn't possibly spread ourselves thin enough to cater to everyone's needs. I required another ESL teacher stat! Mike and I were getting ulcers waiting for administrative approval.

Yet another set of quakes erupted around the question of Jan and me working on the fall play. The elementary school administration had suddenly decided that Jan shouldn't be producing plays because it impeded her work as a Reading Specialist for the elementary students. Mike was our boss, and he advised that neither Jan nor I work on school plays. In Jan's case, he was fed up with the hassle from the elementary offices. And in my case, he reasoned that the ESL workload was far too heavy already.

Mike had a good point in both instances. However, without Jan and me, there would be no fall play. We had already auditioned the students who were eagerly awaiting the results. The ball was rolling. Besides that, this was all extra-curricular work. No part of it interfered with our regular jobs. We both suspected that this tempest had started with Tildy whispering complaints into carefully selected ears, but we remained circumspect.

After an agonizing week of constant meetings and power plays, Jan and I decided to go ahead despite the misgivings of administration. We hadn't been *ordered* not to proceed with mounting a play. We posted the cast list with triumphant smiles. As it turned out, this wouldn't be the only attempt to shut down the play that year.

In the meantime, help arrived in the form of two gracious, skilled ladies. The new fourth grade teacher just happened to be a theatre major so she could help with the play. Hooray! And, even better, I was blessed with a new part-time ESL colleague, Kate—a petite, red-haired Scot with some wicked story-telling skills. Kate turned out to be an excellent teacher, a down-to-earth person, and a good friend. The two of us shared a classroom and worked closely together as a team. There was never a minute of conflict or dissension. We managed to have an excellent collegial relationship and a strong friendship.

With all this worry and conflict in the first few weeks of school, we were left wondering what the rest of the year might hold. How could we lift our spirits? Answer: Apply the Islamabad remedy for all ills—organize some parties. First on the list would be our 25th Anniversary party. We kept the numbers smaller this time, inviting 50 people to our Park Road home.

Khan once again prepared delicious food, and I spent a few hours creating dance cards. Our guests were a bit surprised to receive these as they entered, but hilarity ensued as dance partners were searched out. Warm conversations, crazy dance moves, superb food and drink … And the pièce de résistance—prizes were given to everyone who managed to fill their dance cards. Party season was off to a great start.

Around this time, I was offered a position on the board of RATS, the Rawalpindi Amateur Theatrical Society. This local theatre group was primarily made up of Brits and Pakistanis who staged some excellent community theatre. Almost instantly they decided that I should host a play reading in my home. I did have the ideal layout for at-home performances. In addition to the Romeo and Juliet balcony off the upstairs bedroom, we had a spacious raised entry that ran the length of the living room and dining room, a perfect stage.

About 40 people showed up for a reading of *Love Letters,* fifty years of letters exchanged between a man and a woman that highlight the joys and tragedies of their lives. Khan never batted an eye at serving all the crazy diverse guests we entertained over the years. Our staff's enjoyment of an evening's performance equaled, and at times surpassed, that of the guests.

Thankfully, Julie's school year was off to a flying start. She'd been working out to increase her strength and endurance for the school's annual trek into the Karakorum mountains. The intrepid high school science teacher led this 7-to-10-day arduous journey. We voiced some concerns since Julie had just recovered from a serious bout of mononucleosis. But the doctor pronounced her fit enough to sign up.

The goal of the ISOI trek of 1993 was to reach the Baifo glacier—the world's third longest glacier outside of the polar regions—in the Karakorum Mountains of Gilgit, Baltistan (Pakistan administered Kashmir). This would be a rigorous journey. The excursion was to begin on the same path as the trek to the base camp of K2 but would eventually veer off toward the glacier. In the end, they hoped to reach heights of up to 12000 feet.

To everyone's dismay, the group was dogged with difficulties before the students even got started. Generally, trekkers could board a flight to the city of Skardu and start from there. But there were no flights available. As a result, Julie and her companions endured a 32-

hour bus trip, which included a five-hour stop for a landslide and two flat tires. This was followed by an eight-hour jeep ride on constricted mountain roads—roads with no barriers or protections. I'm sure those kids had visions of plummeting into the valley below a few times in those 40 hours of travel.

After a long harrowing drive, they began their hike. They trekked over landslides, boulders, and rocks. They passed through ancient mountain villages, viewed breathtaking rugged mountain scenery, felt broken and jubilant by turn, and danced with the porters around the campfire at night.

We breathed a sigh of relief when the phone rang announcing Julie's arrival back in Islamabad. Nisar drove us to the meeting point and there she stood, smiling victoriously, dark brown, blistered, and a little beaten up. Nisar took one look at her and pronounced, "Julie, you look like mountain man!"

Julie regaled us with stories about the trek for weeks to come. One story remains a vivid memory. The trekkers had to return to Islamabad the same way they left, via jeep and bus ride. After a few hours on the bus, they had reached the highest point on a mountain pass. It was getting dark, so the driver attempted to turn on the headlights, to no avail. It quickly became apparent that the headlights weren't functioning. Darkness was upon them. What could they do? An immediate solution was required, so one of the extra Pakistani drivers scrambled up the side of the vehicle and parked himself on the hood. He shone a flashlight onto the road and guided the bus along the narrow pass throughout the moonless night.

I'm sure that many of the exhausted trekkers slept through those long hours, a whisper's edge from falling through the darkness. I shuddered at the thought. This was a parent's worst nightmare. And, God knows, we didn't need any more nightmares. Thankfully, we only heard these hair-raising stories well after the fact.

ISOI toasted another successful trek, and then it was time to begin rehearsals for *The Miracle Worker,* the play that I had settled on back in the London bookshop. Julie was cast in the role of Annie Sullivan, the teacher who taught Helen Keller, a blind and deaf girl, how to communicate and read Braille. This wasn't the usual ISOI light comedy or musical. It was a serious play requiring focus and dedication. Everyone involved worked hard right through to December.

I feel that I must add a note here: both of my children got leading roles in ISOI plays, particularly Julie. This wasn't because I, alone, chose them. I always invited my team to help me cast the plays I directed, and there had to be one hundred percent agreement on the final cast list. All actors in the school plays were chosen according to the merits of their auditions. Besides that, I only directed one play in the school year. The band and choir teachers later joined by director Sophia, the talented 4th grade teacher, always presented a musical and Julie managed to get lead roles in those as well. I was (and am) a firm believer in people achieving according to their capabilities.

Warm autumn weather began to encourage outdoor activities and, topping the "most popular" list was ISOI's annual International Day. The community joyfully gathered to sample food and crafts from countries around the globe. Candied apples, muffins, and cookies were on display at the Canadian booth but, sadly, no Nanaimo bars or butter tarts. Maybe next time! Kids enjoyed the usual rides—a hand-operated Ferris wheel and merry-go-round.

The UN club held an evening of dinner and play readings which was well-attended. We patronized the Canadian and American clubs more often as they offered lots of activities, but the UN club provided a nice change. On another evening of gentle breezes, RATS performed *The Tempest* in the British High Commissioner's garden. For a few hours, we escaped into an exotic starlit fantasy.

On the home front, we had another, more personal, fall project. As part of the continuing quest to upgrade the appearance of our home, Wayne and I decided to have the living room furniture reupholstered.

One afternoon we stopped by the shop where we'd originally purchased our sofa and chairs. We received a warm welcome and chose some stylish material in rich shades of blue. The salesperson informed us that we didn't need to bring our furniture to the shop. They would be happy to come to our house and do the work there. We thought this was a bit strange, but it suited us fine. Less to worry about.

About a week later, a crew of men showed up with the material and proceeded to strip off the old upholstery and re-cover our furniture. It was a mess for a while, but they managed to complete the job in one day. The furniture looked gorgeous. They'd done an impeccable job. We paid them and off they went.

Many months later we were shopping near the furniture store and decided to stop by and tell the owner how happy we were with our new upholstery. He greeted us, and we began to effusively praise his workers for their efficiency in finishing such a large task in one day. The shop owner's eyes widened as his voice caught in a soft gasp. He shook his head in dismay. He'd known nothing of this transaction. One of his salesmen had fulfilled our contract on his own and pocketed the money. This had been the nefarious reason for doing the work outside the shop.

Ah Pakistan, never a dull moment!

CHAPTER 29—UNREST AT HOME AND ABROAD

We braced for October. A year ago, this inauspicious month had brought us shock and grief. What was in store for us now? Fortunately, the season began on a positive note.

When the Superintendent of ISOI hosted his annual Halloween costume party, my ESL colleague, Kate, and I hatched a plan. Since both of our husbands would be out of town on the night of the event, we decided to dress up and go together. We each owned burkas, the outer garment worn by some Muslim women that covers the body and face. What a brilliant idea it would be to don them as our Halloween party attire!

Nisar dropped us off about a block away from the Superintendent's house. Incognito because of our burka coverings, we didn't want anyone to recognize the car. We entered the house and observed everyone dressed in a wide range of wacky costumes. They were talking, laughing, and having a great time. Suddenly a hush fell over the room. Everyone stared at us. Their eyes spoke volumes: "Who are these strange apparitions?" "Where do they come from?"

Gradually conversations started up again, but most people avoided us. Some gazed at us in suspicion, while others tried to guess our identity. We used gestures for communication to preserve our anonymity. But soon, the two of us started to feel uncomfortable. This was a festive occasion; our face coverings wouldn't permit us to eat or drink. Even worse was the stigma of being outcasts. These were our friends. We worked with them every day and they were shunning us. Our clever plan had become much more than a Halloween party trick. We were experiencing life inside a burka, and we didn't like it. We viewed the world through a small piece of netting across our eyes. It was like living in the third person; being in the world but not part of it. We were nobody. We were strangers. We'd been rendered invisible.

Finally, I gestured to Kate, and we retreated to the guest bathroom. I whipped off my burka and declared, "I hate this. We can't eat or drink or have any fun. Those are our friends, and they won't have anything to do with us. Please let's throw these burkas in the corner, go out there and enjoy the party." She vehemently agreed. After that night, whenever I saw a woman in a burka, I felt great compassion. I'd found it stifling. Did she feel that too?

Jason called us frequently to let us know how he was doing in California. He enjoyed classes at the college and found his course of studies quite easy. He'd purchased his first car, an old Audi. And my mom had flown down to pay him a visit. She and her travelling companion loved San Francisco and San Jose. They'd just barely managed to stay out of trouble thanks to a random stranger who implored them to turn around one night when they inadvertently wandered into the Tenderloin district. The innocent adventures of two older ladies!

We celebrated Julie's 17th birthday with a cake artfully decorated in comedy/tragedy masks. As a special gift, we gave her a rough-cut ruby necklace and earrings. This may sound extravagant but, as with Jason's graduation gift, prices were unbelievably low for high-quality gems in Islamabad. There were a couple of jewelers in town whose shops we frequented. We'd purchased several sparkling stones from a young Irish jeweler. His family had mines in Afghanistan and Pakistan, and he claimed to have designed pieces for Cartier. Whatever the case, he did some excellent work for us.

Time marched along, and we celebrated Canadian Thanksgiving with our Canadian friends, not to be outdone by American Thanksgiving with American friends. In November I had a ballgown made for the St. Andrew's Ball, an evening of dining, dancing, and pageantry in celebration of the heritage of Scotland. In keeping with this theme, there was a requirement to learn Scottish country dancing. We didn't manage to get to that, and, as a result, we stumbled around awkwardly amid all the complicated reels. Luckily, after a few drinks, nobody cared.

On the flip side of all this merriment, tensions once again gripped Pakistan that fall. There were some deaths in Turkey and Norway that had caused the controversy around Salman Rushdie's book to rear its ugly head anew. There had been a death fatwa (a legal ruling under Islamic law) issued against Rushdie by Ayatollah Khomeini of Iran in 1989 citing blasphemy.

Hostilities flared throughout the Muslim world, particularly in places of budding fundamentalism like Pakistan. Even though Islamabad was a secure city, demonstrations could quickly turn to riots. Mob mentality was tough to control.

Expats were warned to remain in their homes for a few days until the danger blew over. Even though I understood the importance of safety, I was frustrated by stay-at-home orders. I was directing a play. Every day counted. How could I handle this? There was an obvious answer—rehearse at my house. We had a built-in stage, plus there was the bonus of being treated to Khan's baked goodies. Thanks to teamwork extraordinaire we all gathered, worked together, and enjoyed every minute. Those were the days....

After we returned to school, Naila and I had a serious conversation. She, as a devout Muslim, was adamant that Rushdie's book insulted Islamic teachings. I asked her if she'd read the book.

Aghast she emphatically professed, "No."

Then, I asked what I considered to be a logical question, "How can you judge a book if you've never read it?"

She couldn't understand why I would even query her beliefs. The mullahs and those in authority had declared that this book was heresy. Therefore, it was. She would never cast eyes upon evil words. We talked for a long time, but I couldn't convince her of the advantages of independent thought and action. We came from two distinct worlds. Our divergent cultures had imbued us with vastly disparate values. She came from a world of rote learning, a rigid class system, and unquestioning obedience to authority, especially that of religious leaders. I came from a world of meaningful learning and lateral thinking guided toward independence.

The following weekend I took some time to reflect. How did I feel about Pakistan? About Islam? About Pakistanis? I was torn, conflicted. Wayne and I had made some true, faithful Pakistani friends. Wayne's UN team would have dropped anything to help us out. One of them, a doctor, had provided excellent advice and care when I had that excruciating ear infection.

All the merchants treated us with kindness and respect; our household staff was loyal and hard-working. Most Pakistanis weren't in the habit of putting on fake smiles. Friendships were hard-won but lasting. Once our faces were familiar in the marketplace and around town, locals were amicable and trusting. Pakistan was a country of diversity and stunning scenery. Many of its citizens were devout, not fanatical, Muslims. There was a long list of pros.

But the cons were formidable—deceitful police, slippery lawyers, the corrupt judicial system, baksheesh required with many transactions. Not to mention riots, vendettas, and killings if rhetoric got stirred up. Then there were the everyday annoyances that often ignited my anger, the worst of these being the lack of respect for women. Getting leered at had become increasingly galling.

Sorting all this out was challenging, especially if you factored in the background noise. Many in the expat community were critical, negative, and sometimes downright racist when it came to Pakistan and its people. Friday conversations at the Canadian or American club could become a litany of "everything we hate about this country."

Some expats forgot how privileged they were compared to most Pakistanis. Trailing spouses often took the lead here. After all, it wasn't their idea to come to Pakistan. They were only here because of their husband's (or wife's) job. Negative attitudes were far-reaching. If mom wasn't happy, her kids often reflected that at school.

I wasn't a disgruntled spouse. Jason and Julie knew that, and I hoped that they would project positive thoughts and actions at school and amongst their friends. When we'd first arrived and I'd heard some teenage expats spouting racial slurs, I let Julie and Jason know that I never wanted to hear that from them.

All of this was bouncing around in my brain—the pros and cons of life in Pakistan. Where did I stand? I couldn't say. Not then. I didn't condone some of the common practices in Pakistan such as wife-beating, cruelty to animals, extreme religious beliefs. But neither could I condone the economic disparity. A small percentage of the population owned all the wealth, and they had no intention of sharing this with the poor and dispossessed. It was, in many ways, a feudal society, and those at the top weren't interested in educating the masses. They didn't want the underclasses to have access to independent thought. It might make them too powerful. Politicizing Islam (e.g., introducing Sharia Law) became yet another method of appeasing the multitudes.

When I was in the midst of my Pakistan years, I didn't understand how blessed I was to have the opportunity of being immersed in a culture so different, so foreign to mine. It would take me a long time to fully absorb my conflicting thoughts and emotions and understand Pakistan. In the meantime, I would live day to day, keeping my eyes and heart open. Time and distance would hone my insight and wisdom.

On the family front, I was pleased that Julie was healthy and full of energy because this had turned out to be her busiest semester ever. At the top of her to-do list were SAT courses and college applications. In the end, she applied to six universities in the US and Montpelier in France. Of course, she also had one of the lead roles in the upcoming school play plus a heavy academic load. She was taking a few Advanced Placement (college level) classes as well as her regular studies.

So, imagine my surprise when I learned that she'd agreed to teach three levels of ballet classes to young girls every week! The Satellite

Center, where Julie taught, was located off-campus in Islamabad city. It had been created and organized to provide educational, recreational, and social activities for students and adults associated with the ISOI community. Classes, for both adults and children, were offered in tennis, yoga, painting, ballet, aerobics, and more.

The Snack Pit served burgers and shakes and employed ISOI students as waiters and waitresses. This was a much-needed community gathering place for young and old alike. It had taken us a while to become familiar with this center as it had been closed when we first arrived in Pakistan.

Julie did an excellent job of teaching the girls. When her schedule was demanding and last-minute timetable switches were required, some of the parents became frustrated. However, a final showcase lesson where the students performed choreographed routines put a smile on everyone's face. I was relieved and proud to witness this happy ending. Nevertheless, Julie had felt defeated by the parental backlash over scheduling difficulties. She announced that she wouldn't be teaching classes in the next semester. Some of the girls were disappointed, but Julie had made the right decision. There was far too much on her plate in that final ISOI semester as it was.

This conflict of irritations reminded me of a talk that Mike had given to our team in an early PPS meeting. It went something like this: "Expats in hardship postings such as Pakistan tend to feel frustration and anger when life doesn't meet their expectations. They are inhabiting a culture that doesn't always share their values regarding time, efficiency, workplace/family priorities, and a host of other things. But they have no control over any of this. It's not their country.

"Where might they be able to exert some control? Where can they find an outlet for their pent-up anger? The local embassy? Probably not. Embassies and High Commissions carry the weight of authority. Shouting at them could lead to trouble. What about the International School? Bingo! ISOI staff and administration are easy, familiar targets, so don't take it too personally if parents attempt to rake you over the coals. Most of the time you simply represent a useful conduit for their discontent."

Mike wasn't trying to say that parents never had a good reason for grievances. He was warning us about a common problem in overseas life. I shared this wisdom with Julie when she was crestfallen about being assailed by some of the girls' parents. Thankfully, these "tempests in a teapot" quickly blew over in our small community.

At the same time as I was trying to guide Julie through a few senior year issues, my worries about Jason were multiplying. He'd started bombarding us with phone calls and faxes imploring Wayne and me to let him come home. We couldn't seem to extract the underlying causes of Jason's unhappiness. He just kept telling us that he needed to be with his family.

These communications were heart-rending. He was homesick, having a rough time adjusting to life in California. All we could do was reassure him that we'd see him at Christmas. In the meantime, could he please stick it out? I had vivid dreams of Jason jumping on a flight and showing up at Park Road in the middle of the night. Mercifully, this didn't come to pass.

In contrast, this fall season was one of the most positive and productive of Wayne's work life. Early November saw him presenting a paper at a conference in Nairobi, Kenya. While there, he did some touring and visited a game park. He brought home some treasured souvenirs and I made a mental note to add this to my future list of places to see.

While I was knee-deep in report cards, an evaluator travelled from Australia to assess Wayne's project. This report would carry a lot of weight as it was the first full evaluation since the project's inception. On the day of the finalized assessment, Wayne sped home from work and burst into the house with a huge smile on his face. Official UN folder in hand, he exclaimed, "Look at this glowing report. We should gold plate it."

I was beyond happy for him. Pakistan was our first overseas posting. Many days Wayne had driven home from work feeling frustrated and out of his league. Up to now, it had been almost impossible to measure what kind of impact his work was having. This glowing appraisal was just the kind of morale booster he needed. His contract had been renewed until January of 1995. If we were lucky it would be extended beyond that.

CHAPTER 30—COUNTDOWN TO 1994

The final weeks of 1993 … Would it be smooth sailing into the New Year? We could only hope.

Our cast and crew had worked their hearts out, given everything they had for months. And now it was almost time to present the fall play, *The Miracle Worker*. We were about two weeks from opening night. Everyone was nervous and excited. All the pieces were coming together and then …

I was called to the high school administrative offices for an urgent meeting. I couldn't imagine what this was about. As I entered the meeting room my eyes settled on Tildy, sucking all the air out of the room. She was flanked by the high school PE teacher and the high school principal. I was invited to sit.

This meeting had been called to address a problem that had arisen around academic achievement and extracurricular activities. One of my cast members, Andrea, who played the substantial role of Helen Keller's mother, had garnered exceptionally low grades in more than one of her high school courses. Tildy reported this to the high school principal with the recommendation that Andrea be pulled out of all extracurricular activities until she raised her grades.

This was a stinging slap in the face. I had so many questions … Why was this happening now? Hadn't the state of this student's studies been earmarked earlier on? Was it my duty to monitor the grades of all my actors? I was completely at sea regarding the details and rules of academic performance and extracurricular events at ISOI. The high school didn't have a large population and teachers paid close attention to potential problems. If this was a concern, why was it being flagged just two weeks before performance day?

I logged many hours of work doing the school plays. It was all extracurricular—not part of my job. Technically, I wasn't on the high school staff. I belonged to student services. No one had ever told me that I had an obligation to keep tabs on student grades as part of eligibility for plays. I suppose one reason for this was that most students at ISOI came home with excellent report cards. This had never been an issue in the past, at least not during my time there.

I argued that Andrea had a pivotal part in the play, and everything would be ruined if she were pulled just two weeks before opening night. The PE teacher seemed to be on my side. He would never wish this to happen if there was an important game on the line. I also made the point that these circumstances could have been easily remedied one or two months ago but not now. Tildy just kept hammering home that the rules were the rules, were the rules.

My mind was reeling, *This is an obvious manipulation. Tildy is seeking to sabotage the play.* But I didn't dare voice this aloud. I had to wait a couple of days for the official decision. In the meantime, I was keeping my fingers crossed. I'd suggested that the school find some other way of punishing Andrea for slacking off. Surely, they wouldn't destroy this special play that we had all worked so hard to create. This would penalize the entire cast, not to mention the ISOI community at large.

Finally, the edict was handed down. Andrea would be forbidden to take part in *The Miracle Worker*. I couldn't believe it! No one offered any solutions. I felt like I was on a tiny boat in the middle of the ocean with no oars and no lifeline. What could I do?

Then it occurred to me. There was one solution, a long shot if I could just do some convincing. Mary, a responsible senior, had taken on the role of assistant director. She'd been at all the rehearsals helping with directing and feeding actors their lines. As such, she understood every part of the play and had probably absorbed a lot of the dialogue in the process.

So, I asked her if she would take on the part of Helen's mother. It was a big ask. Mary had to learn that part in less than two weeks. She probably hated me for asking, but she did it! And she did it magnificently. She saved all of us. Thank you, Mary!

Why didn't I just let it go? I could have. But so many would have suffered if I hadn't rescued our precious creation. To this day I don't understand how Tildy managed this crippling maneuver. Still, I was lucky. She would have done much worse damage to my endeavours if I'd been her only target. But she went after others too, people with a lot more influence. They were aware and wary. A colleague had recently remarked, "Tildy has the countenance of an angel and the tongue of an asp." Machinations are limited when true character is revealed.

Good news! Our play was a smashing success. The audience was brought to tears every night. Teachers and Pakistani staff had come through splendidly once again with outstanding costumes and a cleverly designed set. ISOI carpenters had even managed to create a second storey bedroom for Annie Sullivan.

The high school principal wrote me the most glowing letter of congratulations I'd ever received. Did he feel guilty? A seventh grader had played Helen, and she was fabulous, really held her own with all the high schoolers. Those kids put their hearts and souls into crafting a powerful piece of work. I was so proud of them. To quote Shakespeare, "All's well that ends well."

Just before the Christmas season, Wayne and I were invited to our first Pakistani wedding. A UN staff member's son was getting married. We didn't quite know what to expect so we dressed in our finest clothing and presented ourselves at their door, gift in hand.

Everyone was sitting outside, men on one side of the garden and women on the other. There was a buffet of food laid out, and the guests were seated in circles chatting. We assumed that we were going to join the crowd. But no. Instead, the two of us were shepherded into a large living room filled with carved wooden furniture. Our host exited and we were left alone, sitting side by side on an unyielding sofa.

Wayne and I stared into space for a few minutes and then two bearers appeared, each with a large platter. In unison, they set the platters on the table in front of us and gestured for us to begin eating. What was this?

Each platter bore an entire roast chicken, a knife, and a fork. Nothing else. There were no vegetables, no rice or potatoes, no curries, no desserts—just the chickens. We looked down at the roasters and up at each other. We surveyed the swinging door. No one in sight. It appeared that this was our dinner.

Being a foreigner and a boss, Wayne was considered an honoured guest. These birds had been cooked especially for us. We had no choice. We gingerly lifted our utensils and began to eat those sizable chickens. This was indeed a challenge. But we did our best.

Forty minutes and two stomach aches later, we were collected by the host. He paraded us past the guests out into the center of the garden. We were to be seated beside the bride and groom on a raised dais. The newlyweds had obviously been told to sit in silence. They stared straight ahead so we followed suit. From the vantage point of their comfortable garden chairs, the guests scrutinized us, sharing juicy observations in Urdu. And we thought eating the chickens was uncomfortable!

After what seemed like an eternity, we were allowed to climb down and sit with the guests—Wayne with the men and me with the women. I found a chair in the women's circle, smiled, and nodded. They all looked at me, smiled back, and then continued their Urdu conversations. No attempts were made to speak to me or even acknowledge I was there after that initial greeting.

I'm sure that these women spoke at least some English. Almost everyone we'd met in Pakistan had, at the very least, basic English conversation skills. Were they being rude? No, I don't think so. These ladies were middle class, stay-at-home Pakistani wives who existed in tight circles of family and close friends.

They weren't part of the diplomatic cocktail circuit; their children didn't attend international schools. Foreigners simply weren't part of their lives. When I showed up in their circle that day, they didn't know what to do with me. A tacit agreement had been made to "proceed as if this strange white lady isn't here." It made for a long evening!

Christmas season was upon us, and we were once again decorating the tree and planning our annual party. Jason would be home soon, and I created a guest list of about 90 friends for our celebration.

I also made sure to engage the high school choir to sing all our favourite carols. In between preparations, we attended the usual round of Islamabad Christmas parties, notably the "Canadian family" party for about 70 guests that included gifts and turkey dinner. It was to be Christmas in Pakistan for us that year, and it looked very promising.

Hopefully, the new neighbours wouldn't pose a problem for our Christmas gathering. There were large, fully occupied family homes on each side of us now. The left-side neighbours were reasonably quiet, but the right-side neighbours were quite the opposite.

Our staff had identified these noisy residents as a government minister and his family. If that were the case, then a lot of family members had been brought into the fold. Some days it seemed like an entire village lived in that house.

An old couple inhabited the lower level. I assumed it was the grandparents. They appeared to have hearing problems. Every night Grandpa enjoyed listening to religious tapes of sermons given by impassioned mullahs, at top volume. At the same time, teenagers on the upper levels loved their Bollywood music, again, at ear splitting decibels.

As if that weren't enough, there were also "wolf on the driveway" sound effects two or three times a week. Wayne and I, curled up on the sofa with an intriguing movie, would be jolted from our evening reverie by plaintive howling. Was there a wild animal in our garden? We would hurry out onto the balcony to try and pinpoint the source of these anguished cries, only to observe our neighbour, standing outside his house, baying at the moon.

Did this guy, who we'd been told was a government minister, have a drug problem? How else could we explain sightings of him planted on his front drive wailing and yelping for 10 or 15 minutes at a stretch? We were at a loss as to how to even start a conversation about this kind of disturbing behaviour.

Wayne didn't want to create a conflict. That house appeared to be sixteen kinds of crazy, and it wasn't difficult to imagine that weapons might be part of the mix. So, on those nights of fiery sermons, Bollywood tunes, and hallucinatory howling, we simply turned our TV up a notch or two.

Just another day in the neighbourhood!

Jason's arrival in Islamabad was a joyous event for all of us. He was thrilled to be back with family and friends. We could finally have a face-to-face talk about his California situation. Why was he so unhappy? In the end, it seemed that the answer boiled down to loneliness.

He was doing well in his courses and achieving good grades, but he couldn't seem to connect with like-minded people. His ISOI friends didn't live in San Jose, and it was challenging to find time to get together. The college did invite him to social functions. However, they were designed for foreign exchange students, many of whom were Japanese with limited English skills. Jason found the gap in culture and language too difficult to bridge.

As well, his landlady had been accustomed to renting rooms to Asian students who required guidance in navigating American cultural practices. Jason didn't fit into that category, and he didn't need a mother. He often felt smothered and misunderstood. But he was still very enthusiastic about taking film courses. He wanted to pursue his dreams.

We empathized with Jason's situation. Unfortunately, we couldn't remove him from his living situation at that point, so we promised him that, if he managed the best he could in the coming semester, we would find him more suitable housing for the next school year. He slowly nodded in agreement. It wouldn't be easy, but he would endure for a few months. With that settled for the time being, we all set out to enjoy every moment we had together that holiday season. Family togetherness was becoming a precious commodity, not to be wasted.

Our Christmas party was a smashing success as always. The four of us attended midnight Mass at the Catholic church on Christmas Eve and woke up Christmas morning to an English breakfast. Khan had outdone himself.

After the oohs and aahs of gift-opening, we settled down to watch Aladdin armed with bowls of crunchy popcorn. Then we dressed for Christmas dinner with two other families. This turned out to be one of our best Christmases ever, in a country that didn't celebrate Christmas!

After a few lazy family days, we boarded a plane for a six-day holiday in Singapore to bring in the New Year. Sadly, Jason would be leaving us at the airport in Bangkok to head back to San Francisco. Our time with him was all too short. I hoped and prayed things would go smoothly for him in the next few months. It's a fragile time when your kids first spread their wings. You want only the best for them.

Singapore embodied a relaxing interlude for the three of us, although I think Julie felt the absence of Jason. She was relegated to spending time with her parents, no goofy side excursions with her brother. Nevertheless, we all relished taking in the sights. This time around there was less shopping and more touring. We explored Little India, Hindu and Buddhist temples, and lush botanical gardens. A cable car ride to Sentosa Island garnered a visit to the World War II museum and their famous aquarium. This was the first time we had ever walked through an ocean tunnel where we could view bull sharks and giant manta rays swimming all around us.

On New Year's Eve, we started at the famous Raffles Hotel, where we sipped on Singapore Slings. Then we joined with some teacher friends at Fatty's to ring in the New Year. We feasted on the ultimate Singaporean dinner—chili crab, pepper crab, BBQ pork, shrimp fried rice and spicy stir-fried veggies. Fatty's left us full, fat, and rolling into 1994.

As Told to Me

The following are a small collection of stories told to me by friends who have lived in Pakistan. They are all true expat experiences.

Barry and Catherine's Toaster Story

In 1971 our cook bearer became the proud user of a toaster, the like of which he'd never seen. He could put the toast in, dial how he wanted it cooked, and then it would miraculously pop up when ready. The news of his acquisition spread far and wide amongst all the neighbouring cook bearers. One by one they crowded into the kitchen to witness this marvellous machine. When Barry arrived home for lunch the cook bearer and his audience had gone through two loaves of bread. They just couldn't get enough of the "pop up."

Tom's Quetta Story

During my years in Pakistan, I had the opportunity of travelling to destinations that weren't often visited by foreigners. The city of Quetta in Balochistan was one such place. Imagine my surprise when, one day as I was roaming the streets of this intriguing city, I came across a sign in English over a doctor's office. It read, "Hemorrhoids and other Sexually Transmitted Diseases Cured Here."

Norma's Stories

The hostess—A hostess bought a large fresh fish for her first dinner party. She stuffed it and instructed her bearer to put parsley in the mouth just before serving. Dinner party conversation stopped when the bearer appeared proudly carrying the fish on an elegant platter—with the parsley in his mouth.

The housewife—A housewife, new to Islamabad, was hurrying out the door to a meeting. She asked her bearer to go to the market early and buy a chicken for dinner. Would he then please put it in the fridge until she could get home to prepare it? Imagine her surprise several hours later when she opened the refrigerator door and found a live shivering chicken staring her in the eye.

The pastor—A pastor travelled from Islamabad back to the US where he spoke to church groups about his work in Pakistan. He outlined some community projects such as the one for *Busti*[45] women living in Sindh. One man in the audience seemed particularly engrossed in his presentation. Afterward, this man stayed behind and approached the pastor. Full of curiosity, he wanted to know more about "these busty women living in sin."

Gail's Stories

Ghosts—The local workers at ISOI thought the campus was haunted. Periodically, there would be rumours of ghosts and witches floating around the quad.

---

[45] Busti is the name for poor Christian sweeper's colonies.

Snakes—There was a school closure for "snake day" when cobras were found on campus.

Land Turtle—We were driving to school early one morning when we suddenly lurched to a screeching stop. A giant land turtle was crossing the road.

Wild boars—Wild boars were ever-present around Islamabad. Nevertheless, they were considered gross and unclean by the devout Muslim population. You can imagine the uproar when one of those boars was spotted on the school grounds. The workers were desperately trying to chase it away when it entered the mosque. Panic ensued.

PART 3
A DEEPER UNDERSTANDING

CHAPTER 31—WILL WE EVER UNDERSTAND?

The general history of Pakistani politics reads like the script from an impassioned, and sometimes violent, nighttime soap opera. Democracy has been allowed to function in varying degrees with frequent interference by the military. Due to widespread poverty and a low literacy rate, the Pakistani population has been challenged in making informed choices in leadership even when they do get a chance. As well, a history of corruption within the electoral system has facilitated the power of the ruling elite.

As expats, we weren't particularly impressed by either one of the alternating governments of Nawaz Sharif or Benazir Bhutto during our time in Pakistan. Sharif's introduction of Sharia ordinances had directly affected our family during the "blood money" negotiations. Throughout Bhutto's tenure, there were constant rumours of corruption, family in-fighting, and suspicions of violent use of force. As far as we were concerned, neither of these leaders took steps to further educational opportunities for their people or alleviate mass poverty.

A brief look back reveals that Pakistan has had a turbulent political history—corruption, assassinations, family feuds, power grabs, accusations of murder … The list goes on. The President is the head of state and commander of the armed forces and the Prime Minister is the head of the executive branch of the government. The President has the power to oust the Prime Minister if that is deemed necessary.

When we first arrived in Pakistan, Nawaz Sharif had taken over from Benazir Bhutto as Prime Minister. Her first term had been 1988-90. Sharif was ousted in 1993 and, after some interim leadership, Benazir once again took the helm. In 1997, Sharif came to power a second time after Bhutto had been ousted. Both Sharif and Bhutto came from wealthy, powerful families, and each of them had alternately been accused of corruption and sentenced to time in prison. The Bhuttos were among the richest feudal landowners in Sindh province, served by many share-cropping families. Asif Ali Zardari, Benazir's husband, was also from a family of wealthy Sindh landowners.

Nawaz Sharif was responsible for furthering Islamization in Pakistan's legal system during his 1990 to 1993 tenure. Considered one of the wealthiest men in Pakistan, he was ousted on corruption charges more than once.

Benazir was the first female leader in a Muslim-majority country. She could have done a lot with that. She was a powerful young woman with an Oxford and Harvard education. Many people, expats and Pakistanis alike, felt that she didn't give much focus to facilitating the advancement of women in Pakistan. Maybe that's unfair. Maybe she tried. All I know is that, from what I observed, the plight of women appeared to remain much the same as always.

The US had a fraught relationship with Pakistan. Americans had needed Pakistan as an ally during the Cold War years, but relations cooled during the '80s and '90s due to the *Pressler Amendment*.[46] As a result, USAID offices in Pakistan were expected to be mostly closed by the beginning of 1995. This was a huge loss on many levels, and resentments build when these connections are lost.

Underpinning both the tensions of foreign relations and the political maneuverings of Pakistan's wealthy elite was the general encouragement and facilitation of religious zealotry. Islamic fundamentalism had grown and strengthened over time in the country's climate of impoverishment and ignorance. Religious organizations often provided the poor with hospitals, education, food, and shelter.

---

[46] The Pressler Amendment banned aid from the United States dependent upon proof that Pakistan wasn't developing nuclear weapons.

Conversely, government leaders had regularly proven themselves incapable of addressing the problems of the masses. Instead, the ruling class exploited religion to give legitimacy and popularity to their regimes. It appeared that their reasoning was that, if extremism were permitted, then maybe the masses wouldn't criticize the corruption and blatant inequities all around them.

Pakistan had been founded as a secular Muslim country. But during the 1970s and '80s, both Zulfikar Ali Bhutto, Benazir's father, and Zia Ul Haq had used Islamization as a tool to legitimize their rule, particularly the latter during his 10-year term as—what most would call—a military dictator. Ul Haq attempted to crush opposition by aligning himself with religious fundamentalism. It is estimated that by the end of Zia Ul Haq's administration there were over 8000 official *madaris*[47] and more than 25000 unregistered religious schools in Pakistan. Poor families would send their sons to these schools so that they would be housed and fed in tandem with receiving religious education.

The mullahs running most of these seminaries were said to be semi-literate themselves. They demanded memorization of the Quran and blindly promoted religious extremism. Financial assistance for these madaris was supplied by wealthy Muslims in Pakistan and abroad. These schools didn't teach terrorism, but they sparked the kind of zealotry in impressionable young Muslim boys that created militant *jihadists.*[48]

The fundamentalism initiated by Zia suited both western countries and other Muslim countries at the time. The main objective in the 1980s, particularly for the US, was defeating the Soviet Union in Afghanistan. Pakistan also had a special interest in launching armed attacks against its archenemy, India, over the Kashmir dispute.

---

[47] Madaris are religious seminaries.

[48] Jihadists are those that war against western corruption and fight to make their version of God's law supreme on earth.

Unfortunately, by the 1990s, fundamentalism, extremism, and burgeoning terrorism were growing beyond government control.

Those of us living in Pakistan were just beginning to wake up and see the potential danger in the mix at the dawn of 1994. Regrettably, we didn't have a crystal ball that predicted the future, but very soon, the sins of the '80s and early '90s—that lethal combination of corruption and fundamentalism—would begin to yield dire consequences.

Against this backdrop of political and religious tension, our family of three headed into another year of adventures in Islamabad.

1994 opened with an enthusiastically received Brahms concert performed by the Islamabad Chorale, an adult community choir of which Julie was a member. Next came the school carnival which included rides in carts pulled by oxen in decorative, rainbow-coloured harnesses as well as *tonga* (light, horse-drawn two-wheeled vehicle) rides.

Rehearsals had started for the spring musical, *Guys and Dolls.* Julie was playing the role of Miss Adelaide and relishing every moment. This would be her last school performance before going on to university. In an amazing stroke of good luck, we had found a teacher, a professional opera singer from Denmark, to give Julie private singing lessons. It was such a great opportunity in the months before she headed out to conquer the world.

My ESL program was running smoothly thanks to the teamwork of Kate, Naila, and myself. I loved my students. Every moment in the classroom with them was meaningful and fulfilling. They were all diligent about learning English, as it was their ticket to academic studies and a wider circle of friends. We had so much fun mounting snippets of Shakespearian plays in our small classroom, reliving momentous times in world history, or just discussing the confusing complexities of the English language.

One sunny early morning I was unexpectedly called to my boss Mike's office. Perplexed, I knocked on the door, "Come in Sharon and have a seat." Seated across from Mike was a slim, impeccably dressed Korean man that I recognized as the father of two of my ESL students. Mike made the introductions.

"Sharon, I'm sure you remember Mr. Kim."

"Yes, how are you, Mr. Kim? Nice to see you."

With a slight bow, Mr. Kim acknowledged my presence and quickly got down to business, "Mr. Mike and Mrs. Sharon, I have come to thank you for accepting my daughters into the ESL program and for doing such a wonderful job of teaching them English."

With that, he reached into the large bag he'd placed beside his chair and pulled out two artistically wrapped gift boxes. He gave one to me and one to Mike.

"These gifts are a token of our family's appreciation for all of your work. It is now time for my girls to exit the ESL program and enroll in all appropriate courses of academic study offered at ISOI."

Mike and I exchanged shocked looks. What?! It was apparent that Mike hadn't known the objective of Mr. Kim's visit to his office either. We'd both been taken by surprise. What was happening here? It was the job of the ESL department to decide when students were ready to move beyond ESL classes based on progress measured by the teacher. It wasn't an arbitrary family decision. Surely Mr. Kim knew this!

Before we could open our mouths to object, Mr. Kim stood up, gave a slight bow, and turned on his heel with a quick "Thank you." He was gone just as quickly as he'd arrived.

Mike and I sat there stunned, gifts in hand. Mr. Kim had been very polite and very firm. The problem was that neither of his daughters was anywhere near ready to exit the ESL program. That simply wasn't going to happen.

This was one of those times when we had to dig deep to find cultural understanding. We had many Korean students in the ESL program as Daewoo had been granted several road construction projects in Pakistan. Mike and I had to figure out why Mr. Kim had made this request and how we could diplomatically steer him back onto the ESL road. Fortunately for me, this was part of Mike's job as the valiant leader of PPS. He would need to be tactful, firm, and persuasive. In the end, I don't know what magic spell he wove, but the girls remained securely in their ESL classes. Working at an international school was often an exercise in diplomacy.

Life seemed to be rolling along smoothly. Wayne and I were lulled by the Pakistan-style, peaceful rhythms of daily living. But one Saturday evening, while watching a movie in the family room, we were quickly brought up short.

Julie exploded through the front door, dashed up the stairs and into her bedroom. Seconds later she reappeared, ran down the stairs, and back out the door. This had all taken place in a matter of minutes and her only words to us as she breezed by were, "Just have to get something …" We wondered what was going on.

Julie had been dating Paul, a young man whose father worked for the British High Commission. Paul was already pursuing post-secondary education in England but had come to Pakistan for a while to be with his parents. On this Saturday evening, Julie and Paul were invited to dinner at a friend's house. They had an enjoyable evening but left early as Julie had to finish a school project.

On the way home, Paul and Julie were stopped at a red light when two policemen approached their car. Paul was perplexed by this as he was driving his father's vehicle which had diplomatic license plates. The police knew that they were to stay away from cars with those plates. Paul nonchalantly rolled down the window thinking to remind the cops that this car was off-limits. Then he saw the metallic glint of their raised guns. Paul broke into a sweat and Julie started shaking uncontrollably. What did these guys want? There was no reason for the police to engage with them, particularly with brandished weapons. These guys didn't care about approaching foreigners with diplomatic plates. This was dangerous!

One on each side of the car, the two cops leaned in. The one on Julie's side pressed his gun to her head. With a leering smile, he slowly scanned her body. He brought his mouth close to her ear and, once again, demanded money. It was clear what he would do to her if he didn't get it.

In a quiet voice, Paul announced that they didn't have much money in the car. Then Julie had an idea. Despite the panic rising in her throat, she blurted out, "I have money at home. What if we leave something of value with you, go and get the money and bring it back to you?"

Much to Julie and Paul's surprise, the cops agreed to this. They asked for Paul's driver's license and his watch. Having searched through the ID cards in Paul's wallet, the police reminded him that they knew where he lived. If Julie and Paul didn't come back with the money, they would find them.

At that point, Paul hit the gas and drove straight to Julie's house. She dashed in, got the rupees she had saved up in her room, and dashed out. Strangely enough, the cops accepted the money, returned Paul's possessions, and let them go. When Julie returned to the house for the second and final time, we sat her down and she blurted out the whole story.

Shocked and upset, we laced into Julie for not stopping to tell us what was going on when she came home the first time. What was she thinking? She could have been badly hurt. We could have intervened. In hindsight, I can see that she was in a state of shock that night. She wasn't thinking straight. All she knew was that she needed to get the money to the cops so they would leave her and Paul alone. After Jason's accident, she'd had a ringside seat to family negotiations demonstrating the power money had to pacify the police.

A cold chill crept up my spine. I tried not to think about what could have happened to Julie that night. Wayne and I were both horrified at this incident. We'd just recovered from Jason's traumatic accident only to be confronted with another ordeal. We immediately called Paul's dad, who worked in the upper echelons of the High Commission, and he set things straight very quickly, much to our relief. It turned out that those "cops" weren't even real policemen despite their uniforms. They were security guards for a wealthy family. When they saw Julie and Paul, they decided that two young foreigners were easy marks for a little extra cash. We had some good fortune that time around. Paul's father had a powerful position and was able to bring the matter quickly to a close.

The phony cops were arrested and put in a local jail cell. Paul's dad and Wayne were called down to the station to observe that justice had been done. In an eerie twist of fate, Wayne immediately realized that the policemen who'd arrested these two guards were the same police that had harassed us for months after Jason's accident. That day, they bent over backward to be polite and subservient to Wayne. Would we ever figure out Pakistani ways?

We closely watched over Julie after her scare and, thankfully, she recovered well. She came to realize that she and Paul had been confronted by two bullying idiots. The three of us thanked our lucky stars every day for having dodged another bullet. Julie had been through so much in a few short years—debilitating illness, the consequences of her brother's accident, the break-up of her first romance, a serious bout of mononucleosis, and now this. Of course, she'd had many amazing experiences and unique opportunities as well. We could only hope that some of the trauma didn't mar her future. I continued to keep my eyes open for changes in her emotional state.

CHAPTER 32—SPRING BREAK HIGHS AND LOWS

March ushered in a season of music festivals for Julie, one in Dhaka, Bangladesh, and one in Dusseldorf, Germany. As I mentioned earlier, when students travelled regionally in South Asia for festivals or sports events, they were always housed with other international school families. ISOI families, including us, kept students from visiting international schools too.

During her time in Bangladesh, Julie was billeted with one of the wealthiest families in the country. They lived in an enormous mansion, and Julie's room, near to that of the host daughter's, was located inside spacious private quarters. I'm not sure if Julie even met the girl's parents. She lived a few days of luxury beyond her wildest imaginings—gourmet meals set before her, private cars for shopping trips, etc.

What a difference between this experience and Wayne's first visit to Dhaka where he saw workers sitting on the road in the blazing sun smashing bricks to make gravel. Or spreading piles of grain stalks on public roads so that vehicles would run over them in threshing season. This level of disparity was mind-blowing, even for those of us that were witness to the Pakistani wealth gap on a daily basis.

A few weeks later, Julie and other specially selected ISOI students landed in Dusseldorf for the Honour Band and Choir Festival. They stayed at the Hilton hotel, did some castle tours, and sang their hearts out. We watched a recording of the final concert—spectacular! These events attracted some of the most gifted, dynamic musicians and teachers in the world. Attending an international school continued to open up worlds to Julie that she would never have experienced in a Canadian lifetime.

Winter and spring in Islamabad were once again punctuated by the usual rounds of dinner parties. The stand-out of the season was a progressive dinner organized by some ISOI teachers. Anything coordinated by teachers, known to be master planners, is guaranteed to be a success.

Guests were invited to a different house for each course of the evening meal. The first course, appetizers, was formal, and we all wore tuxes and sequins. After that, we jumped into our vehicles, raced home, changed clothes, and arrived at the next home for the soup and bread course. This house had been transformed into a "soup kitchen," and we all dressed as down-and-outers. The hosts, dressed as a priest and a nun, served us as we lined up for soup.

The main course was an outdoor barbeque with a country and western theme. After another quick-change trip home, we arrived as cowboys and cowgirls and two-stepped the night away. After that, it was time to relax and savour a final course of dessert. We all donned our jammies, grabbed our teddy bears, and packed our swimsuits. This was a house with a backyard hot tub. Late into the night, with full tummies and lifted spirits, we sleepily found our way home. This was one for the memory books. Islamabad in the '90s—best parties of our lives.

Spring break arrived, and while Julie was in Dusseldorf, Wayne and I attended the NESA (Near Eastern Schools Association) teacher's conference in Colombo, Sri Lanka. NESA encompasses international schools in the Middle East and Asia, so teachers from Egypt, Turkey, the Gulf countries, India, Pakistan, Bangladesh, Nepal, and more were in attendance. Experts from all over the world were brought in as speakers and presenters.

The keynote ESL specialist was an American professor who had travelled widely setting up language programs. As I was absorbing the creative energy and learning from the best, I was also granted the honour of chairing an idea exchange session. These conferences were inspirational and energizing, elevating all of us beyond our circumscribed environments. I loved every minute, and Wayne attended a few sessions as well.

But before the conference began, Wayne and I took a little Sri Lankan road trip. First, we travelled south to the resort town of Hikkaduwa, known for its strong surf and long, sandy beaches. Driving conditions in Sri Lanka were harrowing. Their citizens would be in close competition with Pakistanis for the most dangerous drivers' trophy.

Despite a few near misses, we enjoyed the roadside scenery—tropical gardens, fishing villages, women in saris, men in sarongs. We stopped to watch toddy tappers climbing more than 100 feet up into the palm trees with no protective gear to extract sap which is made into palm wine or *toddy*.

As evening approached, we managed to get a room overlooking the ocean at a little out-of-the-way resort and found a thatched-roof village restaurant for dinner. All of the seafood was fresh from the ocean, and that night, we ate the largest, tastiest prawns of our lives, cooked on a modest makeshift grill. We seemed to be the only foreigners around, and locals were intent on capturing us in conversation. Our evening passed quickly with alternating bouts of laughter, a glass or two of toddy, and curious questions.

The next morning, we hoped to lounge for a few hours by the ocean before travelling on. We rose early, or what we assumed was early, only to find all of the beachside chairs covered in towels and reserved with personal belongings. How could this be? We queried the front desk.

"Oh, we are so sorry sir. All of our other guests are German tourists. They rise at five in the morning, reserve the chairs by the ocean, and then go back to bed until the sun rises. You have to wake up early to get ahead of the competition. Again, our apologies."

This was our second experience with German tourists in Sri Lanka. We appeared to have lost this round, but lesson learned. Maybe we would become the "German tourists" of the future.

We decided to pack our bags and drive farther on to the seaport of Galle on the southwest coast. Beaches and palm trees surrounded the 16th Century Portuguese-built Galle fort. The rest of the city boasted 17th Century Dutch era houses, shops, mansions, and museums. We had a leisurely stroll, took in the sights, visited a stately old Dutch Reform Church, and sipped our morning tea on the verdant, tropical grounds of a colonial hotel overlooking the ocean.

Rejuvenated and relaxed, we were excited to get back to Colombo for the conference and enjoy dinners out with friends— French cuisine at the Taj hotel, Chinese cuisine at the Ramada Renaissance, and great Sri Lankan food everywhere.

After the conference, our Islamabad group boarded a flight to the Maldives for a paradise-style vacation in the Indian Ocean. The Maldives is a chain of about 1200 small coral islands with pure white sand beaches, clustered in small groups or atolls. Our plane landed on a tiny island which was the dedicated airstrip. My heart jumped into my throat as we descended onto what looked like an aircraft carrier. Fortunately, the plane stopped just short of the ocean.

This three-day reprieve could only be described as glorious. The sand was like talcum powder, and the reflective blue sea was crystal clear. We had a beachside room on the island of Faru at a Club Med resort. Alas, we heard that it burned down a few years later.

This was my first experience snorkelling, and I was a bit nervous. However, I couldn't have picked a better place to start. After a few lessons in the swimming pool with a very patient Jan, I joined the others on daily ocean excursions to observe colourful fish of every shape and variety while floating over vibrant coral reefs.

The stunning scenery in the depths of the ocean helped me to forget that I was breathing through a tiny tube just inches above the water! When we returned to dry land, we found our evenings jam-packed with shows, disco dancing, and participatory entertainment.

We bid our goodbyes to a final flaming pink and orange-streaked sunset over curling waves. Wayne and I thought to get back for a longer holiday, but that just never happened. Nowadays, the Maldives is considered one of the most expensive and luxurious holiday destinations in the world. We were so lucky to have experienced its beauty before the prices got out of reach.

Shortly after we returned to Islamabad, it was reported that a few of the hotels in Colombo where we'd eaten had been bombed in the ongoing Sri Lankan civil war. More violence and needless injuries! With a morbid expat sense of humour we all expressed relief—the terrorists had waited until we left. As I look back, I realize that this may seem to be a rather shocking, blasé reaction given the gravity of the events. Of course, we took these bombings seriously. We empathized and mourned for the needless loss of life in that exotically beautiful war-torn country.

However, all of us had learned to live with the implicit threat of danger. Living in Pakistan was living with risk. Some countries in that part of the world were worse, some better. If you lived in a potentially threatening environment, you had to learn how to cope. Morbid humour, parties, community support, helping out where possible ... These things were the balm that soothed the frightened, disillusioned soul. Some days if you didn't laugh you might just break down in uncontrollable tears.

In our attempts to get back to "normal," we quickly got back into the swing of Islamabad activities. Our Canadian Club organized a golf tournament at the beautifully manicured course in Pindi. I reluctantly agreed to take part. Wayne was a good golfer and the sporty one in the family. I was the opposite. People always tell you that these events are "just for fun" so I joined. I did have an enjoyable day, but my scores were a disaster, and my team came in dead last. I was never sure how much "fun" that was for my teammates.

The spring musical *Guys and Dolls* opened to rave reviews in April. Miss Adelaide is an eccentric character, and Julie thoroughly enjoyed playing that role. Shortly after the final performance, I was accompanied by 12 students and Sophia, the fourth-grade teacher/drama specialist who brilliantly directed the high school musicals, to the Art and Drama Festival in Karachi. Julie captured the best actress award for Instant Rapport which Jason had won the year before and ISOI performed some scenes from *Guys and Dolls* to an enchanted audience. I presented a well-received drama workshop.

During this time in Karachi, we were all going full bore from 7:30 a.m. to 10 p.m., alternating between outdoor oppressive heat/humidity and indoor frigid air conditioning. I caught a bad cold, and it took some time to kick it. As I look back, I realize that this was the beginning of a pattern. I would operate at full capacity and beyond until my body finally rebelled with bouts of colds or influenza. It would be many years before I learned how to slow down and apply some self-care.

CHAPTER 33—ACCOLADES

In April/May of 1994, I wasn't slowing down for anything. Back home on Park Road, I hosted an Easter dinner for two other families, and at school, I became one of the sponsors for the International Thespian Society, thereby arranging ISOI's first induction ceremonies. I was excited to give out Thespian stars to all my deserving students.

There was a disappointing side note to this event—a few of the students didn't show up to receive their awards. I was perplexed and spoke to one of the parents. She gave me an aggravated look and said, "My daughter and a few of her friends decided to boycott the induction ceremony because they felt it should have been held on the upcoming school awards night, not as a separate event. Those who take part in plays and musicals are being left out of receiving wider acclaim."

I was baffled by this explanation, "True. We couldn't manage to be included in the school awards night for this, our first, year. But I tried to make it special for everyone, and this 'boycott' didn't have any impact on the school administration. It just cast an air of dismay over the ceremonies that the rest of us had worked so hard to make happen."

This mom's eyes widened, "Oh dear, I'm sorry about that. The girls were talking to Miss Tildy who suggested that they boycott the proceedings. She convinced them that they would be fighting for a cause."

Ah, Tildy! I was getting so tired of her manipulation. But there was no use fighting it. I never had and never would. I wasn't about to involve myself in any kind of feud. I searched out the girls to give them their awards and left it there. I did wonder how and when the next blindsiding episode would take place.

May events took on a special poignancy for Julie as her final school year wound to a close. One of our friends hosted a Mother's Day high tea in her bountiful rose garden. A small string section of talented Islamabad musicians played classical music as mothers and daughters performed shared poetry readings. Flowered dresses and big hats were the order of the day.

Another friend hosted a runway fashion show on the spacious grounds of her back yard with both local Pakistani and expat models. Western and South Asian collections were on display. Julie and I each bought flowing, formal shalwar kameez ensembles.

The end of May ushered in some significant events. Once again, we found ourselves munching on picnic dinners as we sat among our community of ISOI families and enjoyed the annual Concert in the Park. Everyone reveled in the finale of songs and dances from *Aladdin* as faces glowed in the setting sun.

An incident on the home front was a bit more unsettling. It was a Saturday morning, and Julie was due to have her weekly piano lesson with Eric, the Performing Arts Director and Band teacher at ISOI. As Wayne and I were getting ready to go shopping, we noticed a couple of bees flying around the living room. We asked Peter to get rid of them and didn't think much more about it.

An hour or so later we arrived home to Julie and Eric's vociferous complaints about all the bees buzzing around their heads during the piano lesson. We looked up and, sure enough, the number of bees in the house had multiplied considerably. What was going on?

Wayne and Peter went outside in search of a hive. After a while, they found a gas pipe hole that had never been properly sealed at the side of the house. It led to the back of the living room bookshelves. Bees appeared to be flying in and out of this hole. Wayne and Peter rushed inside and listened closely. There was a consistent humming sound coming from deep within the wall behind the bookshelves. A closer look revealed dust-covered bees crawling out of tiny cracks in the wood into the living room. We were being invaded!

There was no way to save this hive. It was beyond our reach. Either we had to put up with an increasing population of sickly lethargic bees overrunning the house or get rid of the hive altogether. Wayne and Peter proceeded to spray poison into the hole and seal it as well as taping over the inside cracks. The rest of the afternoon was reminiscent of a scene from a horror show as hundreds of bees panicked and set upon a deafening maniacal drone that abruptly ended in deathly silence. We sat down to dinner sorrowful and sick.

On a happier note, the day of Julie's Senior Prom had finally arrived. During our Canadian vacation, Julie and I had purchased red velvet and satin fabric. The tailor stitched together a gorgeous velvet gown with satin shoulder straps. We had shoes made to match and Julie wore her rubies.

I'd questioned the practicality of wearing velvet in the heat of Pakistan, but Julie looked gorgeous as she slowly descended the stairs, hair smoothed into an elaborate chignon, the rippling ruby folds of her velvet gown reflecting the setting sun. My heart swelled at the same time as my eyes filled up with tears.

Our baby girl had become an elegant young lady. Soon she would be leaving home. I wanted to hug her, squeeze her tight, and keep her close. But that would only have embarrassed her in front of her new boyfriend, Tariq.

Julie's eyes shone the next morning as she described how they had been crowned Prom King and Queen. I smiled and applauded her happiness. These moments were bittersweet for me, but I kept the looming "empty nest" sadness to myself.

Awards night followed soon after, and I was proud to present performing arts awards to all my deserving students. Julie ended up with quite a collection of awards—Choir, Thespian, and the Outstanding Performing Arts Award. The latter was for all her work in acting, singing, dancing, and piano during her time at ISOI. Academically, she received awards for outstanding achievement in both English and French. And from the PE department, she received a physical fitness award.

Back in January, we'd promised Jason that he could come home for Julie's graduation. It had been part of the agreement we made when he promised to persist in his California studies until we could find him better lodgings for the next school year. He'd also convinced us that the family would never be the same after Julie graduated, so he travelled from San Jose to Islamabad and back again for a one-week visit with the family.

I've never regretted this decision. Jason beamed with pride as Julie marched up to receive her diploma. She was Salutatorian for the class of '94. Wayne and I were called up to put the medal around her neck. In addition, she got the Faculty Award for best all-around student and a Presidential Academic Fitness Award signed by President Clinton. Jason gave her a bag of goodies in preparation for college, and we gave her the complete works of Shakespeare.

As a special treat, I took Julie to the beauty salon. We'd never experienced eyebrow *threading* (thin, twisted thread rolled over areas of unwanted hair and removing it at follicle level) and this was our chance to try it out. South Asian women used this technique instead of plucking or waxing. It was a successful, if quite painful, treatment. Sacrifices had to be made for beauty, but we never tried that again.

Jason brought us copies of his transcripts from De Anza, and we were pleased to see that he was doing very well. He especially enjoyed his Philosophy and Anthropology courses. He told us that he would like to finish out his second year in San Jose and then transfer to Vancouver, B.C. in Canada to attend film school. He was still determined to follow his dreams.

After graduation, Julie remarked that this must be the pinnacle of her life. She didn't see how things could get much better. All those awards! And her final report card revealed that she had finished off with an excellent academic record. Of course, none of this happened by magic. Julie was intelligent and talented, but she worked harder than anyone I'd ever known. I was hoping she might take it easier in university, maybe enjoy herself a little.

She'd been accepted to five universities, four in the US and one in Montpelier, France, due to her impressive French grades. Wayne wanted her to study for at least a year in France, but she was over the moon about being accepted to New York University based on her academic scores and a taped audition.

In addition to academic courses, she would be studying at the Stella Adler (Tisch) Studio of acting. Many famous actors had studied there. The tuition and the cost of living in New York were steep for us, even with the help of the UN. However, Julie had worked so hard for this opportunity, we would do our best to provide support.

We wanted both of our children to have the best education possible. This had been one of our goals in moving overseas. The time had arrived to help them make their dreams come true.

CHAPTER 34—HOT TIMES: SUMMER IN THE CITY

School was out and most of our friends were packing up and preparing to leave. Not us! We'd elected to stay in Pakistan that summer of '94 for several reasons—Wayne was deep in the demands of his work, it wasn't a home leave year, and we had costly college tuitions looming. Wayne and I were apprehensive about this decision at first. In June we were already experiencing record temperatures of up to 115 degrees F and a water shortage. But the four of us were going to be together, and that was a five-star bonus.

I'd made some summer plans in advance. First on the agenda was a water aerobics class at the American Club pool, a great way to beat the heat and take care of my health. The second activity was far from a favourite holiday pastime but necessary in any case. I was badly in need of some dental work, a couple of root canals and some crowns. This required a string of judiciously spaced appointments with the dentist lasting most of the summer.

The good news was that Islamabad had a couple of excellent dentists housed in well-appointed offices surrounded by lush tropical gardens. Not only that, but dental costs were less than half those in Canada. I was more than aware of my privilege. I didn't have to sit in the street and wait for the guy with the pliers.

Julie had started work at the Satellite Center taking charge of six-to-eight-year-olds enrolled in summer camp. A Canadian family requested that she tutor their fifth grader in spelling and math before school started again in August as well.

While Julie enjoyed these jobs, that summer she'd found a new hobby that would ultimately become a lifetime passion. She was creating eye-catching necklaces and bracelets from beads she sourced in the local markets. Her pieces became popular with expats and

Pakistanis alike, selling like hotcakes at the international clubs and venues around town.

Jason was due to arrive in Islamabad mid-July and would stay until the beginning of September, the UN was talking about sending Wayne to Bangladesh for a month in August, and I needed to accompany Julie to New York in September. Faced with the daunting task of juggling all the different family agendas, Wayne and I decided to sneak in a little break. It was only a three-hour flight to Dubai, and we'd heard all about the gold *souks* (bazaars) and other attractions from our travelling buddies. Julie went to stay with friends and off we went.

We certainly didn't choose Dubai with the motivation of cooling off. At 105 degrees F, it was just marginally cooler than Islamabad. No problem! The hotel was fully air conditioned, all the swimming pools were chilled, and ocean dips were bathtub warm. Our state-of-the-art accommodation on the beach had several bars, restaurants, and lounges as well as a top floor disco. The beach restaurant served romantic seafood dinners complete with live entertainment every night of the week. Heaven!

Dubai is located in the United Arab Emirates which borders the Gulf of Oman and the Persian Gulf (also known as the Arabian Gulf) between Oman and Saudi Arabia. Situated in the Arabian Desert, it has a natural harbour and has been a trading port since ancient times. During our 1994 stay, we found Dubai to be clean and ultra-modern with shopping malls, office towers, superhighways, fancy cars, exclusive shops, and sleek architecturally designed hotels. Ensuing years seem to have propagated more of the same.

We saw many white flat-roofed homes with marble features and manicured gardens. Tons of water were required for all the gardens and golf clubs due to the desert location. This didn't appear to be a problem. Dubai was rich, as were most of the cities in the Gulf countries, and the main source of fresh water was derived from *desalination.*[49] With its upscale shops, restaurants, and supermarkets, much of Dubai, minus all the high-rise buildings, reminded us of Palm Springs in California.

In contrast to the majority of the Persian Gulf countries, the UAE didn't depend exclusively on oil revenue. Rather, it relied on tourism and trade. As a result, even though the UAE was an Islamic country, it was much more tolerant of westerners and western ways than other Gulf countries such as Saudi Arabia, which didn't allow the presence of non-Muslim foreigners unless they had work permits. In Dubai, alcohol consumption was sanctioned for foreigners at licensed venues such as hotels and tourists could eat pork products as well.

Like most citizens in Gulf countries, people in the UAE hired outsiders to do the work. There was a kind of class system in Dubai organized around employment. Pakistanis and Yemenis were the labour class, Indians were the merchant class, Sri Lankans and Filipinos worked in the households. Filipinos also worked as shop clerks, and most of the bands and singers came from the Philippines. People from western countries worked in schools, embassies, and various business projects.

This freed up the Arabian population of Dubai. The men seemed to spend hours on their phones making deals. This was the first time we were exposed to the widespread use of portable phones—a novel, rich man's pastime. These local men usually wore a long loose-fitting cotton garment known as a *dishdasha* with a head covering (*ghutra*) held in place with a black cord. Sometimes they wore western attire.

The women were either at home or shopping. Local women often covered themselves with an *abaya* (a long black cloak) and a voluminous rectangular scarf. Some of them wore a metallic-looking face mask called a *batoola* or *burka*. The first time I saw a woman with this 'golden mask,' I was immediately transported to super-hero comic books. After a few takes, I got used to it.

---

[49] The term desalination refers to removal of salt and impurities from seawater.

Depending on family values, the amount of covering was a personal decision. Foreign women wore western clothing and some even wore shorts. This would have been considered a shocking abomination in many Muslim countries especially in other parts of the Gulf. The variety of clothing styles worn by females was a testament to Dubai's tourism tolerance.

At the hotels, there were some unexpected hard and fast rules concerning clothing. A sign at the swimming pool proclaimed that no one was allowed in the water unless they wore a swimsuit. Street clothing was prohibited in the pool. At first, we thought this was an odd rule, but then we remembered all the people in Karachi frolicking in the waves fully clothed.

Devout Muslim women considered swimsuits to be too revealing. The hotel, however, catered to tourists and wouldn't allow women to wear abayas for swimming. It was dangerous and unsanitary. This "clothing" rule was a bit of a worry for me though. I burned easily and needed to wear my t-shirt in the pool for protection from the scorching desert sun. My concern about being chastised was ultimately outweighed by my fear of burning. Thankfully, no one called me out for throwing on the t-shirt.

Dubai had long been known for its electronic and gold souks, however we didn't find the deals we were expecting in the electronic shops. This probably had something to do with massive bulk purchases made by a newly rich business class of Russians who were spending their fortunes.

In the mid-90s they were shuttling back and forth from Dubai buying 10 or more televisions at a time, as well as large quantities of other electronic devices, to sell back home. There was much speculation as to how these Russian buyers procured their vast sums of money, but Dubai merchants weren't complaining.

The gold souk was a different story. A sizeable section of downtown Dubai was devoted to a maze of covered walkways that encompassed store after store with thousands of glittering gold bracelets and chains on display. After a breathtaking first glance, we slowly adjusted to the treasure trove around us and bought some gold jewelry, including a necklace with my name in Arabic. Dubai was a duty-free port with the best gold prices in the world. We couldn't pass up that opportunity.

Besides shopping, bouncing in the ocean waves, and eating, we took part in an afternoon of dune bashing followed by an evening picnic in the desert. At first, we had a bit of trouble signing up for this adventure. A concerned Indian booking agent called our room one night as we were getting ready for bed.

Tour operator: "Hello, Mrs. Bazant? I'm calling to suggest changing the day for your desert trip."

Me: "Oh, is there a problem?"

Tour operator: "Not exactly. We just think it would be better for you and your husband to take the tour on Thursday instead of Wednesday. You would have more privacy."

Me: "We don't mind touring with others, and we don't want to pay extra money for a private tour."

Tour operator: "There will be no extra charge. We want to change your day because of the Russians."

Me: "What do you mean?"

Tour operator: "On Wednesday there is a group of Russian tourists signed up for dune bashing and picnic. Our experience has been that they drink a lot of vodka and become very loud and unruly. You and your husband will not have a good time. I strongly recommend that you change the day."

Me: "Ok, no problem. See you Thursday then."

Oh, those Russians!

Our trip into the surrounding desert was everything we had hoped for. Dune bashing in a Land Cruiser was a roller coaster experience, as the driver tackled the massive dunes at top speed. It made for stomach rolling fun. Along the way, we identified what we assumed was an optical illusion of palm trees and water. It turned out to be a natural oasis populated by Bedouin families (visions of *Lawrence of Arabia)*.

We also spotted several camel caravans. The beating sun, vast desert and plodding camels made us feel like we were in a scene from an exotic movie. The reality is that camel racing is a popular sport, and camels are kept in the desert outside Dubai. Our final sighting was a massive palace being constructed in the middle of nowhere. A wealthy prince had decided that an isolated desert life would protect his family from the scourges of the world.

Toward dusk, we parked in a sand crater and were treated to barbeque chicken and ribs, *tabbouleh* (salad), *baba ghanoush* (smoked eggplant), and *taboon* bread, a special local recipe. After dinner, Wayne and I climbed a small dune, watched the sunset over the shifting sand, and marvelled at the star shine. We cherished this moment in time, two small figures enveloped by the immense, stark beauty of the desert.

We arrived back in Islamabad recharged and ready to meet Jason at the airport. After a quick "hello," he repacked and joined Julie and a group of friends for a trip to India to see the Taj Mahal. There were five of them, all college students except for Julie, and they shared one Delhi hotel room to save money. They enjoyed shopping for bargains and admired the imposing beauty of the Taj Mahal, even if they did practically burn off the bottoms of their bare feet on the scorching marble floors, a consequence of visiting this site in one of the hottest months of the year.

Then they encountered a problem. The flight from Delhi back to Islamabad was cancelled. They had already blown most of their money on purchases and a gourmet meal at the Bukhara Restaurant. In order to get cheaper eats, they talked their way into the Delhi American Club on the strength of their Islamabad memberships. They counted their pennies as the skies burst open in monsoon rains until, soaked and jubilant, they were finally able to board a flight home. "Broke in India" was not the quest they had planned.

After all the travel excitement, our family settled into a routine. Every weekend we ordered warm buttery chapatis from the guy down the street with the underground oven. Julie continued to work at the Satellite Center and her other jobs, as well as slotting in time for singing lessons. Jason managed to get a job as a waiter at the Satellite Center.

Most nights they went out with their friends and Jason did a lot of filming. He wanted to record all the precious memories. Soon everyone would be headed back to college. They would be moving on. Would they ever see each other again? Would they miss their Pakistan days?

For the moment, we were all dealing with monsoon season and Islamabad was prone to flash floods. One day Nisar was driving along, running office errands, when water suddenly engulfed the car. He managed to extricate the car from the situation but not before the vehicle partially filled up with water. Our poor Honda! It took quite some time to remove the overpowering musty odor.

There were other hidden dangers during monsoons. One evening, as the skies were darkening, Wayne and I decided to take a walk. We were deep in conversation when a Pakistani man stepped in front of us. He raised his hand and implored, "Stop now. Turn around and go back home. It's dangerous out here. Large snakes are crossing the road just a few meters ahead." We took his advice.

At the beginning of August Wayne prepared to go to Bangladesh. He would be gone until the end of the month and Jason was due to leave at the beginning of September. It was time for a long talk.

Jason sat us both down and broke the news that he'd decided not to go back to De Anza. He wanted to take a gap year in Canada and continue with his education after that. Whatever the case, he didn't want to spend any more time in California.

Nonplussed, we asked what was behind this change of heart. He told us that his movie-inspired childhood dreams of living in California had turned into a bitter disappointment. Not only was he lonely and finding his housing situation difficult but the cultural environment had fallen well short of his expectations. San Jose had some gangs and that was a little scary, especially if they invaded college parties but the biggest problem for Jason was what he described as "living in a police state."

Police were everywhere and wielded a lot of power. Jason had the impression that citizens lived in fear of being targeted by the police, especially people of colour. Many of his friends were of mixed race. He had personally experienced police corruption and abuse of power in Islamabad. Jason didn't want to live with that. He wanted to get back to Canada where people weren't so fond of their guns and the police had a more respectful attitude.

We certainly didn't want to force Jason to attend school in a negative environment. At the same time, we worried that he wouldn't pick up his education again. We let him know that if he went back to Canada to live and work, he had to manage on his own. He agreed to that. We didn't know where this was going, but hopefully, he would find his way. In September he would fly back to California, pack up and drive to Alberta to start a whole new chapter. At least he would be among family and friends.

Time started to fly. New people were arriving in Islamabad to work at the High Commissions and Embassies. ISOI was getting a brand new administration as well—a new Superintendent, a new High School Principal, and a new Business Manager. I invited all of them and their families for a summer lunch of ham (a delicious Dubai purchase) assorted salads, and cheesecake. Based on the camaraderie of this get-together, it looked like it was shaping up to be a great school year. I took the opportunity to host a few more dinners before I had to start ESL testing. I needed to choose a fall play as well.

All of this needed to get done before I left for New York with Julie on August 23. We had decided to take some mother/daughter bonding time, spending three nights in Istanbul, Turkey, on the way. Both of us were researching the history of that region, from the Sumerians to the Byzantine Empire and beyond. We were immersed in the stories of Sultan's palaces, belly dancers, bazaars, and ancient mosques. This was going to be an exciting trip! My mother would join us for a few days in New York, and I hoped to be back in Islamabad by September 7, just in time to say goodbye to Jason. Then we would be empty nesters.

How did that happen so fast?

CHAPTER 35—EMPTYING THE NEST

The time had arrived. Julie had her room sorted and her suitcase packed. I'd made all the arrangements to be off work for two weeks. We were finally ready to board the plane in Islamabad bound for New York to get Julie settled in university. First came a three-night interlude in Istanbul.

Istanbul is the only city in the world that sits on two continents. It straddles the Bosphorus Strait which separates Europe and Asia. Ferries and bridges connect the European and Asian sides of the city. The European side is further divided by the Golden Horn, a natural estuary, which separates historic Istanbul from the modern city. Boasting a skyline studded with domes and minarets, Istanbul invites visitors to travel back in time and partake in a few days of romance and adventure. We could walk the streets where crusaders once marched, admire ancient mosques, peer into Sultan's harems, explore the Grand Bazaar, and shop to our heart's content.

Julie and I fell in love with everything Istanbul, and our time there was a great end-of-summer/college send-off. We stayed at the Citadel hotel built into the old wall of *Constantinople*,[50] right on the sea, where the Bosphorus met the Sea of Marmara.

In the morning, a cozy café welcomed us to a breakfast of tomatoes, cucumbers, olives, feta cheese, rolls, and Turkish coffee. A perfect way to start the day. In the evenings we would lie in bed and watch the ships sail between Europe and Asia.

We packed as much exploration as possible into the short time we had. First on the list was a visit to Hagia Sophia, a Greek Orthodox church from the Byzantine Era, 350 to AD 1453, converted

---

[50] Constantinople was the name of Istanbul during the late Eastern Roman Empire.

to a mosque when the Turks captured Constantinople and made it part of the Ottoman Empire. In the 1930s, Hagia Sophia became a museum, and in 1985, it was declared a UNESCO World Heritage Site. This renowned place of worship had long been famous for the Byzantine mosaics that decorated its interior walls. Some of them were considered masterpieces of Byzantine art with motifs of imperial portraits and religious images.

Next, we visited the Blue Mosque and the Sulaymaniyah Mosque, both still active. The Blue Mosque was constructed in the early 1600s and was named for the hand-painted blue tiles that adorned the interior walls. At night it was bathed in blue light which framed its five main domes, six minarets, and eight secondary domes. It was considered to be the last great mosque of the Ottoman classical period. The Sulaymaniyah Mosque was built in the 1500s by the Sultan of the same name. It was an architectural masterpiece meant to glorify the greatest and richest of the Ottoman sultans. Both of these massive structures boasted giant chandeliers. The Blue Mosque chandelier had a unique feature: the architect had come up with the idea of placing ostrich eggs among the glass bowls to repel spiders. The odour emitted through the shell deterred spiders and was undetectable to humans.

After this, it was time for some palace exploration. Topkapi Palace, the first palace of the sultans, housed the most amazing collection of jewels we'd ever seen including the Spoonmaker's Diamond, an 86-karat pear-shaped diamond that was the subject of folkloric legend, and the Topkapi Dagger, an emerald-studded sultan's dagger sometimes featured in heist movies. It was an incredible museum filled with jewel-encrusted gold and silver pieces, Ottoman clothing/weapons/religious relics, and the world's largest collection of Japanese and Chinese porcelain.

We also visited the opulent 19th-century Dolmabahce Palace, the largest in Turkey. Its 285 rooms, 46 halls, 6 baths, and 68 toilets included elements of Baroque, Rococo, and Neoclassical designs blended with traditional Ottoman architecture. We had never walked through rooms of such extravagance and luxury—gold, crystal, and marble at every turn.

Here we visited the harem and the *Turkish baths*, domed rooms covered in marble with a central raised platform. We were familiar with the concept of harems from our explorations of ancient India and Pakistan, but the baths intrigued us—an intensive wash, scrub, massage experience. Sadly, we didn't have time to surrender ourselves to spa pampering in Istanbul.

Julie and I took a quick peek at what was left of the ancient *Hippodrome*, the Colosseum of the Byzantine period, a stadium for horse and chariot racing. The movie, *Ben Hur*, had been filmed here. Just around the corner, we had the very modern experience of watching the Prime Minister land in her private helicopter.

We loved the exotic blend of east and west that was Istanbul. European Istanbul reminded us of Athens with upscale clubs and shops. Asian Istanbul had carpets, hookahs, spices, and mosques. We were awe-struck by the large Roman aqueduct bridge that spanned Ataturk Boulevard, a left-over of the Aqueduct of Valens from the late 4th Century. Turkish architecture and catacomb-like marketplaces intrigued us as well. The Spice Market (1600s) and the Grand Bazaar (1400s) were huge domed emporiums dating back to the Ottoman era. They were colourful, fragrant, and full of bargains. I bought a Turkish tea set and *Turkish delight* (sweet, chewy candy). Some merchants made great efforts to sell us a carpet, but we had no trouble resisting. They didn't realize that we lived in Islamabad, an oriental carpet paradise.

One afternoon Julie and I took a cruise up the Bosphorus to the Black Sea. The boat slowly floated by gorgeous waterfront mansions or *Yalis*, traditionally built from wood, from the 18th, 19th, and 20th centuries. Yalis were first popularized during the Ottoman Empire as second holiday homes for the wealthy. The shores were also dotted with ancient forts and historical sites. It was a relaxing, if very windy, afternoon.

That night, after choosing fresh fish to eat outdoors, we decided to check out a row of nightclubs along the sea. People were laughing, socializing, dancing to live rock music, having drinks and snacks with their friends. This was an eye-opening experience for Julie and me. Here we were in a Muslim country where men and women could socialize in public places, dance, and drink alcohol. What a difference from Pakistan!

We couldn't leave Istanbul without exploring the dress shops. Julie bought skirts, blouses, dresses, winter boots, and a winter coat for less than a third of North American prices. The salesclerks were friendly and helpful. We found most Turkish people to be warm and outgoing.

One cultural practice shocked us, however. Everyone smoked everywhere. And I mean everywhere! Taxi drivers smoked incessantly, and we were asked if we wanted a cigarette with every cab ride. Shop clerks smoked as well, even those in clothing stores. They would be puffing away even as they were carrying outfits back and forth from the change rooms. I'd never seen so much smoking by so many.

I have been informed by tourist friends that, in recent years, Turkey has banned smoking in many public places including bars, cafés, and restaurants. It's good to see that beautiful country moving in a healthier direction.

On our last night in Istanbul, we went to Orient House, an enormous restaurant/nightclub with tables of patrons from all over the world. Little flags denoted where each set of guests were from. We had Russians on one side of us and Scots on the other. The Scots were friendly and sociable. The Russians spent the evening knocking back shots of vodka. It was a dinner of stereotypes.

The show was truly entertaining. It started with Turkish songs and went on to highlight folk dances, tribal dances, wedding dances, and harem dances interspersed with belly dancing. Audience participation was encouraged, and Julie took part in the belly dancing contest. We still laugh and reminisce about that night! The MC rounded out the evening by singing songs from every country represented in the room, which turned out to be most of the world.

We were sorry to be leaving Turkey. Nevertheless, on the final morning, we showed up at the Istanbul airport well within the designated arrival time. The terminal doors opened to pandemonium. What should have been a routine embarkation process turned into an instant nightmare. Hundreds and hundreds of people were frantically trying to secure boarding passes. Ticketing agents were situated around a huge elevated oval desk. Passengers could approach any agent, no matter which airline or flight they were taking. We attempted to stand in line. The problem was that there were no real lines, and no one knew what they were doing. We stood in three different "lines" because computers kept breaking down and we were told to see another agent. Every time we moved, we wound up farther back in the line. I feared that we would miss our flight. People were shouting and fighting with each other everywhere.

Julie and I frantically tried to get an agent's attention, but they all ignored us. I finally walked to the front of the "line" and became very assertive (lesson learned courtesy of Pakistani airports). The agent had no choice but to take the tickets I was waving in her face.

As she was processing our tickets, some New Yorkers behind us asked how we managed to perform this magical feat. Even their Turkish travel guide couldn't get anywhere in the airport mayhem. I turned to our ticket agent and shouted above the fray, "These people are with us. Please give them their boarding passes as well." She obliged and we were on our way!

We were all so grateful to board that airplane, especially our New York friends. When we landed at Newark Airport, as a gesture of thanks, they drove Julie and me to our hotel. This saved us money, especially in luggage charges. Julie had large, heavy cases, and it took at least two strong men to wrestle them between vehicles and carts.

It was fabulous to be in New York once again. This time we had a full agenda. Julie only stayed one night in the hotel with me, moving into her NYU (New York University) Greenwich Village residence the next day.

Julie introduced herself to her two roommates, both, like her, Tisch School of Arts students. Then we were off and running—purchasing bedding, personal items, and a computer. I remember it well, the two of us sweating and laughing, treading the crowded Manhattan streets burdened with armloads of purchases.

Unfortunately, we had a rather negative banking experience. I wanted to set up an account for Julie and deposit a substantial amount of money to cover her first-year expenses. It never occurred to me that a bank wouldn't want our money. But much to our surprise, we were treated like foreign scum by every bank we entered until we were finally welcomed by the Chase Manhattan bank. The biggest problem seemed to be that most of these institutions didn't understand, or wish to understand, our situation.

One bank gave us a particularly hard time. I explained that we were Canadians living in Pakistan and our daughter had a visa to live in the US and attend NYU. The banking officer gazed at us suspiciously and tapped her long, square translucent nails on the desk, "You claim to be Canadian citizens?"

"Yes."

"If you live outside of Canada you can't be Canadian citizens."

"Of course, we can. There are people all over the world living outside their countries. They still have citizenship in their country of origin."

"No, that's impossible. I can't set up an account for you because you aren't citizens of any country."

"That's absurd. Let me speak to your manager."

Speaking to the manager made no difference. No matter how much ID I presented, they simply wouldn't accept the fact that we were Canadian citizens. This level of ignorance was appalling.

Other banks didn't make this claim. They just didn't want anything to do with non-Americans. I hadn't had this problem in California when I set up an account for Jason. Was this a New York issue? I never knew. In the end, all I could do was say, "Thank you Chase Manhattan. Because of you, our daughter was able to live in New York."

Julie and I took a little downtime after all the stress of getting set up for school. One afternoon we met Wayne's New York boss at the Daily News building and caught the train out to his home on the Hudson River. He and his wife told Julie that she could contact them if she ever needed help. Their kindness was reassuring after some of the Manhattan gruffness we'd encountered.

Julie signed up for NYU orientation tours—harbour cruise, comedy clubs, Central Park picnic—while I was shopping for Pakistan necessities. We both went to our familiar Upper West Side doctor for medicals and he referred me to a podiatrist. I was still having problems resulting from that fall in Thailand. I needed to resolve my limping pain.

My mother flew to New York for a few days, and the three of us savoured our moments together shopping, double-decker bus touring, and taking in a Broadway musical. The fun ended far too quickly. Mom left one day, and I was due to leave the next. Lamentably, Julie and I didn't part on the best of terms.

In our final few days together, Julie had begun to anger easily. She downplayed any concerns I expressed about her being on her own in a big city or finding her way around a large university complex in the heart of the busy streets of Greenwich Village. She was making new friends in an exciting new city and her mom was out of the loop. I was crushed by her irritability and dismissiveness.

Julie obviously had separation anxiety, but that didn't make things any easier for me. This hadn't happened with Jason when he'd ventured out on his own. Then again, he was a boy, the oldest, and much more prone to hiding his feelings. I left New York feeling forlorn and alone. I hoped and prayed that this misunderstanding between Julie and me would sort itself out.

My flight home couldn't have been more exhausting—nine and a half hours to Istanbul, nine hours of sitting in the dingy airport, a six-hour flight to Karachi, another five hours sitting in that airport, and a two-hour flight to Islamabad. I had never been more grateful to set my cases down at Park Road. Home at last! I flopped face down on the bed and slept until the next morning when I was due back at ISOI.

Two days later, Jason left for California. He took a long look around the house and bid a fond farewell to his room filled with movie posters and teen idols. I think he sensed that he wouldn't be returning to Park Road. He cherished the good memories and let go of the bad ones. After a few deep sighs and lots of big hugs, we sent him on his way.

Wayne, not long back from a month in Bangladesh, was off to Vienna for a week. I found myself sitting alone in our 7000 square foot empty nest. Tears flowed as I wrote in my diary:

My dearest children,

It's 6 p.m. and I'm listening to Billy Joel. I played his songs so much when you were little—my fair-haired boy and my dark-eyed girl. You are everything I envisioned before you were born and more.

Jason, you are a caring, loving person. You are easy to be with, loads of fun, and generous to a fault. I'm proud to call you my son.

Julie, you are intense and talented, a Renaissance woman. You drink deeply of life and it responds in all its lights and shadows. I'm proud to call you my daughter.

What am I going to do without the two of you? Where did the time go? The years have gone by in a flash. The house is so quiet without your voices.

Will I still share your victories and defeats? Will you still need me? I know I can't rewind the clock. But if I could, I'd make every moment count.

I feel a deep pain like something has been wrenched from my heart. I will always be here for you. Never forget that.

I love you, Mom

These were the secret musings, buried deep in my diary and my soul. Jason and Julie would never know the overwhelming sadness I felt when they left to live so far from home. They had adventures ahead of them, new vistas to explore. They had to leave childhood behind them.

Chapter 36—Off Balance

We were gradually adjusting to living with no children. Jason had packed up his California life and taken a scenic drive back to Alberta. He would soon get a job and find a place to live. Julie called to say that she was settling into university with acting, writing, and dancing classes.

Her dark mood from those final days we were together in New York had blown over. Much to my relief, she was as chatty and loving as ever. She shared the news that she'd joined a choir and found time to hit a few hot spots with new friends. She was enjoying the celebrity sightings as well. When she got lonely, she would pick up the phone and call Jason.

Our Canadian family and friends asked if we worried about Julie living in New York City on her own. The answer was an unequivocal "No!" I was always concerned for her safety as a young woman in Pakistan, especially after Jason left for college. I felt that she was infinitely safer in New York.

Wayne and I were both busy with our jobs. I was preparing to launch my next play, and Wayne had just returned from long days of work in Vienna, being left with the impression that his Pakistan contract would be renewed for another year. He surprised me with a gorgeous gift when I returned from New York. During his time in Bangladesh, he'd purchased natural pink seed pearls. Our jeweler strung them into an exquisite necklace with a morganite cabochon— it was a memorable gift of love to begin our empty nest years.

Fall months at home began in the messy chaos of interior house painting. It was a nerve-wracking process as the workers strung rickety ladders together with bits of rope and climbed high into the ceilings. We couldn't wait for these heart-stopping antics to end and for the dinner parties to begin. The vines that crawled up the exterior of our home were turning deep red, and the colours and scents of autumn were swirling in the air.

Over the years, Nisar and I'd had lots of strange happenings as he transported me around Islamabad. Once, as we were slowing for an intersection, a young man on a bicycle smacked head-on into our car. The boy was fine, but our car was dented up a bit. Pakistani bicycles were heavy, cumbersome machines.

On another occasion, we had stopped at a red light and a small Suzuki truck rolled right into our back bumper. It was as if the driver had no idea how to use the brakes. These weren't large accidents by any means; just a result of every day careless Islamabad driving habits.

One of the most disconcerting incidents during an outing with Nisar happened on an October afternoon soon after the house painting had finished. We'd driven to a small market near Park Road as I wanted to purchase some new fabric for our living room cushions. Nisar was walking ahead of me and I was preoccupied with searching for the fabric shop.

I was absorbed by displays of offerings in the shop windows when I suddenly felt a close presence. I turned my head and there was a Pakistani man in a white skullcap standing directly in front of me. His crazed eyes bore into me with a menacing stare. Rooted to the ground, I could only focus on the large blue/black bruise in the middle of his forehead.

What did he want? My stomach turned over. Did he have a knife? Time lurched into slow motion. He suddenly began bellowing at me in Urdu.

At the moment Nisar turned to see what was happening, the man punctuated his venomous tirade with a violent arc of spit, contaminating me with his contempt.

Nisar was quickly at my side to make sure I was alright, his eyes scanning the surroundings. But the raving interloper had vanished just as quickly as he had appeared.

I couldn't stop shaking. My innocent shopping trip had been viciously disrupted by hatred so thick that it sat in the air like a ghostly presence even after its bearer had left.

I didn't understand all the vile words that had been thrown at me, but I understood that this man had an aversion to me, to foreign women. He wanted me to disappear. Unnerved, I asked Nisar to drive me home. I was no longer interested in shopping—not that day or in the foreseeable future.

Who was this irate man? I didn't know. But I did know that he considered himself to be pious. What I thought of as a bruised forehead was something known as a *zebiba* or prayer bump. This is a callous that has developed due to the friction generated from the repeated contact of the forehead with the prayer mat during daily prayers. It's considered a sign of being devout.

Showing off is prohibited in Islam, but religious zealots were certainly proud of their prayer bumps. These guys scared me. It seemed that there were more of them around Islamabad that fall. I'd lived in Pakistan for almost four years at that point without ever being verbally attacked, let alone spit on. What was happening? Slowly and steadily times were changing. There was a different order of things creeping up on all of us. The shifts were still subtle. But they were there.

From that day on, my Islamabad outings were charged with a kind of hyper-awareness.

In the autumn months of 1994, a new name was being bandied about on the dinner party circuit and over afternoon drinks—the Taliban. Who were they? What were they doing? Believe it or not, when the Taliban first reared their ugly heads, they had some public support. A few in the expat and diplomatic community believed that this could be the answer to restoring order in Afghanistan, a country plagued with violent in-fighting.

When the Russians had finally pulled out of Afghanistan, they left a vacuum. Those that had taken up arms against the Russian invaders quickly re-formed into sectarian factions fighting for territorial control. The country was torn apart by warring *mujahideen*[51] warlords. Corruption, brutality, rape, and murder were all on the rise. The Taliban were predominantly ethnic Pashtuns. Many Afghans, as well as Pakistanis, studied at Madaris (plural of Madrasa) in Pakistani territory. Senior leaders of the Afghanistan Taliban had attended a well-known Madrasa in Pakistan. The man who ran this seminary was often referred to as the "Father of the Taliban." In this way, Pakistan provided the Taliban with a constant flow of recruits.

Many speculated that the ISI (Inter-Services Intelligence), the premier intelligence agency in Pakistan, supported the Taliban and that Pakistanis provided them with a diplomatic and economic lifeline.

Whatever the case, the Taliban had deep, strong ties with Pakistan which had long welcomed religiously based opposition groups onto their territory. Pakistan, by now, had a history of facilitating Islamic fundamentalism. Afghans, weary of lawlessness, corruption, and chaos, welcomed the Taliban when they first appeared on the scene because they initially brought things under control and allowed commerce to flourish. Even though their mandate was clear—restore security and enforce their austere version of Sharia (Islamic) law once in power—many Afghans, as well as international diplomats, blindly welcomed Taliban intervention. Western nations were strangely quiet when the Taliban began their reign of repression, which started with stripping away the rights of women.

I wasn't comfortable when some of our Canadian expat friends expounded on the virtues of having Taliban rule. Bearded, prayer bump fanatics both frightened and repulsed me. Men that wanted to enforce Sharia laws and throw women in the corner didn't strike me as benevolent rulers. I could sense an unsettling tension in the air. I

---

[51] The mujahideen are guerilla fighters in Islamic countries.

filed these misgivings in the back of my mind for the time being. I had a backlog of work at school as well as rehearsals for *The Nerd*, another hilarious play by Larry Shue that we would present in December. Thanksgiving celebrations came and went as well as ISOI International Day, music concerts, and parent/teacher interviews. School and social events were a little hollow without the presence of Jason and Julie.

Nevertheless, a whole group of us got all decked out in our sequins and tuxes for the annual Marine Ball at the American Embassy. This was considered one of the best parties of the year and it was loads of fun—military ceremony, banquet, and dancing the night away. Alcohol flowed freely and people let their hair down. This type of party was important in a hardship posting.

Wayne and I didn't have an aversion to drinking alcohol by any means. But we noticed that booze played a, some would say, necessary leading role in expat life. Living in Pakistan as a foreigner wasn't always easy, and many expats had a jaded view of the Pakistani lifestyle and values. Getting together for drinks smoothed over the bumps.

Needless to say, spirits didn't raise people's spirits or fix attitudes. In fact, commiserating over drinks often reinforced negatives. It could also lead to drinking problems, and we saw plenty of those. Maybe it was the small community or maybe it was the rigors of a hardship posting, but during our Islamabad years, we observed more extreme drunkenness and issues around alcohol than ever before.

People arrived at prestigious formal functions in tuxes and gowns, and sometimes things went south very quickly. The inebriated man sitting beside you at the banquet table would suddenly get up to go to the bathroom and come back with streaks of vomit on his brand-new crisp white tuxedo shirt, only to order another round of drinks. Or you might see a very drunk embassy official sitting on her own and ask the whereabouts of her husband.

She would point down. He was passed out under the table. It was only 10 p.m.

There were many stories like this. There were whispers of drunk driving incidents and brushes with danger. These were wild and crazy times. For the most part, what happened in Islamabad stayed in Islamabad.

December ushered in the opening night for *The Nerd.* The community had high expectations for ISOI performances, so we were all relieved when our play was hailed as a hit. Putting this together had presented challenges. I had a talented group of actors and a skilled crew. However, a couple of students were extremely difficult to work with, and this affected the mindset of the entire cast. After a few altercations, I finally fired my student assistant director and we pressed on.

Alas, this cast a permanent pall over the show. Rudeness and clashes of chemistry pervaded our rehearsals, an unusual circumstance at an international school like ISOI. After the final performance, everyone took their bows, and I thanked them for all their fabulous work. Despite some bumpy roads, the show had been a success. I was proud of our creation and let bygones be bygones. Our struggles had faded into the past and we could move on and look forward to the next show.

It was time for the usual round of Christmas parties and concerts. Wayne had to travel to the UAE to review their addiction treatment services, so he missed a few soirees. The good news was that he managed to get in some excellent Christmas shopping at the duty-free malls.

One of my favourite parties that Christmas season was the progressive dinner we had for my boss Mike's 50th birthday. Each house had been transformed into a different decade (the '50s, '60s, '70s, etc.) in décor and music. I was the only one who dressed for each era, after all, I was a drama teacher. I didn't have a really good outfit for the '70s, so I stuffed my shirt and went as a pregnant woman, my real-life look for that decade.

Wayne arrived home from the Gulf just in time to finish out the season of Christmas parties. We enjoyed the tempura at the Japanese Embassy celebration of the Emperor's birthday as we had enjoyed the festivities at the Korean Embassy a few months earlier.

The Japanese party was particularly well-attended as they were serving Chivas whiskey by the case. These were standing room only cocktail parties which we had become accustomed to—our legs were much stronger than when we first arrived in Pakistan. I had an especially large number of Japanese and Korean students, and we were honoured to be invited to their embassy functions.

As Christmas approached, Wayne and I were getting excited to start our holiday trip. We were scheduled to meet Jason and Julie in Egypt. Jason was sharing a condo with two friends in his hometown in Alberta and detailing cars for a living. His gap year was turning out to be hard labour, but he had a girlfriend, and he seemed content. He still missed his family, though, and couldn't wait to get on a flight to Egypt.

Julie was enjoying her classes and New York, but she was looking forward to trading the hustle and bustle of that city for the splendour of Cairo. Because of the movement in USAID, we now had a few American friends living in Egypt as well. This Christmas was going to be a nostalgic reunion of family and friends.

CHAPTER 37—THE WONDERS OF EGYPT

Christmas in Egypt was a captivating treat. I would highly recommend it!

We started out in Dubai where we did some Christmas shopping at the duty-free mall. Laden with gifts, we finally touched down in Cairo and settled into our room at the historic Marriott Hotel. Its central wing was initially built as a palace in 1869 to host Napoleon III and his wife during the opening of the Suez Canal. It was converted to a luxury hotel in 1894.

Used as a hospital during World War I, it became a private residence for many years and re-opened as a hotel in the 1960s. The original architect had been asked to copy the design of Versailles in France. We were impressed with the wide staircases, marble features, and sparkling chandeliers. The lobby was hung with authentic paintings of the opening ceremonies of the Suez Canal. We both relished the historical significance and loved our luxurious modern rooms.

Once settled, our good friends Anna and Tim, now expert residents of Cairo, took us on a shopping trip to Khan el-Khalili—the oldest market in Cairo dating back to the 14th Century. In the beginning, it was built to revitalize the city after the ravages of the Black Death. Portions of it displayed the original Islamic Mamluk architecture featuring great archways and vaulted ceilings.

Our friends guided us to the best shops for silver, papyrus paintings, copper, textiles, and the famous delicately crafted Egyptian perfume bottles. Some of the oldest cafes in Cairo were housed in the bazaar, where we sampled our first bites of Egyptian food. Kushari, the national dish, was a delicious blend of rice, macaroni, and lentils topped with spicy tomato sauce, chickpeas, and fried onions.

Cairo was founded in AD 969 but the land in and around it had long been the site of ancient capitals, remnants of which are still visible in Old Cairo. It is associated with ancient Egypt as the Giza Pyramid complex and the ruins of Memphis (circa 3100 BC) are located in the same geographical area. Over time, it has been ruled by the Fatimids, Saladin (the first Sultan), the Mamluks, the Ottomans, and the British colonials until 1952. Eventually, it became the largest city in the Islamic world.

When we visited Cairo, we saw a sprawling metropolis with narrow streets, old broken-down buildings, and lots of garbage. Garbage had overtaken the rooftops. From the air, Cairo must have looked like one big garbage dump. Chokingly thick pollution hung over the city as well. Every taxi ride was a breathing challenge exacerbated by the head cold I'd developed just before our vacation.

That said, it was also a fascinating cosmopolitan city. Our hotel had a casino (unheard of in many Muslim countries), and alcohol was sold at hotels and tourist facilities. Travel into the countryside would reveal more conservative, fundamentalist Islamic practices. Starting in 1992, a terrorist Islamic group had launched a campaign of attacks on government and tourist targets, and before our arrival in December of 1994, there had been a deadly attack on a sight-seeing bus. As a result, tourism was at an all-time low.

In Pakistan, we'd heard that this attack had taken place in a rural area off the beaten track. Despite the negative press about travel to Egypt, and travel warnings, we decided to take our chances. After a few days of kicking around Cairo, we felt relatively safe. Our friends who lived in Cairo didn't feel that they were in any danger either, so we took advantage of the lower prices and lack of tourists. Living with potential danger on a daily basis had changed our perspective on what was "safe."

Jason arrived at the hotel on December 23. He was happy to see us and excited to meet up with his friends who were also home from college and visiting their families for the holidays. On the 24th, we met Julie with her gigantic suitcase and burgundy hair at the Cairo airport. The four of us found our way to Maadhi, the section of Cairo where most of the expats live, for Christmas Eve dinner at the home of Jason's good friends. Their dad was a gourmet cook and we had a yummy turkey dinner with all the trimmings.

Despite having been out until the wee hours partying with their friends the night before, Jason and Julie rose early Christmas morning to exchange gifts with us. We were tired but filled with joy, sipping orange juice, and sharing Christmas hugs. Later in the day Anna and Tim invited us for Christmas dinner. They invited another ex-Islamabad family as well. These were our friends, and all the kids were buddies too. We might as well have sung *I'll Be Home for Christmas*. We felt like one big family around the table that day.

December 26 found us once again at the airport waiting for the flight to Luxor in southern Egypt where we'd board a ship for a five-day Nile cruise, an exploration of ancient Egypt. It seemed as though there was a story with every airport, and this one didn't disappoint. Our flight was delayed, and when we were finally able to board and get seated, we were immediately asked to get off the airplane and wait for a while longer. Aargh!

Grumpy and exhausted, we finally arrived in Karnak/Luxor, the site of stupendous temples and pharaonic structures. There were rows of sphinxes and colossus-sized statues of Ramses II. As we walked around these towering ruins, our guide translated the *hieroglyphics*[52] and symbols on the *obelisks.*[53] We were fortunate to have a guide from Aswan, who had graduated with a degree in Egyptology from the University of Chicago. He had been working with tourists for 17 years.

Artifacts and ruins in Egypt are awe-inspiring and overwhelming. Much of what we saw on our cruise was 3000 to 5000 years old and gigantic. Everywhere we turned there was another ancient painting or

---

[52] Hieroglyphics are pictographic script.

[53] An Obelisk is a four-sided tapering monument with a pyramid shape at the top that symbolizes the sun god *Ra*.

carving. A huge scarab commemorating the coronation of Alexander the Great graced a large section of one Luxor wall.

Cruising the Nile was like going back in time. We watched peasants harvesting grain and herding cattle on the banks of the river. Since Egypt was mostly desert, Egyptians had historically lived along the Nile.

We soon arrived at the Valley of the Kings and Queens. In the dry mountainous area across from Luxor, tombs of ancient kings, queens, and nobles (1539 BC to 1075 BC) had been excavated. Pharaohs were buried with jewels, gold, and worldly treasures, but due to the work of ancient grave robbers, the tombs had long ago been cleared of these riches. As we advanced underground, deep into the tombs, we were awestruck by the magnificent murals and hieroglyphs depicting daily life and the land of the gods. The Valley contained approximately 63 of these exquisitely decorated tombs that were rotated for public viewing so the paint wouldn't deteriorate due to rampant tourist traffic.

The famous Tomb of Tutankhamen (King Tut) was completely intact. It had been discovered in 1922 filled with golden treasures, most of which had been moved to the museum in Cairo. The Funerary Temple of Queen Hatshepsut was bigger than most palaces, and operas had been staged there in modern times.

Each stop on the cruise revealed amazing temples and artifacts:

- Esna—Halls and columns built by Roman Emperors;

- Edfu—Enormous carved depictions of trips into the underworld;

- Kom Ombo—Paintings of vultures on the ceiling, Greco-Roman architecture, and mummified crocodiles;

- Aswan—Aswan Dam and the island temple of Philae, which had been removed from a submerged island and reconstructed.

The cruise was relaxing, with musical evening entertainment. Woefully, all the passengers, including us, got sick. We went down like dominoes—one by one. This was our introduction to an Egyptian stomach bug, as opposed to the familiar Pakistan variety. It was brutal—with projectile vomiting, diarrhea, sweating, and body aches that kept a person curled up in a ball for 24 to 48 hours. Even Jason, the family member with the strongest constitution, was down for a day or two.

We'd been told that people often got sick on Nile cruises, but we thought that meant "seasickness." We didn't realize that food and water sources in rural Egypt could pose such a problem.

Upon our return to Cairo, weak but mostly recovered, Wayne and I decided to take a tour of the city with some friends. The first stop was the Citadel, a medieval Islamic fortification that was the seat of the government and residence of its rulers from the 13th to the 19th centuries.

My favourite visit that day was to the Gayer Anderson Museum, a multistorey house deep in the old city, one of the best-preserved examples of 17th-century domestic architecture left in Cairo. The carpets, screens, and furniture dated back to British colonial days, and a James Bond movie had been shot there.

One evening our family took a glorious *felucca*[54] trip up the Nile with all of our Islamabad friends. We snacked, drank, and reminisced about Pakistan days together, both good and bad. We didn't sail very far up the river due to lack of wind but that did little to dampen our enthusiasm. There was nothing better than watching the sunset on the Nile with old friends.

Then it was on to the Cairo museum, full of jaw-dropping collections. We viewed 4500-year-old statues, multiple gold sarcophagi of King Tut plus his famous mask and golden throne,

---

[54] A felucca is a traditional wooden sailing boat with lateen sails.

mummified monkeys, and partially unwrapped mummies of the pharaohs with real hair and skin, preserved after all this time.

We travelled on to Saqqara outside Cairo to view Djoser, the oldest of all the pyramids (2650 BC) which more closely resembled those in Mexico. There was nothing much left of the ruins of the ancient, once vibrant, capital of Memphis except a few scattered rocks.

That day we also visited a carpet factory. We were shocked and upset to see that they were using child labour, even though they assured us that these children were taken out of poverty-stricken homes and provided an education. We were skeptical.

Wayne and I took a short excursion past "The city of the dead," an ancient graveyard upon which local Egyptians had established a village, to Coptic Cairo. The Oriental Orthodox Christian (Coptic) Church was based in Egypt, Africa, and the Middle East, said to have been founded by St. Mark in AD 42.

The Coptic church diverged from other Christian churches during the 5th Century due to differing beliefs about the nature of Christ. Coptic Christians in Egypt have suffered a long history of persecution. These first Christians in Egypt spoke the Coptic language, and the scriptures written during those times are still used by Coptic churches everywhere.

This was the oldest, most run-down part of Cairo. We wound our way through dirty cobblestone streets until we found a small door in a wall that opened to a beautiful old courtyard with stately trees and ornate churches—an aura of tranquility prevailed. In St. Sergius, the oldest and smallest of the churches, there was an underground crypt where the Holy Family was said to have rested on their journey into Egypt. This peaceful place of courtyards and churches was intriguing, and we wished we had more time to explore.

The final trip for the four of us was to the famous Pyramids of Giza. We acquired two camels and rode around the three pyramids— Cheops, Chephren, and Mykerinus, the sphinx, the digs, and the boat.

Riding camels had a similar feel to riding a horse, albeit bumpier. The scariest part was the beginning. After having mounted the kneeling camel, we felt a rather violent and sudden lurching forward motion as this awkwardly gracious animal attempted to stand up. I wondered how many novice tourists had been thrown face-first into the baking desert sand!

Judging by the ear-to-ear smiles on the four of us riding camels in Arab headgear, I would say this was one of our best family excursions. We had lunch at the hotel across the road. Our kids described it as having *Princess Bride* architecture—carved Egyptian screens, ornate chandeliers, and long dark, red-carpeted hallways dotted with palm trees. It was an epic afternoon for all of us.

There were many delicious meals and warm get-togethers in Cairo for Christmas and New Year's Eve. On the last night, we had a Vietnamese feast at the home of family friends from Islamabad. The three of us said our teary goodbyes to Egypt and Jason, who was staying on for a few more days with friends before making his way back to Canada. Then it was time to hop on a flight back to Islamabad.

CHAPTER 38—AN UNSETTLING ENLIGHTENMENT

Could it be 1995 already? Where had the time gone? Were we old hands at living in Pakistan by this time? In some ways, perhaps. Ironically, the more we learned about the subcontinent, the more we realized just how much we didn't know. Learning, it seemed, was a never-ending cycle of expanding our knowledge and exposing our ignorance. Each time we were caught in the darkness, we found the light just around the corner, only to be caught once more in a patch of darkness. The light was always there. We just had to search for it.

Julie was with us for a couple of weeks before returning to NYU, and together we arranged the first Bazant party of the season, a January Blues Party for 125 people. This was our largest party to date and there was still room for more guests. Everyone wore blue, and all the food had "blue" connections—blueberries, blue cheese, etc. Glasses were lifted as we celebrated reaching the middle of the decade.

Being home with us for a while was good for Julie. Of course, she enjoyed party planning and hanging out with us. She also came to understand that she'd moved on, not from her family but from Islamabad. Many families had been posted to other countries and her friends were all in college. The life she'd known no longer existed. New York was Julie's new home, although she would connect with the family wherever we lived. We didn't know it then, but this would be the last time she walked through the door at Park Road.

After Julie left, it was time for me to prepare for the Arts Festival in Kathmandu, Nepal. My students and I practiced long and hard, rehearsing a short play and some oral recitations for the 6-day event.

Somehow, I was talked into leading a three and a half-day Collective Creation workshop as well, during which groups work together to create a theatrical piece. I received excellent feedback for my work, but I hadn't bargained on how exhausting it would be to guide and direct workshops for more than half of the festival. Why did I do this to myself? Maybe I needed to learn to say no.

All told, our festival contributions were deemed a success. In addition to receiving kudos for my workshop, one of my students won in the best couples' category of Instant Rapport. Now it was time for some Nepal adventures.

Kathmandu was a peaceful city of friendly, bowing people deep in a valley of the misty Himalayas. Nepal bore a resemblance to both India and Tibet with its mixture of Hindu and Buddhist temples. Our little group took in the sights—an eclectic marketplace full of shouting vendors, saffron-robed monks, half-naked Saddhus with painted faces and matted hair, dancing cobras, sharp sweet incense, shawls/jackets made of the finest wool, semi-precious stones such as turquoise, amber, and coral. Pagoda-style temples graced the perimeter of the squares and restaurants served a wide range of food, everything from pizza to German cuisine and Nepali delicacies. Men in pointy *Dhaka topi hats*[55] rode donkeys, motorcycles, and rickshaws through the early morning streets.

There were lots of local activities such as jungle walks on offer, but the most famous activity of all was mountain climbing. Not just any mountain climbing—this was the home of Mount Everest. Many had journeyed here to conquer its heights. The lure of the majestic snowcaps of Everest was the forever background of Kathmandu.

A closer look revealed another side of Kathmandu. It was dirty, polluted, and full of garbage. The river ran filthy. Old hippies that had lived in Nepal for years would say that it was a matter of where you looked. If you looked down, you saw the garbage. If you looked up, you saw the temples and the blue sky. It was all a matter of perspective.

---

[55] A dhaka topi hat is cotton hat which is part of the national Nepali dress.

I looked up and down and became instantly captivated by Kathmandu. I could feel the deep peaceful spirituality that pervaded all activities. I'd long been interested in Tibetan Buddhism and many Tibetans had migrated to Nepal after the Chinese takeover of their country.

One night after a late festival coordinators' meeting, I hopped on the back of a fellow teacher's motorbike. We wound our way through the narrow Kathmandu streets on that starry night entranced by the tinkling music of the temple bells. This is my enduring memory of Nepal.

Our group arrived back in Islamabad, weary and proud. I was feeling a bit under the weather from days and nights of hard work, but my ESL classroom was calling. Wayne welcomed me back with a pair of deep blue lapis earrings that he'd had specially made. It was his way of saying "You are valued." For all the years we lived in Asia, he would surprise me with pieces of gorgeous jewelry as tokens of his love.

Islamabad made world headlines just a few short days after I returned. Ramsi Yousef, who had escaped after the 1993 World Trade Center bombing, was found in a guest house not far from where we lived.

During his time as a fugitive, he'd planned and attempted bombings of airliners and was suspected of an aborted assassination attempt on Benazir Bhutto. The agents who arrested Yousef found children's toys packed with bomb components in his room. He was taken back to the US and ultimately sentenced to life in prison.

His activities and arrest became an integral part of the story of the expansion of terrorism in South Asia and beyond. Yousef was born in Kuwait to Pakistani parents, had pursued post-secondary education in the UK, and returned to Pakistan in the early '90s where he allegedly studied bomb-making at a terrorist training camp in Peshawar before embarking on multiple acts of terror. (His maternal uncle, Khalid Sheikh Mohammed, also Pakistani and now imprisoned at Guantanamo Bay, was named the principal architect of the 9/11 attacks in 2001.)

The expat community was both shaken and relieved by the capture of Yousef. Wayne and I were shocked to discover just how close we'd been living to a terrorist. We had to accept that others were likely hiding in plain sight around us. This was an eerie realization. Nevertheless, we filed it under the heading of "just another danger lurking at the edge of our daily lives."

Benazir Bhutto and Bill Clinton were working on warming diplomatic relations between their countries, and this arrest was considered a big win. Fundamentalist groups and radicals in Pakistan saw it differently, though. This extradition compounded their hatred of western policies and values. Tension was building. We were beginning to awaken to some hard realities. Maybe Pakistan was a terrorist training ground. At the beginning of March, we gave our heads a shake in an attempt to rid ourselves of frightening thoughts about what might be emerging from under the surface of our relatively peaceful Pakistan days. Nonetheless, our next trip took us to what many believed was a terrorist haven. At spring break, I accompanied Wayne on a jaunt to Quetta, Balochistan.

Back then, the Balochistan province of Pakistan wasn't a well-known part of the world. On the map, this empty space with camels running across it bordered Iran, Afghanistan, and the Arabian Sea. It was the largest province in Pakistan but the least inhabited and the least developed. Quetta was its high-altitude, semi-arid capital city close to the Afghan border and situated near the Bolan Pass, which provided entry to Afghanistan through the Kandahar region. I wrote my first impressions in my diary:

> *Here we are in Quetta. Dry brown mountains overlook a dry brown desert. It's a lawless tribal city full of fierce-looking men and women in purdah. We are staying with an Australian who works on the drug enforcement border patrol. He welcomed us with these words, "Quetta is not the end of*

the earth, but you can see it from here." I guess he doesn't like it here.

Quetta scared and fascinated me all at once. The striking Serena hotel had been designed to match its desert surroundings with an adobe look and woven textile hangings. They sold tribal jewelry and richly textured carpets. Outdoor markets featured mountainous piles of the finest quality pine nuts, pistachios, walnuts, and raisins.

We walked through a large square in the center of town, inhabited by severe-looking bearded men wrapped in dark clothing carrying AK47 assault rifles. There were no women anywhere, except for me. Some of these men were squatting in a circle playing a gambling game that involved breaking, or attempting not to break, eggs. They gestured for Wayne to join them. I stared at the ground and shivered. What were their other pursuits? Killing their perceived enemies? Smuggling drugs? In subsequent years, Balochistan faced continuing waves of violence from insurgents and terrorists. 1995 was the tip of the iceberg. After 9/11, we would never have dared to set foot in that market.

Upon returning to Islamabad, I was asked by the Canadian High Commission to speak to a group of Afghan refugees that were emigrating to our fair country. I was more than happy to oblige. I'd worked with many refugees in Canada, and I understood what adjustments they would have to make upon arrival. Besides that, I loved working with immigrants and refugees. They were so grateful to find a home in their country of choice. They often became the best and most loyal citizens.

I'd consistently found Afghans to be warm open people, and this group didn't disappoint. I spoke to them for about 45 minutes, and then it was their turn. They served our Canadian contingency some mouth-watering dishes and peppered me with questions, devouring every morsel of information. I made it clear to the High Commission that I would be happy to return any time in the future.

And then another incident rocked our world. On March 8, in Karachi, two American diplomats were killed and a third was injured when gunmen opened fire on their van as they drove to work. Karachi was known to be violent, but this was the first time westerners had been targeted by terrorists amid all the political, religious, and ethnic upheaval. Investigators believed that the attack was payback for the capture of Ramsi Yousef in Islamabad the previous month. Security tightened. A shadow had been cast over the Bhutto government's ability to control violence in the country as well as her imminent visit to the USA.

None of us knew what might happen next. How safe were our Islamabad diplomats? How safe were we on those weekends spent at the American Club or the Canadian Club? How safe was the school? We needed to push these thoughts aside. It did no good to speculate on something that was essentially out of our control. We had to trust the protections we had in Islamabad, the seat of the government and home of diplomats. Could we do that?

This episode didn't stop Hillary Clinton. In her capacity as the US first lady, she landed in Islamabad on March 25, as part of her ten-day, five-nation tour of South Asia. She met with Benazir, toured the Faisal Mosque with Chelsea, and hosted a reception at the American Embassy. My colleague Kate went to hear her speak and was unexpectedly impressed. I wished I could have attended but it was for Americans only. Hillary's visit was a gesture of good faith in tumultuous times. It helped all of us to feel just a little bit better.

CHAPTER 39—BLACK COMEDY

Despite a background of recurring conflict and tension, everyday life continued as usual. I'd been chosen to perform in a community RATS play, *Black Comedy*. As if I didn't have enough to do with ESL classes, community work, festivals, and dinner parties, I'd decided to further expand and exercise my acting chops. Of course, as a theatre major, I'd taken roles in many plays earlier on in my life, most recently performing with an amateur theatre group before moving overseas. But my Islamabad friends had never seen me as an actress. I hoped that I would live up to community expectations.

The next two months comprised solid rehearsal time for me and a lot of travelling for Wayne. His itinerary included trips to Delhi, Beirut in Lebanon, and Colombo in Sri Lanka.

He found Beirut, to be a city of fascination and contradictions. In 1995, much of it was still rubble, and citizens were working hard to rise from the ashes of a civil war that had only ended in 1990. In the 1960s, Beirut had been considered the Paris of the Middle East. Sections of the city that had been rebuilt revealed some of its former glory.

Wayne delighted in fabulous food at five-star restaurants with European prices to match, was treated like a special guest, and brought home an intricate carving made from the famous Cedars of Lebanon. He was fortunate, as a Canadian, to be able to travel and work in Beirut. At that time, Americans couldn't get security clearance.

Meanwhile, the day arrived for my debut performance in Islamabad. On a warm May evening, our RATS play opened to great anticipation in a pitch-black theatre. The audience was confused. Then the lights went up. In a suspension of reality, the light was meant to signify darkness—the power had gone out in the interior of the onstage home. At the end of the play, when the stage lights went down, the lack of light symbolized restored electricity. This clever device encouraged the audience to imagine that all the characters were operating blindly in the dark adding to the chaos, mistaken identity, and madcap hilarity of the play.

I played a middle-aged spinster, a teetotaler, who accidentally imbibes alcoholic beverages. She gradually becomes very drunk resulting in some crazy uninhibited behaviour. I thoroughly enjoyed this character and the company of my castmates. My friend and colleague, Sophia, and her husband were in the play as well. We had a diverse cast—Pakistani, American, Canadian, Dutch, British. Despite the long days of working my regular job and rehearsing the play, I loved every minute. One night I got a standing ovation after my drunken monologue. It's such a great feeling to be appreciated by your community!

In stark contrast, a senseless tragedy occurred that May in Islamabad. Pakistani staff at the American Club were cleaning up and fooling around one night after the restaurant had closed. One of them stumbled or was accidentally pushed, into the swimming pool. The victim couldn't swim; neither could his fellow staff members. As he went under, struggled, and gasped for help, his mates were paralyzed with fear. Assistance didn't arrive in time to save their friend from drowning.

Pakistan suffered many needless deaths as a result of ignorance, carelessness, lack of safety standards, or, as in this case, lack of basic skills. Pakistani staff at foreign embassies, houses, or schools often became part of a big family, so we all mourned this heartbreaking loss.

Time stops for neither the tragedies nor joys of this life and it seemed be flying by faster and faster with every school year. Before we knew it, we were sliding into end-of-year activities—final exams, performing arts awards, thespian inductions, concert in the park. My bucket was full and overflowing. There were the usual rounds of teary goodbyes. I hosted a UN lunch as well as a tea for ISOI colleagues to say farewell to all those leaving for other postings. Khan and I were getting good at making those fancy little cucumber and cream cheese sandwiches.

The last day of school was a tough one. Cutbacks and reorganization carried out by the new administration had resulted in hard feelings. Tempers were frayed and gossip was high. Many people felt that they'd received unfair treatment.

My ESL department hadn't escaped the chopping block. Naila was reassigned to the middle school assistant position she'd had before joining our team. This was upsetting for both of us. She'd been an integral part of the ESL program, and I would sorely miss her.

We all valued our assistants, especially in the Student Services department where many of them helped out with individual students. They were not only colleagues, but good friends. Most of the teaching assistants were women and, due to their status in a traditional Muslim society, their personal lives sometimes collided with their work lives.

In the final months of the school year, Sakina, one of Jan's assistants, had been missing from work for a few days, with no word as to her whereabouts. Days passed and worries heightened. Sakina had been upbraided by other assistants for "immodest behaviour" in the past. These infractions included wearing tights to a party and speaking freely in front of westerners, especially men. We all knew that she'd been beaten more than once by her father for pursuing a clandestine relationship over the telephone.

News finally reached us. Sakina had run away with her boyfriend and embarked on a forbidden journey, a love marriage. Her family had disowned her. None of us at school heard from her again. It was as if she'd disappeared into thin air. We kept her in our thoughts and prayers. If these marriages didn't work out, there were disastrous consequences for a woman in Pakistan. Society would shun her. Being used goods meant no man would have her in the future, and her family would most often reject her. At best, she would end up in the streets. All of us hoped that Sakina would have a long, happy life in a marriage filled with love. The alternatives were too horrific to consider.

Besides the loss of Naila and the disappearance of Sakina, Jan and I found ourselves entangled in yet another outcome of departmental change and restructuring. Jan invited me into her classroom for a chat one day, and I plopped down in a chair, relaxed and happy to have completed another successful year at ISOI.

With downcast eyes, Jan spoke softly, "Sharon, I won't be helping with the play for the next school year."

"Why?" My heart caught in my throat. What was she trying to say?

"I will be head-down-bum-up next fall since my position as Reading Specialist has been expanded to include a lot more work. I just won't have the time or energy to produce the show."

"What!? I understand. The extra work is a huge weight. But what am I going to do without you?"

"I'm sure you can find someone else to help. I'm not indispensable. You'll do a great job as always."

I left her classroom with a hollow feeling in the pit of my stomach. Could I do this without her? I was quite sure that she was indispensable. I tried to push down the creeping dread. That reckoning was still three or four months away. Maybe a miracle would save me.

Why didn't I march directly into the administrative offices and announce that I wouldn't be directing any more plays? I certainly had no obligation to proceed on my own. I don't know why I didn't do that. I guess I felt obligated to the students and the community. I still hadn't learned how to say no, it seemed.

As it turned out, a miracle did save me … just not any miracle I could have imagined.

I slowly walked back to my little room so Kate and I could get busy packing up. After four years of campaigning for a larger workspace, we were finally being moved out of our cozy corner into a sunny spacious classroom. "Hooray!" This was one positive outcome of all the reorganization and reallocation. We'd had to give up our assistant in exchange for a better space. We wanted both but decided to surrender and count our blessings.

In our dining room at Park Road, I recounted the tearful departure of some of my beloved ESL students and my end-of-the-year disappointments. Wayne reminded me that we had more pressing issues. It was time to pack for our Canadian summer reunion with Jason and Julie. We would travel via Vienna and try to assess what the future held in store for us.

Wayne's contract was due to expire in January of 1996. Would we stay in Islamabad for another year? Would we be posted elsewhere? Positions were coming available in Bangkok, Delhi, New York, and Vienna. What next?

I opened the closet, pulled out the suitcases, and ruminated on the first half of 1995. Dark days and tears had been shot through with laughter and light. It dawned on me that, without realizing it, we were becoming warriors.

CHAPTER 40—DISCOVERY

The first leg of our home leave trip took us to Vienna for a quick check-in. Wayne kept his appointments with the head office, and we commiserated over rich Viennese coffee and cakes. It looked like we would be heading to a new posting come January of '96, but there was no firm decision. We would just have to wait. Dealing with the unknown was difficult for Wayne but I was sure that life would unfold as it should. Nothing was written in stone. I relished the exhilaration of standing on the precipice of a new chapter.

As we were winging our way to Canada, I sat in the blurry darkness of the aircraft cabin amongst fitfully sleeping seatmates and reflected on our family evolution. Who had we become, and where were we going?

Our roots would always be in Canada. We were born there. Our people were there. But we didn't quite fit anymore. Our families and many of our friends found it difficult to understand our "new identities." They had no relative benchmarks or connections to our experiences.

It seemed that we were on our own, disassociated from what once had been familiar. On trips back to North America we spent a lot of time keeping quiet and pretending to be "the same old Bazants," but that felt off-kilter, inauthentic.

At the same time, we didn't belong to Pakistan. By now, we understood many aspects of that culture and we had made ourselves a cozy abode, but we weren't Pakistani. Although we were long past Pakistan culture shock, we were still jolted by unexpected behaviours and events from time to time. That would never change.

We had broadened and expanded our world views. We were getting comfortable with visiting places where the language, dress, and overall culture was very different from ours. Sometimes we were more comfortable in these situations than we were in our Canadian "home."

So where did we belong? We'd travelled to many other countries and discovered exotic practices and warm, welcoming people. But we didn't find a home in those places either. Books have been written about this phenomenon; a feeling of belonging everywhere and nowhere at the same time. We were starting to feel that. Would we feel it for the rest of our lives? For the moment we had to put aside these complicated questions. Our identity journey had only just started.

We touched down in Alberta groggy but happy to once again be spending time with our adult children. Our eyes brimmed with tears of joy as we hugged Jason and Julie. Jason was finishing up his last few months of work at the detailing garage. For the first time in his life, he'd been confronted with a gruelling, physically demanding job. That said, he looked happier than I'd seen him for some time. He was surrounded by close friends and our families were a mere bus ride away.

A gap year and manual labour had been good for Jason. It helped him to see the future more clearly, and that future still included film studies. In late August he and a couple of friends were planning a move to the coast—Vancouver, British Columbia. He'd enrolled in Capilano College with an eye on eventual admittance to Vancouver Film School. His eyes brightened with excitement as he shared the details of his prospects.

My heart burst with gratitude. I thanked God and the universe for guiding him back from the trauma of his Pakistan accident. My most fervent aspirations had always been for my children's happiness.

Julie had adopted New York as her true home. She loved the Greenwich Village location of NYU and had already memorized the subway system that allowed her to visit museums and art galleries on the weekends. She was working hard at academics as well as at singing, acting, and dance classes. With all this, she still had the energy to enjoy a full social life with her new friends. Julie loved being busy, and the hustle and bustle of New York City fed her creative spirit.

For the three-month break, she'd moved in with Jason and his roommates while working at a seasonal job overseeing concessions for the City of St. Albert in Alberta. Julie relaxed into the hot sunny days of summer with family and old friends. It was wonderful to see her cheerful and contented, even if Jason did have to remind her to keep her voice down from time to time. She'd already adopted the tenor and volume of a loud New Yorker.

Both Jason and Julie were able to take a few days off so that the four of us could spend some time together in Banff and Jasper, Alberta. The Rocky Mountains were near and dear to us. We'd spent many summer vacations there when the kids were growing up. The sharp sweet scent of the evergreens, crisp morning air, the penetrating heat of the hot springs pools—we were in family heaven.

Before long, it was time to say goodbye. I travelled back to Islamabad knowing that my children were going to be fine. I could stop holding my breath. Life was on our side, at least for this moment in time.

We would always feel nostalgia for our old life in Canada. Going back for holidays, tasting favourite foods, and visiting old friends and family would be necessary highlights during our overseas years. Connecting with our children would warm our hearts wherever we might be.

My heart was filled with excitement for the new school year ahead. I loved my work, and it had become that much easier in the past year. The new administration wouldn't let Tildy get away with any of her destructive machinations. She'd made a couple of futile attempts at back-stabbing, but those had died a quick death. Peace prevailed. I could live and teach and create without fearing her surprise attacks. What a wonderful gift!

After unpacking and unwinding, Wayne and I were once again knee-deep in work and fall activities. ISOI was bustling along with autumn events. Wayne was captured in the photo booth at the school carnival sporting a red boa.

But as was often the case in Islamabad, these episodes of frivolous antics were short-lived. We were all caught off-guard by a clandestine middle-of-the-night mission that took place in the first months of school. A lovely young American middle school teacher married to a Pakistani man had failed to arrive at work. Where was she? We soon learned that, with the help of her close friends, she had escaped on a late-night flight out of Islamabad with her baby daughter. Her life in Pakistan had become intolerable. This was a situation in which many western women married to Pakistani men found themselves.

There was a common thread to these stories. A couple would meet in North America, or some other western country, where the fascinating young Pakistani man with South Asian swagger was working or studying. His starry-eyed classmate or co-worker would become captivated by his dark good looks and exotic charm, igniting an intense, whirlwind romance.

Most often, the two would be married in North America, although sometimes there was a Pakistani wedding. The latter was rare because most Pakistani families strongly disapproved of love marriages to foreigners. For this reason, marriages between Pakistani women and foreign men were extremely rare as females were more controlled by the family's cultural values. Eventually, the time would come for the Pakistani man to return to his country. His new wife happily accompanied him, excited to explore a new place and become part of the cultural tapestry. But there was so much she didn't understand. Most Pakistanis lived in extended households, and the bride was expected to live with her husband's family. As the blissfully happy couple settled into his family home, their lives would often begin to unravel. As matriarch, the mother-in-law was in charge of the house and all domestic matters. She also set the tone for family values. There is a saying in Islam, "Heaven lies under the feet of your mother." This is a meaningful and important proverb. It's also practiced according to personal interpretation.

If a son conscientiously worshipped at the feet of his mother, then his wife became a secondary partner. In a traditional Pakistani household, the daughter-in-law was subservient to both her mother-in-law and her husband. Add in the possibility of the mother-in-law behaving like a dictator, and you had a familial ticking time bomb. Most women from western countries weren't accustomed to living in extended families nor were they taught to be subservient wives. The Pakistani man they had fallen for had been a free spirit living outside the confines of his cultural structure and norms. Once he got back home to Pakistan, he naturally settled back into the customs with which he'd been raised and expected his wife to adapt and conform, so the young western wife found herself living under the authority of her husband's family in a very conservative Muslim country.

Giving birth to a child frequently resulted in further alienation, as children were considered to belong to the father, especially boys. She was then faced with an unbearable, inescapable dynamic. Leaving Pakistan by herself was a daunting prospect. Attempting to leave with a child was next to impossible. Her husband and father of her child could, and often would, go to any lengths to hunt them down no matter where they went in order to take back the child. As far as we knew, our friend and colleague had made a successful escape. The baby was a girl, so perhaps the father was less interested in pursuing them.

I knew and worked with several western women married to Pakistanis. Not all of them suffered a difficult situation. Some Pakistani men had independently adopted more western thinking. They lived separately from their extended family members and treated their wives with respect. I knew at least a couple of strong-willed western women married to Pakistani men who were in loving, equitable relationships.

But I knew or heard of just as many, if not more, situations where this was not the case. Some of the foreign spouses of Pakistani men had a downtrodden, defeated look. It seemed to me that they had grudgingly accepted their situation or perhaps they were abused in some way. I never knew for sure. This was just my instinct.

Many foreign families didn't want their daughters to date Pakistani boys. Generally, it wasn't a racist thing, but a cultural thing. Pakistani boys were commonly raised with the mindset that western girls were to be used and discarded. And, if a serious relationship did result, what was the future prognosis? It was better to distance your daughter from all those potential minefields.

In her last term of high school, Julie had dated a Pakistani boy. We didn't object because Tariq was a good person, and he treated her well. Wayne and I liked him a lot. But we did come to learn that his family knew nothing about him dating a foreign girl. He was boarding with another Pakistani family in Islamabad for his senior year at school and his mother and father lived in a different city. He hadn't informed them about his Canadian girlfriend. We never knew if they eventually learned about Julie or not. Once Tariq went back home, the bond with Julie slowly dissolved, which was probably for the best.

There was a heartbreaking story connected to another American woman I knew. After we'd left Pakistan, I heard through the grapevine that she had departed her Pakistani life and gone back to the US. As an adult, one of her sons, who had eventually come to live with her in the US, became brainwashed by Islamic extremism. He was shot and killed in an attempted terrorist attack in Texas in 2015, a tragic ending for everyone involved.

I hadn't known her sons when we lived in Islamabad. They were much younger than my children. But she was a kind and gentle lady. I just couldn't comprehend what might have caused that boy to embrace terrorist fanaticism. He wasn't poor or oppressed. Nor had he ever attended a madrasa. He'd had all the benefits of any westerner in his teens and twenties. Did this happen because he felt like a misfit? Had he internalized warring cultural values? I would probably never understand. There were just too many crisscrossing threads of influence in one short lifetime. I could only imagine the pain and suffering his mother had to endure.

CHAPTER 41—MEANINGFUL MOMENTS

As the fall season in Islamabad progressed, I took on more community involvement. Once again, I travelled to Pindi to talk to the Afghan refugee group and attend their graduation from the "English/Learning about Canada" program. I encountered such mixed feelings from the group. They'd been selected to emigrate by the Agha Khan Foundation in Canada, and they were excited to start a new life there. On the other hand, they felt a deep sadness in leaving this part of the world. They had left a war-torn chaotic country. Would they ever return to the beloved Afghanistan of their youth? Probably not.

Those of us who have been fortunate enough to grow up in peaceful democratic countries have no idea how it feels to be displaced, to never again return to the spot you call home. This privilege of birth leads us to believe that it couldn't happen to us. We can't see ourselves fleeing from war or famine or strife. But that is some magical thinking.

Kabul, Afghanistan was once considered the "Paris of Central Asia." In the 1970s, Afghan women not only attended university, but they did so in miniskirts. Tourists visited from all over the world and remarked that Afghanistan was one of the most beautiful places they had ever seen.

What a difference from the Afghanistan of the '90s and into the 21st Century. Life can turn on a dime. Families can suddenly be torn apart due to natural or manmade disasters. It can happen to anyone, anywhere, at any time. I hope that optimistic group of Afghans found peace and prosperity in their chosen corner of Canada.

Our lives continued to be marked by milestones, both big and small. Wayne's softball team was enjoying continued success, even if he did spend a few weeks with the imprint of the ball tattooed on his bicep. Baseball injuries abounded in the expat community but never seemed to slow anyone down.

We celebrated a more international milestone with a formal reception in celebration of the 50th Anniversary of the UN. Lots of dignitaries were in attendance including Benazir Bhutto.

I will never forget the much more dramatic dinner party that Wayne and his colleagues hosted for a group of Iranian men. They were on an observational tour to learn about UN drug and enforcement projects in Pakistan. On the last evening of the visit, the UN officials included their wives at the farewell dinner.

It was common practice in Pakistan to form a reception line to greet honoured guests at these functions. As the Iranian men proceeded down the line, we wives extended our hands. In a clear gesture of repugnance, these men stepped back, crossed their arms, and flattened their hands against their chests.

All the women glanced around in shock and dismay. None of us had ever experienced being so thoroughly rejected when offering to shake hands. They'd treated us like we had some horrible disease. Apparently, it was the disease known as "being women."

This behaviour was alarming to us because we had all lived in Pakistan for a few years, some had lived in other Muslim countries as well, and had never come across this type of aversion. Even though modest conduct was expected of women in Islamabad, Pakistani men had never refused to shake hands.

Was this the mindset of all Iranian men? To save us all further embarrassment, the women ate dinner in a separate room that night.

Soon after this, Wayne took a UN-related trip to Uzbekistan and Kyrgyzstan. This was an eye-opener. Accompanied by an interpreter at all times, he made some important discoveries.

According to his observations, these countries possessed more difficult living conditions than Pakistan. That fall of 1995 he observed that many people in Tashkent, Uzbekistan, and Bishkek,

Kyrgyzstan, lived in small communist-era cinder block houses that were baking hot in the summer and freezing in the winter.

Nevertheless, these were interesting, diverse cities, and the countryside boasted some spectacular scenery. There were no flights into Bishkek the day of his appointed visit, so he was driven for eight hours along the bumpy roads from Tashkent.

Wayne had a rather unusual stay in a very stark Bishkek hotel room. At the entrance to every floor in the hotel, there was a floor lady—part nurse, part house mother, part cop—who watched over the premises, guarded the room keys, and answered questions.

He arrived back at the hotel late one evening and noticed a group of six or seven young women sitting next to the floor lady's desk. As she handed him the keys, she spoke in slow broken English and asked if he wanted to "rest" with any of the young women. He politely declined, went back to his room with the fly-blown walls, chuckled to himself about the peculiarities of the world, and fell instantly asleep.

The next day he managed to get a flight out in a rickety old Russian airplane that he boarded from the tail. All seats were vintage sofa chairs and luggage was thrown into a big box. He prayed that he would reach his destination safely as the plane chugged and rattled its way to Tashkent.

Wayne returned from this trip with a massive "Bubba Gump" sized cold sore and a Matryoshka/Russian Nesting Doll, something I'd never seen before, with eighteen increasingly smaller parts. It sits on my shelf to this day. My grandsons love taking it apart and putting it back together.

The end of October found Wayne and I standing in front of the mirror admiring our costumes for the Canadian Club Halloween party. I had a pile of traditional nun outfits at school from *Sound of Music* days and Wayne enlisted the tailor in making him a priest costume. It was a very politically incorrect evening as we kissed, hugged, and danced the night away as a priest and a nun. People did a lot of double-takes—we looked very authentic! All expats were welcome, and we partied with many of our good friends. Creative costumes abounded. Vampires, pirates, waitresses, pumpkins, Saudi princes, witches, devils, and even burka-clad ladies took a spin on the dance floor.

Soon after this, the Canadian High Commissioner hosted a dinner for all the Canadians in Islamabad. Back home, an October referendum for Quebec sovereignty, separation from the rest of Canada, had been narrowly defeated. After toasting and celebrating this defeat, we all sang *O Canada* and shed a few tears. Living so far away and observing the strife in other countries had affected all Canadians in that room. A united Canada meant everything to us.

That same night Jaffrey, manager for the Canadian Club, showed us the small brass plaque with our names engraved on it that had been mounted on the bar among those of the many other expats that had lived and worked in Islamabad. Proud Canadians abroad, one and all!

Chapter 42—End of an Era

At the beginning of November, we got the news. We were being posted to Thailand. Wayne was to start work in Bangkok in January. As we had some vacation time coming, we would be leaving Pakistan at the end of the school term in December.

So much to do and so little time. Suddenly, moving was a reality, and it was all happening at lightning speed. I was caught up in a labyrinth of thoughts and feelings.

I was ecstatic to learn that we would be living in Thailand. We'd visited twice and loved it both times. From my perspective, there were no negatives on that side. Tropical breezes, friendly soft-spoken people, modern shopping centers and convenience stores, proximity to some of the world's best beaches … The list of positives could go on and on.

At the same time, I'd called Pakistan home for five years. We'd had our ups and downs, extremes at both ends of the spectrum, but there was so much we had come to appreciate and love. Our domestic staff, our colleagues at work, our friends, the parties, the camaraderie, trusting relationships with Pakistani friends and merchants, adventures in exploring this country with its stunning, majestic scenery, our Park Road house. These were just a few of the things we would miss. It was a strange feeling of being filled with jubilance and sorrow all at once.

I gave my notice at ISOI much to the chagrin of the administration. Of course, leaving half-way through a school year wasn't ideal, but there was a bit more to this story. When we'd arrived back at school in late August the two teachers that were in charge of the school musical had asked to trade places with me. They were leaving Pakistan at the end of the second term and needed time to prepare and pack. In light of that, they wished to present the musical in late November. Could my play be mounted in the spring?

I agreed, especially since they had already approached the administrative offices for approval. I couldn't tell anyone that I might be moving because Wayne and I'd had no official word from his head office at that point.

Now that I was officially leaving before the second term, there was a big question mark about what might happen with the spring play. I'd already chosen *The Good Doctor* by Neil Simon, but who was going to direct it? Even more importantly, who was going to take over my position as the Secondary ESL teacher. I felt some guilt, some responsibility, and I worried about all of it. But I had no control. Wayne's contracts lined up with actual Gregorian calendar years, not school years. This was always a problem when teachers weren't married to other teachers.

We made plans to take a whirlwind trip to Thailand toward the end of November to find a place to live, and, hopefully, line up a teaching position for me. Before that, there was lots to take care of.

In what would turn out to be our last Park Road party, I hosted a Mexican-themed dinner for 40. Khan outdid himself in preparing delicious Mexican cuisine. This was a planning session for the 1996 SAISA (South Asian Inter-Scholastic Association) Festival being hosted by ISOI in February, and teachers from other cities in Pakistan as well as from India, Sri Lanka, and Bangladesh would attend. I was to have been instrumental in spear-heading this festival. However, that was not to be. Hosting the dinner would be my only contribution, and I made the best of it. Sharing ideas and making plans with creative arts and drama teachers from all over South Asia was inspirational and fulfilling in itself. I was happy to have been able to make those connections.

Satisfied and relaxed after another successful event, I failed to see the sharp turn in the road ahead.

November 19, 1995, 9:30 am. Kate and I loved our spacious sunny classroom with large windows that overlooked the quad. That morning we were both focused on teaching our respective ESL groups when a loud thump and rattling noise captured our attention. It was a brief, intense disruption that had us running to the windows looking for the bird that might have accidentally flown into the glass. There was nothing to see. Puzzled, we got on with the day.

At the same time, Wayne was driving from his office to the main UN building in the diplomatic enclave. When he got to the entrance of the enclave a policeman was blocking the way. He didn't give this much thought as police blocked off roads regularly in Islamabad for a variety of reasons. He knew the area well and zigzagged his way along an alternate route.

Something was odd, not quite right. What was it? Then it slowly dawned on him. Leaves were thick on the ground, crunching under the tires. The trees were naked, bare. What kind of fierce, ghostly wind had ravaged the landscape? As he was driving by the Egyptian Embassy, Wayne became aware that the gates to the compound were gone. Strange. He slowed down for a closer look. The front façade of the embassy had disappeared.

It was like looking into the interior of a ruined dollhouse. Debris was scattered everywhere. What was this? It felt like an eerie, slow-motion, silent movie. Where were the people? He had the sensation of floating toward his destination, suspended in space and time.

Wayne pulled up to the UN Headquarters just in time to see people streaming out of the building. He stopped the car, jumped out, and ran to ask what was happening.

"Don't you know? How could you have missed the blast?"

"What do you mean?"

"A bomb just went off at the Egyptian Embassy. We have been ordered to evacuate."

He paused to survey the surroundings. All the glass on one side of the UN building had shattered and imploded into the hallways.

The garage doors of the British Compound houses across the street were buckled as if a giant had squished them like a coke can. People were running out of buildings everywhere. Police and civilians were converging at the scene.

Wayne had no idea why he hadn't heard or felt the impact of the blast as he was driving toward it that morning. It must have happened just before he arrived. Chills overcame him as he realized how close he'd come to the explosion.

ISOI was eight or nine miles distant from the enclave and the blast had seriously rattled our classroom windows. Kate and I could never have imagined that a fleeting early morning interruption was the result of the force of a bomb. What might have been the results of a closer encounter?

Islamabad slowly began to piece together the story behind the early morning bomb blast. We learned that this attack had been perpetrated by the Egyptian Islamic Jihad and planned by Ayman Al-Zawahiri, the Egyptian terrorist that ultimately took over al-Qaeda after the death of Bin Laden. According to Zawahiri, they had wanted to attack the American Embassy or other American targets, even other western embassies.

All of that proved too difficult for one reason or another so they concentrated on the Egyptian Embassy. The Egyptian government was fighting against fundamentalism and Pakistan had agreed to extradite several known terrorists to Egypt. This was established as the main reason for the attack. Some Pakistanis believed that at least part of the motivation was retaliation for the extradition of Ramzi Yousef to the US.

Whatever the reason, it was a devastating blow. Two men managed to kill the security guards. Then, a taxi with a 250-pound bomb rushed the compound and blew off the gates. After that, a second vehicle with a larger bomb detonated and the side of the building crumbled. Embassies and buildings nearby were also damaged by the forceful explosions.

The two bombers, Second Secretary for the embassy, three Egyptian security guards, and 12 others including Pakistani security guards, civilians, and diplomats were killed. In the end, the tally was 17 killed and more than 60 injured. This was considered a win, a great success, by jihadists.

In looking back, I have a greater understanding of the brush with danger that many of us were blithely unaware of at the time. American interests in Islamabad included the school, the Satellite Center, and several other institutions. Rattling windows were a slight distraction.

That day was a powerful tragedy as it was. But I think of how many more of us might have been lying in the rubble if all of the terrorist's plans had come to fruition. It was the stuff of nightmares for many weeks to come.

Still reeling from the jolt of this event and its tragic repercussions, we got set to board a flight for a five-day visit to Bangkok. For a short time, we could escape the horror and bloodshed of the bombing.

This was no holiday. I had two job interviews lined up, and we were also embroiled in an extensive search for a place to live. Happily, we were successful on both counts. It wasn't easy to secure a teaching position half-way through a school year, but I managed. I would be working at one of the bigger international schools in Bangkok teaching ESL classes to young children. Not my ideal situation. Nevertheless, I was willing to see what might pop up in the fall. In the meantime, I had a job.

We were overjoyed with the new home we chose, a 2800-square-foot furnished apartment with glowing hardwood floors, teak woodwork, two balconies, and a fully equipped kitchen. We were selling most of our Pakistani furnishings, so this fit the bill and made the transition much easier.

The best news was that it was a five-minute walk to my school. Wayne had a bit of a commute, but he would be out of the country a good deal of the time, as he was to be in charge of multiple projects in the region.

Walking in the streets of Bangkok dressed in light summer clothing, sleeveless top, and shorter skirt caused me some conflicting emotions. I kept looking around to see if anyone was staring at me. It felt strange to walk so freely amongst others on my own in an Asian country without being leered at or harassed. I also felt the need to keep my guard up. To be aware of any danger that might lurk around the corner. After a few days of prickly tension, I finally realized that I was safe. I couldn't believe it! This would take some adjustment. I'd become accustomed to living on the edge. Would I miss that? Would it be boring to live without the gunfire, the earthquakes, the flash floods, the power cuts…?

It wouldn't be overseas living if we didn't manage at least one dinner party or celebration during our trip. This short jaunt was no exception as we shared a sumptuous Thanksgiving dinner with Islamabad friends who had recently moved to Bangkok.

As well as reminiscing about good times in Islamabad, they shared their perspective on the positives and negatives of living in Thailand, particularly Bangkok. We looked forward to our move with great anticipation. Jason and Julie would be meeting us on the island of Koh Samui for Christmas.

Upon returning to Islamabad and ISOI, I was relieved to find that an excellent ESL teacher had been found to replace me. She was actually an ESL specialist, so the school was getting an upgrade. A few people had also agreed to work together in directing and producing the spring play; they would share the workload. The show would go on without me, a testament to the fact that no one is indispensable.

We attended the fall musical, *Little Shop of Horrors*—the last ISOI show for us—and it was absolutely excellent. Sets, costumes, and props were integral to this production, and they were superb. In all my years of teaching, even to this day, no one has ever done these three things better than ISOI. I missed that for many years after we left.

Next up, our final Marine Ball. Once again, out came the tuxes, glittery gowns, and fancy jewelry. We enjoyed a few hours of dancing the night away, my favourite pastime. I closed my eyes and made a wish that these nights of light-hearted camaraderie would still be a part of our future in Bangkok.

Then came the wind-down. Wayne hung up his glove for good as slow pitch season came to an end. Laughter and tears marked a final concert in the park. We hosted our last dinner party for a new family settling into Islamabad.

With most of our possessions sold, the movers came to pack us out. They gently wrapped up my Noritake China from Sri Lanka as well as all of our other worldly possessions and staggered under heavy loads of overpacked boxes out to the waiting truck. We would stay at our friends' house for a couple of weeks until the school term ended.

Kate and her husband Ben hosted a farewell party for us. Over 100 people attended. There were speeches, songs, skits, readings, and tributes. Wayne had received gifts and accolades from his UN colleagues and staff earlier on as well.

My fine arts collaborators presented me with gorgeous brass drama masks as a parting gift. Our friends had stood by us in the best of times and the worst of times. They touched my heart. I still have a portion of the speech I made that night.

Pakistan ... Everything has happened to us here. Our children graduated from school. I rediscovered my directing abilities. Jason had a terrible accident that turned our family upside down. We have hated here. We have loved here. We have learned that we are survivors and warriors. We rekindled our family love and support. We shed our Canadian naiveté here. We have lived shoulder to shoulder with murder, tragic deaths, bombings, corruption, and disease. We have been threatened and treated like kings. We have wined and dined with friends, colleagues, ambassadors, diplomats, and prime ministers.

Sometimes the phone didn't work, sometimes the lights didn't work, sometimes it seemed like the whole country didn't work. We have lived in a beautiful home and closed our eyes to the leaks and the cracks. We had a cook that stole our towels, one that served steak topped with mustard, pepper, and syrup, and one that made the best Chinese food in the world. Pakistan doesn't want us to leave now. Somehow, we've become part of it, part of all the contradictions. How can we forget all this? We won't. We can't. Pakistan will be part of us forever. Now we must move on.

The next morning, Wayne and I did a final walk-through at Park Road, the house that had echoed our joys and sorrows for five years. Now we only heard the echoes of our voices as they reverberated between the pillars and balconies. Above the window in Julie's room, we found our fat gecko friend. I smiled at the memory of my first encounter with a gecko back in the guest house. This one belonged to us, to Park Road. He'd lived there since he was a baby. Suddenly his protection of draperies was gone. Sitting on that bare wall in an empty room, he looked lost and abandoned.

My heart burst and my eyes welled up with tears. How could we leave? This gecko needed us. I had to tell Wayne. We needed to call back the moving truck. We needed to get Khan and Peter and Rafique and Nisar back from the jobs we'd secured for them. We needed to get Jason and Julie back in their rooms listening to music. We needed to sing Christmas Carols with our friends around the tree. We needed to fill Park Road with love again. Wayne found me and hugged me tight. Then he took my hand and walked me out. We gently closed the door behind us.